BY STEVEN RINELLA

The
MEATEATER
OUTDOOR
COOKBOOK

The
MEATEATER
OUTDOOR
COOKBOOK

WILD GAME RECIPES FOR THE GRILL, SMOKER, CAMPSTOVE, AND CAMPFIRE

Steven Rinella

WITH KRISTA RUANE

Photography by John Hafner
Additional Photography by Seth Morris

Random House
New York

Published in the United States by Random House, an imprint
and division of Penguin Random House LLC, New York.

RANDOM HOUSE and the HOUSE colophon are registered
trademarks of Penguin Random House LLC.

LIBRARY OF CONGRESS CATALOGING-IN-PUBLICATION DATA
Names: Rinella, Steven, author. | Ruane, Krista, author.
Title: The MeatEater outdoor cookbook: wild game recipes for the grill,
smoker, campstove, and campfire / with Steven Rinella and Krista Ruane.
Description: New York: Random House, [2024] | Includes index.
Identifiers: LCCN 2023034189 (print) | LCCN 2023034190 (ebook) |
ISBN 9780593449035 (hardcover) | ISBN 9780593449042 (ebook)
Subjects: LCSH: Outdoor cooking. | Cooking (Game) | Cooking (Wild foods) |
MeatEater (Television program) | LCGFT: Cookbooks.
Classification: LCC TX823 .R46 2024 (print) | LCC TX823 (ebook) |
DDC 641.5/78—dc23/eng/20230728
LC record available at https://lccn.loc.gov/2023034189
LC ebook record available at https://lccn.loc.gov/2023034190

Printed in China on acid-free paper

randomhousebooks.com

9 8 7 6 5 4 3 2 1

First Edition

Book design by Debbie Glasserman

FOR JAMES, ROSEMARY,
AND MATTHEW—
DIRT UNDER YOUR NAILS,
LOVE IN YOUR HEARTS

CONTENTS

INTRODUCTION

Recently I was reading about the Blackfoot tribe of the northern Great Plains. They would make an energy-rich food called pemmican by mixing dried and shredded buffalo meat with tallow and grease extracted from buffalo bones. They'd store this mixture inside fresh buffalo skins sewn into oblong bags. As the buffalo skin dried, it would shrink so tightly over the pemmican that the package would achieve, as one observer put it, "the solidity and weight of a rock." I may find zero inspiration in the technology and innovation that goes into something like an iPhone, but I'm routinely blown away by the amazing things that our species has figured out when it comes to feeding ourselves.

We humans have been developing innovations in outdoor cooking for a staggeringly long time. So long, in fact, that we were doing it back when we weren't the only human species. Archaeological evidence links multiple human species with at least limited use of fire dating back some eight hundred thousand years. By three hundred thousand years ago, our own distant *Homo sapiens* ancestors were using fire on a daily basis, as were Neanderthals and *Homo erectus*. Imagine for a moment that you're a time traveler visiting Spain about fifty thousand years ago. You approach a campfire at night and detect the unmistakable smell of roasting meat. Just as you might wonder what type of animal is being cooked, you'd also have to wonder what type of human is doing the cooking—or being cooked.

Since then we've made a lot of nice progress toward a civilized existence, but in our fervor to advance, we've made some terrible mistakes. Our taming of the planet brought about inestimable environmental damage as we leveled forests for building materials, drove dozens of wildlife species to extinction, gutted the earth for minerals and oil, and poisoned our lakes, rivers, and oceans with industrial pollutants. Our intimate and personal relationships with nature have suffered as well. For millions of years, hunting and fishing fueled within us a deep, visceral bond to nature. Our evolving lifeways and interests have pushed us away from these disciplines. In California, the most populous and perhaps most influential state in America, only about one-half percent of residents hold a hunting license. So in a random sampling of two hundred Californians, you'd find only one who might still know the hands-on joy and beauty of deriving their own sustenance from the breathtaking menagerie of wild birds and animals that have supported human life since our beginning.

Hunting and fishing are admittedly extreme examples of engagement with nature. When taken seriously by an individual, they tend to assume the characteristics of a discipline or lifestyle. But even our more casual relationships with nature are dying. In 2005, the author and journalist Richard Louv introduced the term *nature deficit disorder* as a description of the human costs associated with an increasing alienation from nature. He recognized that our divorce from nature began long ago, with the introduction of agriculture. However, he recognized that it accelerated greatly in recent years due to the "proliferation of electronic communications; poor urban planning and disappearing open space; increased street traffic; diminished importance of the natural world in public and private education; and parental fear magnified by news and entertainment media." Louv's writing focuses on children, but a lack of time spent outdoors is a major problem for adults as well. The average American spends 87 percent of their time inside buildings, and 7 percent inside vehicles. That leaves about one half of one day per week that's spent outside. It's an astounding statistic, especially when you consider the dozens of studies over the last several decades linking disengagement with the outdoors to everything from depression to obesity to environmental apathy. While writing about similar findings in my own book *Outdoor Kids in an Inside World* (2022), I pointed out to my readers that the results of such research shouldn't sound particularly surprising. We don't need academic studies to tell us that we feel better when we step outside.

Nor do we need someone to tell us that food tastes better when it's cooked outside. This is something I've recognized ever since I was a little kid. One summer, when I was nine or ten, my dad put me to work with a hammer and chisel removing the old mortar from a pickup-truckload of red bricks that he'd salvaged from a demolished building. I was then tasked with stirring batches of fresh mortar with a garden hoe while my dad and a friend named Eugene built a gigantic fire ring in our backyard down by the lake. For the next decade or so, that fire ring served as a sort of laboratory for adolescent experiments in outdoor cooking. Through an endless litany of burns and scalds on our hands, my neighborhood buddies and I fine-tuned the making of sassafras tea (add lots of sugar), botched multiple attempts at roasting whole chipmunks, incinerated dozens of foil-wrapped potatoes that were buried beneath the coals for too long, fried countless bluegill caught from the lake, and made so many "hobo pies" (nowadays, these are more politely referred to as iron pies) that we'd frequently drain a tub of margarine in a single cooking session and then melt the polypropylene container over the heat of the fire because we liked the crazy zipping sound that the material made when it dripped into the flames.

All of it tasted amazing! Even the burned and desiccated potatoes were a treat once you became accustomed to the grittiness of wood ash. But the actual flavors and textures of the meals had little to do with how much I loved them. Instead, I was drawn to the labor, ingenuity, and ever-so-slight danger involved with outdoor cooking. And I was inspired by the environment. While cooking outside, the walls and ceiling of a conventional indoor kitchen were replaced by the open sky and the lake. A humming exhaust fan and the background noise of TV became wind through the trees and birdsong. While cooking in that environment, with smoke in my eyes and the fire's heat on my arms, I couldn't help but feel connected to something deep and eternal about my own human experience. It drew me into the present and opened me up to the past. When roasting a raw-in-the-middle-but-burned-on-the-outside chipmunk, it was easy to imagine the exhilaration that might have come from flipping a rack of mammoth ribs. And when sharing the concoctions with friends and family, it was easy to imagine walking through the woods toward the firelight of a distant camp in order to share appetizers with that friendly band of Neanderthals that had recently moved into our territory.

Both personally and professionally, I've continued to chase those same outdoor cooking adventures and lessons that I cultivated around the fire pit of my childhood home. Early on, I was focused on the regional favorites of my home turf in western Michigan. Around there, major occasions were often celebrated by roasting a whole hog with the skin, feet, and head intact. I provided the meal for my own high school graduation party by staying up all night to cook a 125-pound pig in a fuel-oil drum that my neighbor had converted into a charcoal-fired roaster. A couple of years later, my college buddy Andy and I borrowed that roaster again in order to attempt something bigger and better. We stuffed a large hog with the bone-in quarters of a whitetail deer that had been run over by the car in front of me while I was driving home from fishing salmon on Michigan's Pere Marquette River. Years later, while living in Brooklyn, New York, I wanted to attempt an even more technically complex underground hog cooking strategy that I'd witnessed in Hawaii. I started by digging a giant hole in the backyard garden space of our apartment building. The first step was generating a deep bed of coals in the bottom of the hole. The plume of smoke that developed as I

pitched in armloads of oak firewood resembled something from an urban warfare news dispatch. I got nervous when I heard the distant scream of fire truck sirens. The nervousness blossomed into full-on panic when two ladder trucks pulled up in front of our building. Five or six firemen poured through the front door of my apartment and then out the backdoor into the garden space. When I explained what I was fixing to do, the captain said, "That's a great idea, but you're gonna need to put that out. Right now."

My adventures in hog roasting demonstrate a familiar pathway that I've taken with many other outdoor cooking strategies: Investigation leads to inspiration, which leads to experimentation, which leads to innovation. Or at least *attempted* innovation. This path of discovery has led to some of my most unique and memorable outdoor cooking experiences. Some were mighty short, such as the one initiated by the journal of a hunter who mentioned flavoring raw buffalo liver with the animal's own bile. I tried that once, in Sonora, Mexico, and once was enough. (If you like the alkaline-goodness of pressing a nine-volt battery to your tongue, you're gonna love bile.)

Another lengthier journey was prompted by a visit to an archaeological site in northern New Mexico. Known as the Folsom site, it's a location where Ice Age hunters corralled at least thirty-two bison in a box canyon and killed them using stone projectile points. A peculiarity of the site is the lack of tail bones in the bone bed that contains the butchered remains of the animals. Researchers have postulated, reasonably so, that the hunters hauled away the hides with the tails intact—which is how it's still done today. While archaeologists recovered jaw bones showing distinctive cut marks where the hunters removed the animals' tongues, there were no femurs recovered at the site. These were likely hauled away to a nearby camp to be boiled for bone grease and then smashed open for the marrow. (As I mentioned with regards to the Blackfeet, grease and marrow were used in the making of pemmican.) You might wonder, as I did, how an Ice Age hunter would go about boiling something. After

all, they had no metal pots or other large vessels that would withstand the direct heat of a fire. I researched this question and found multiple references to other indigenous hunters using animal hides to line shallow pits dug in the ground that were then filled with water. They would heat rocks in a fire, then give the rocks a quick rinse before dropping them into the hide-lined cauldron. The heat from the rocks would then bring the water to a boil.

It's not that I necessarily doubted these accounts; it's just that I had such a hard time imagining what it looked like to see a rock bring water to a boil. I thought about it for a couple of years, until one day, in west Texas, I lined a head-sized hole with the stomach of a javelina (also known as a collared peccary, these small pig-like critters are fairly common in the deserts of the Southwest) and filled the makeshift pot with water and a few strips of javelina meat. I then dropped in a few porous lava rocks that I'd heated in my campfire, and voilà! The water hissed and steamed, and a profusion of bubbles spread forth from where the rocks had disappeared. That night, lying in my sleeping bag with a belly full of boiled javelina meat, I luxuriated in the knowledge that old recipes never die.

Ultimately, the cookbook in your hands represents the future of outdoor cooking more than it represents the past. You're holding a modern but timeless take on everything from preparing charcuterie to cocktails in the great outdoors. But before we get to that, I want to explain one last culinary adventure that exemplifies what I love most about the subject of outdoor cooking. This story, perhaps more than any other, is to thank for the fact that this book now exists. It begins with me reading *The Oregon Trail,* Francis Parkman's journal about his travels on America's western frontier in 1846. In what is now Wyoming, Parkman and his companion were honored by their Oglala Sioux hosts with the meat of a puppy that was plucked from a nest of its littermates in the back of a teepee and knocked over the head with a stone mallet. Parkman describes how the woman responsible for cooking the dog held it by the back foot as she waved it through the flames

of the fire in order to burn off the hair before cutting the animal into pieces and dropping them into a kettle to boil, skin and all. It was a startling passage for me, especially since I'd been raised in the constant presence of my own pet dogs. It forced me to reckon with my personal taboos. And, in a roundabout way, the passage from Parkman's book eventually led me to northern Vietnam in order to write a magazine story about the tradition of consuming dog meat during the Lunar New Year celebrations. Dog meat, thit cho, is regarded as a "warming" food that has the power to change one's fortunes.

It was on that trip, while riding a rented moped into the mountains, that I encountered a shirtless Vietnamese farmer who had just killed a small animal with an air rifle. At first I thought it was a squirrel, but it was actually some kind of arboreal marsupial—think of a small opossum. He already had a fire burning. Holding the critter by the back foot, he waved it through the flames in order to burn the hair off. I was reminded, immediately, of the passage from Parkman's book that had initially sent me on this journey.

I sat down on a stump to watch the man prepare his meal. As he scraped away the burned hair, a golden-colored skin emerged that reminded of a perfectly roasted hog. He went to his garden plot and gathered a handful of thin red peppers, a large banana leaf, a green herb that I didn't recognize, and a few stalks of lemongrass. Working with a small machete that had been forged from a vehicle's leaf spring, he prepared his collection of ingredients and layered them in the center of the banana leaf with a splash of rice wine. He laid the animal atop the ingredients and then rolled the banana leaf into an envelope-shaped package. He folded the package into an old piece of crumpled-up and blackened aluminum foil that he smoothed back out for reuse. This he set into the fire.

What emerged from the coals, an hour or so later, was the most delicious meal that I ate during my time in Vietnam. In fact, taken as a whole, it was the most memorable meal that I've eaten in my entire life. The fork-tender meat occupied a space between squirrel and chicken thighs. It was perfectly sweet and hot and exotic, with that magical bit of wildness that comes with game meat. Even better, the meal brought together every element of outdoor cooking that I've come to love. It captured the adventure of travel and the thrill of the hunt. It expressed the continuity of ancient skill sets. It contained the heat and smoke of fire and the pragmatic ingenuity and elbow grease that are integral to working outside. Yet the ruggedness was balanced with careful attention to detail and an awareness of the primacy of flavor. The meal was built with an acknowledgment that it needed to taste perfect in order to honor all of those constituent elements that went into its creation.

This book was built in the same spirit as that meal. It's my hope that this spirit flows through to you as you prepare these meals for your friends, family, and loved ones. Here's to the smoke in your eyes, the burns on your fingers, and the flavor on your plate.

« Roasting whole small mammals like this marmot on a fire is an ancient cooking technique that still persists in some cultures around the world.

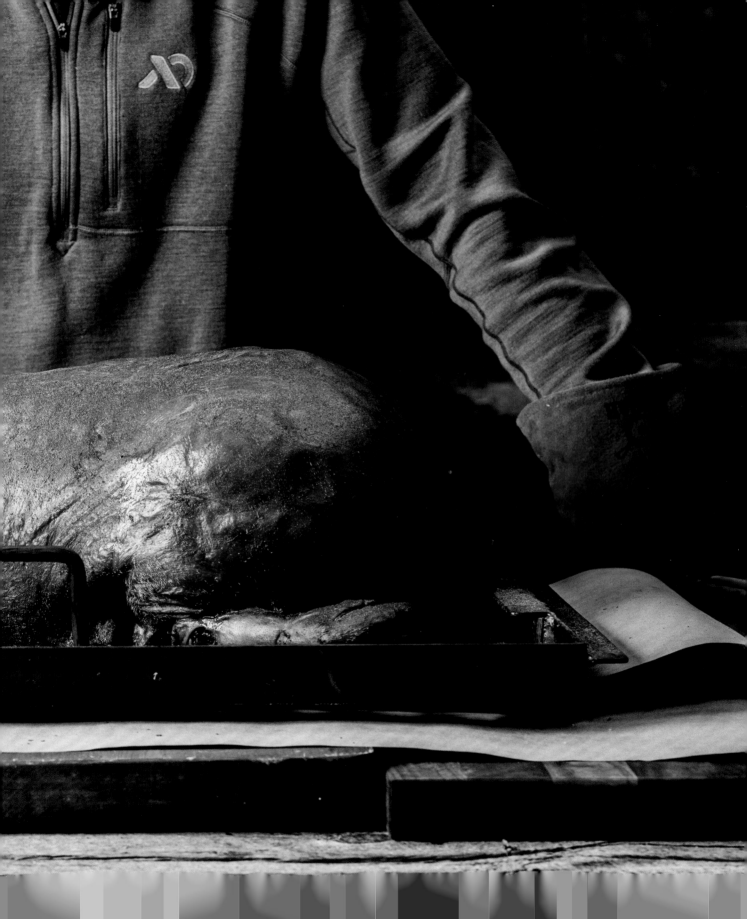

USING THIS BOOK
A NOTE ON VARIABILITY

There are an estimated 20,000 species of fish in the world, 10,000 birds, and about 5,400 species of mammals. We're certainly not recommending all of them as food items, but the numbers help illustrate how hard it is to list every possible protein source that might work for the preparations found within this book. If we have a recipe that calls for halibut, what we're really saying is that it works for things that are halibut-*like*—meaning it works for larger specimens of firm, white-fleshed fish. So if you're looking at this halibut recipe and you say to yourself, "Dammit, all I have is a big redfish," you shouldn't despair. There's a good chance that these two fish species would both work for the same thing. Likewise, moose, caribou, and elk are all members of the deer family, and all of them have relatively lean red meat. Using the same recipe and method of cooking, you can expect to get the same basic results from all three species—and any other member of the deer family, for that matter.

To help you navigate the endless possibilities around ingredient selection, we use a heading called *Also works with* in our recipes. When you see this, you're looking at some of our suggestions for possible substitutions, both wild and domestic, that would work for that particular recipe. If you see a recipe for quail, we might point out that the same preparation would still be pretty damn good with chicken, pheasant, or grouse. Of course, you might have to apply a little common sense to the cooking process. You might need to adjust certain ingredient measurements to account for the increase in size, or perhaps increase the cooking time a bit, but it'll work.

On the subject of variability, we'd also like to point out that there can be as much variability within a species of game animal as there is between different species of game animals. Meaning, the meat from two whitetail deer might have greater differences in quality than there are between the meat of a particular elk and that of a particular moose. Factors such as health, age, diet, and other uncontrollable variables can greatly impact the flavor and texture of an animal's meat; a yearling whitetail doe will almost certainly be more tender than an old buck, but the buck will likely have a more robust flavor. So if a recipe doesn't turn out as planned, consider the possibility that you might get different results the next time you try that recipe with the meat from a different critter.

Likewise, fish and meat that is harvested in nature has tremendous variability in terms of size and weight. While we list ingredient weight and size in our recipes, don't get hung up on the details. A couple of 1-pound beaver thighs will work just as well for the Beaver Confit Toasts with Grilled Figs and Balsamic-Honey Glaze recipe (page 20) as the single 1½- to 2-pound thigh that's listed. And, if your protein weight is a little over what we've listed, proportionally increase the other ingredients to match.

To sum up, think of these recipes as guidelines. They have all been tested and retested in various conditions to achieve desired results. Our instructions will guide you toward a good outcome, but it's best if you meet us halfway by keeping your wits about you and trusting your instincts. This is a collaboration. We promise to uphold our end of the deal.

RECIPE ICONS

Anyone who has spent a little time camping, fishing, or hunting should be familiar with the icons on maps that identify places like campgrounds, trailheads, and boat ramps. Because these symbols are so embedded in the culture and traditions of American outdoorsmen and -women, we're using a similar icon system that will allow you to navigate the recipes in this book.

While some of the recipes in this book were developed with a very specific type of equipment and outdoor location in mind, many can be made pretty much anywhere with just a little tweaking and flexibility. You may see recipes with just a single icon or they may have more than one. For instance, smoking a wild hog ham on a wilderness backpacking trip isn't realistic, but you can cook bratwursts or burgers over a campfire just as easily as you can at home on a propane grill.

BACKYARD

Best suited for an outdoor space right outside your home, such as a backyard or deck. You may need access to a proper kitchen, an extensive ingredient list, or specialized pieces of cooking equipment.

CAR CAMPING

Designed for camping trips where you can carry a decent amount of gear. Think cars, campers, boats, and even pack-horses. These may require coolers, utensils, pots and pans, and cooking systems such as two-burner campstoves, portable fire-pit grills, or Dutch oven tripod setups. You'll find most recipes include make-ahead sauces and rubs or components that can be cooked in a home kitchen and assembled on-site.

BACKCOUNTRY

Suitable for wilderness or backwoods cooking. While remote camping usually involves meals such as instant oatmeal and freeze-dried entrées, these recipes can help you step up your wilderness cooking game with a few packable or freshly sourced ingredients and a minimal amount of gear.

OUTDOOR COOKING APPLIANCES AND KITCHEN SETUPS

When I was in high school, a guy named Brian moved into a rental house down the road from us. We became buddies. One of the things I liked about his family was that they did more outdoor cooking than anyone I knew. Their outdoor "kitchen" consisted of a patch of gravel beneath the carport and was equipped with a simple charcoal kettle grill and a sack of Kingsford briquettes. One spatula, one set of tongs. They had that grill fired up three or four nights a week, and they knew how to use it. It was a good place to be invited for dinner. They roasted chicken, smoked pork butt, and grilled locally caught salmon from Lake Michigan—all on that same setup.

I think of that family and their simplified outdoor kitchen every time I walk into a big home and garden store and get greeted by the latest display of utensils, grills, smokers, and wood-fired pizza ovens that look like Star Wars robots and come with a user's manual as thick as your hand. All too often, I see friends splurge on these ultra-sophisticated gadgets that end up rusting away beneath the eaves of their house with a family of mice living in the pan where the wood chips are supposed to go. Meanwhile, Brian's family is probably still slinging burgers off that same grill they owned twenty-some years ago.

That's not to knock innovative outdoor cooking equipment. Now and then, they come out with stuff that is pretty damned nice, and I do like to keep abreast of the trends. I remember dismissing pellet grills when I first heard about them, because it seemed like sourcing the pellets would be a pain in the ass. And besides that, you had to have a place to plug them in. That just goes to show how wrong I can be. My pellet grill is now my second-favorite piece of outdoor cooking equipment. (My new commercial-grade deep fryer really is a sight to see.)

The point I'm trying to make here is that you should be honest with yourself about your intentions, skills, dedication, and time constraints when selecting outdoor cooking equipment. If you typically have twenty minutes to prepare dinner at night and all you want is a hamburger, don't buy a smoker that takes two hours and an engineering degree to heat up. And you can certainly take a minimalist approach to camp kitchens, too. This is something you should keep in mind as you go through this section that details some of our favorite outdoor cooking appliances and kitchen equipment. In other words, think of this section as more of a conversation starter than a shopping list. And when considering a piece of gear, look through the recipes in this book to make sure you're drawn to the sorts of preparations that the appliance can be used for. America's backyards are full of unused outdoor cooking equipment. There's no need to add to the pile.

Throughout this book, you'll see some uniquely designed DIY cooking rigs, like the rotisserie trompo grill on page 252 and the whole-hog roaster on the opposite page, that were built by friends. Though these contraptions are precious to me, the truth is they typically get used on special occasions for preparations that I like to call showstoppers. Here's a more practical list of what I'd consider to be the essential, everyday workhorses for outdoor cooking.

OUTDOOR COOKING APPLIANCES

Propane Grills

Gas grills are a fast, simple, convenient tool for outdoor cooking. And with easily controlled heat settings and add-ons like side burners, rotisseries, and wood chip containers, you can cook just about anything on them. I like a propane grill with enough surface area to cook meat and vegetables at the same time or to make a big batch of burgers for a group of neighbors and friends. Look for a grill with durable cast-iron grates. You can't go wrong with Camp Chef or Weber grills.

Charcoal Grills

The big knock against gas grills is they don't impart natural smoke flavor. That's certainly true, but charcoal grills aren't for impatient chefs or time-starved parents. A charcoal chimney starter gets you cooking faster, but charcoal grills don't heat up instantly with the turn of a knob. And controlling the temperature requires moving hot coals around. Then there's cleaning up all that burnt ash to consider. But despite all the extra work, charcoal grills are definitely worth having around. Even a simple hamburger tastes better cooked over smoldering briquettes. For my money, it's hard to beat the simplicity and functionality of the original Weber kettle grill.

No matter the brand, you can use standard machine-formed briquettes, lump hardwood charcoal mixes, or a combination of the two. The flavor and intense heat from natural hardwood charcoal surpasses manufactured briquettes; however, briquettes usually burn longer. The varieties of charcoal now available in stores have expanded significantly in the past few years. If you're into doing some experimentation, it's worth exploring how each one cooks. What we don't recommend are charcoal briquettes pre-soaked in lighter fluid. Sure, the chemicals burn off eventually, but the nasty flavor of the fuel does penetrate into your food. Plus, by using a chimney, you can skip the lighter fluid.

Fire Pits

Before I got my hands on one of the portable double-walled metal fire pits that are so popular these days, I was pretty skeptical. I didn't buy claims of smokeless wood fires, and I certainly didn't consider them a must-have piece of outdoor cooking equipment. In fact, they didn't strike me as much more than a glorified version of a chopped-down 55-gallon drum that you'd use to burn trash. Man, was I wrong. I like these things so damn much that I've got two of the Breeo models—a big one that lives on our porch and a smaller one that goes wherever our camper goes. They really do cut way down on smoke, and they put off an amazing amount of heat on cold nights. These types of fire pits also provide a safe place for a contained fire in a small backyard or at a crowded campsite. Best of all, with a few super handy attachments like a grill grate, griddle, and pothanger, it's a joy to cook directly over a wood fire.

Electric Pellet Grills

These grills burn pellets made of food-grade pulped hardwoods that add rich, smoky flavors to food. Pellet grills bridge the gap between a regular grill and a conventional smoker. Although most can't reach the extremely high searing temperatures that gas and charcoal grills can attain, some can hit 500°F and operate as low as 150°F. In other words, you can quickly grill a steak to medium-rare at high temperatures and you can precisely maintain lower temperatures for smoking salmon or ham. And pellet grills are ideal for roasting big chunks of venison backstrap and round roasts. Many pellet grills are programmable and can be run remotely with wireless controllers. Keep in mind, pellet grills do require regular maintenance and cleaning, and you have to keep a supply of wood pellets on hand. GreenMountain and Camp Chef both manufacture quality pellet grills in a variety of sizes.

Chamber Smokers

Chamber smokers smolder wood chips to create smoke. They do a great job of smoking and drying jerky, fish, and summer sausage. When I was a kid, it seemed like half the people I knew had an old Smokehouse Big Chief smoker in their garage. You'd just plug it in, put a pan of wood chips on the hot plate, and you were smoking. There are still plenty of electric smokers on the market today, including the Smokehouse Big Chief, and some are pretty slick. You can get programmable models that operate on autopilot with preset start and stop times. Despite the ease of electric smokers, I prefer propane-fired chamber smokers, such as the Camp Chef Smoke Vault. They have a wide temperature range, and you don't need a nearby power source. I also like the presence of the flame, if only for aesthetic reasons. Get a tall one (I use a smoker that's about 28 inches high) with heavy gauge metal walls to hold the temperature and plenty of shelves for smoking large batches of fish, jerky, sausages, mushrooms, and whatever else you want to cram in there. You can also remove the shelves and hang large items like hams and venison legs.

Deep Fryer

You might not think of a deep fryer as an outdoor cooking appliance, but experience has taught me that outside is the best place to use your fryer. Frying outside means you won't have to contend with grease splatters and oily smells inside your house. Just make sure you've got a covered spot where you can store and use your fryer out of the weather. There are all kinds of small deep fryers made strictly for the at-home chef, but most of them tend to be cheaply built and generally don't last very long before something breaks or the heating element burns out. I have had good luck with a Breville Smart Fryer, but your best option is a heavy-duty stainless steel commercial-grade countertop fryer. You can buy them from restaurant supply businesses online in gas or electric models. For at-home use, electric is the way to go. A good one might cost you a few hundred dollars, but over the long haul, the increased durability and added features justify the investment. With proper care, a commercial fryer should last a lifetime. Look for a double basket model from Globe or Vollrath with a 10-pound grease vat.

Outdoor Cookers

You'll see these things categorized as turkey fryers, crayfish boilers, or just plain old outdoor cookers, but most share the same basic design—a large single burner that sits on four steel legs or a pedestal and connects to a 20-pound propane tank. Many are sold as kits with a 30- to 100-quart pot, a thermometer, and a steaming/frying basket. These setups have long been a mainstay in coastal communities, and they came into wider popularity with inlanders during the deep-fried turkey craze. I find that they're a very useful and versatile part of my outdoor cooking equipment lineup. At our fish shack in southeastern Alaska, we use our outdoor cooker nearly every day to steam crabs, boil shrimp, and deep-fry large quantities of fish and sea cucumbers. They're also useful for big pots of gumbo and chili meant to serve large crowds. On a side note, outdoor cookers are also a handy tool for scalding game birds for easy plucking and cleaning up big game skulls for mounts. Companies like King Kooker and Bayou Classic produce simple, quality outdoor cookers.

Car Camping Grills

Small, portable gas grills that run off green single-use 1-pound propane canisters are super convenient for quickly cooking typical car camping fare like burgers and brats. Due to wildfire restrictions, cooking over a campfire isn't always an option. But Coleman and Camp Chef make affordable, lightweight gas grills that are often legal to use when open fires are strictly outlawed. If fire restrictions aren't a concern and you prefer grilling over briquettes, there are downsized versions of charcoal grills that work well for car camping. But no matter the fuel source, grills do have their limitations. Yes, it's possible to use one to steam some veggies in a foil pack or warm up a pot of water for instant coffee, but there are much better options for things like boiling and frying.

Propane Stoves

A two-burner propane stove will cover the vast majority of your cooking on a car camping trip—and again, it will be indispensable when fire restrictions forbid open flames. If you're looking for something basic, reliable, and highly portable, go with a small, lightweight stove that runs off 1-pound propane tanks like the Coleman Classic Propane Camping Stove. It won't take up much space in your vehicle, and I've even packed one along on canoeing trips. Camp Chef and other manufacturers offer models with an integrated griddle system that adds some valuable versatility. The beauty of these things lies in their simplicity, but be aware that they don't have burners with super-high Btu (British thermal unit) output. It takes time to get a big pot of water boiling, especially in cold, windy weather. Most also lack the space to accommodate two large pots or pans at the same time.

If you're willing to haul around a heavier appliance, consider one of the portable stand-up gas stoves that run off full-size 20-pound propane tanks. With an increased surface area that will accommodate full-size pots, skillets, and griddles over high-Btu burners, models like the Camp Chef Pro 16 come close to matching the convenience of cooking on your range at home. The sturdy folding legs with levelers allow you to set up anywhere, the windscreen ensures the burners don't blow out, and the side shelves provide extra working space.

Campfires

It's easy to forget that there was a time when cooking a camp meal meant making a fire. These days, a propane stove may be the best tool for the bulk of your camp cooking, but it's fun to slow down and do at least some of your cooking over a campfire. With the right equipment, there's a lot more you can do than roast marshmallows and hot dogs on a stick. Most developed campsites, and even some primitive ones, have a metal fire ring with an attached cooking grate. But you shouldn't count on it, especially if you're boondocking where there aren't any designated campsites.

At the very least, you'll want to bring a basic metal grill grate that can be rested on a base of rocks or logs. You can salvage a grate from a retired barbecue grill, but if you want a grate that's going to last and doesn't get all bent to hell, buy a heavy-duty one made out of cast iron or a similarly durable material. It should support the weight of a cast-iron skillet or Dutch oven while also allowing you to cook directly on the grate. Or go with one of the metal Breeo fire pits mentioned earlier (page xxvi). That way you don't have to worry about digging your own fire pit, and they're genuinely safer and less smoky than open fires. Sure, they're a little bulky and heavy, but the grate, griddle, and pot-hanger attachments score big points for ease of use.

Finally, you can do a lot with a Dutch oven nestled among hot campfire coals, but a cast-iron tripod makes it even more versatile; tripods are an indispensable tool for making big batches of stew, chili, and gumbo.

Backcountry Cooking Equipment

When you're tired and hungry after hiking all day in miserable weather, you want to be able to quickly and easily make a meal that carries a heavy payload of calories. Backcountry camping means you're limited to carrying everything you need in your backpack. So you'll want a stove that's lightweight, compact, and works reliably in wet or windy conditions. Jetboil stoves are very popular with backpackers, and they work very well, but over decades of backcountry hunting, I've experimented with all manner of backpacking stoves, and I've settled on the MSR Reactor and MSR PocketRocket as my two favorite options.

The Reactor's enclosed burner is impervious to wind and gets a pot of water boiling in about ninety seconds. It's also a very stable cooking platform, with three different pot sizes available. And the stove and fuel canister pack neatly inside the pot, which has a locking lid to keep everything secure. While there's not a better stove for quickly making coffee and rehydrating freeze-dried meals, I've used my Reactor to cook everything from Chinese hot-pot ptarmigan to hunks of bear meat fried in bear fat. If you're looking to shave a few ounces from a heavy pack wherever possible, try the MSR PocketRocket Deluxe stove kit. The ultralight stove, cooking pot, pot handle, bowl, and fuel canister all pack neatly into the pot. Be aware that the PocketRocket doesn't boil water as quickly or handle wind as well as the Reactor, but that's the price you pay for a stove that fits in the palm of your hand and weighs less than 3 ounces.

Of course, on some backcountry expeditions you may also want to do some campfire cooking. If you can find some green willows or other suitable wood, you can fashion some skewers or a makeshift grill grate with your pocket knife. But a metal grate designed specifically for backpackers can be a real time-saver. There are various sizes and iterations available, from ultralight wire mesh designs to larger, sturdier versions with folding legs that weigh a couple pounds. Your choice will ultimately rest on how much extra weight you're willing to carry and how much pack space you're willing to sacrifice.

OUTDOOR KITCHEN KITS

Some of our backyard recipes require you to have access to a full at-home kitchen equipped with blenders, food processors, ovens, and occasionally a slow cooker or a pressure cooker. As you get more and more interested in backyard cooking, you may want to add a few pieces of specialty equipment that allow you to work comfortably around flames and other heat sources without needing to worry about ruining your indoor gear. When stocking up on outdoor cooking accessories, avoid the temptation to buy one of those grilling kits that pop up in home and garden stores every spring; they're usually composed of useless trash you don't need along with cheap, poorly designed tools that won't last more than a summer. Invest a little more and buy sturdy, stainless-steel tongs and spatulas. If need be, spread out the cost by buying them one at a time. We also recommend getting a quality coal rake for moving hot coals around in charcoal grills, fire pits, and campfires. And make sure to save some money for a good pair of grilling or welding gloves made from thick leather. Your hands will thank you.

BACKYARD KITCHEN KIT LIST

- Large carbon-steel or cast-iron skillet, cast-iron griddle, cast-iron Dutch oven
- Large boiling/deep-frying pot
- Long-handled metal tongs, spatula, ladle
- Wire fish basket
- Paella pan
- Metal skewers
- Charcoal chimney(s)
- Coal rake
- Spray bottle(s)
- Basting brushes
- Heat-resistant leather grilling gloves
- Wire grill brush
- Meat thermometer
- Propane tanks, wood pellets, charcoal briquettes
- Propane fire-starter torch
- Heavy-duty aluminum foil
- Cooking twine
- Baking sheets

On camping trips based out of a camper, car, or boat, you have the ability to create a functional hybrid of your indoor and backyard kitchens. My basic car-camping kitchen kit lives in a couple of Action Packer plastic totes. Prior to leaving on a trip, I usually tweak it based on the number of people in the group, how long the trip will be, and the simplicity or complexity of the meals I'm planning to make. Generally, the items in my kit are either tools that are necessary for a very specific duty or that serve as multipurpose workhorses that allow me to pack less and do more. For instance, a quart-sized water bottle can also serve as a measuring cup. A nylon cutting board works just fine as a serving tray. For cookware, seek out carbon-steel or cast-iron sets (Lodge is the king of these) that consist of a deep cast-iron pan with a lid that can be in-

verted to be a skillet—more tools in one. With this setup you're covered for a wide range of cooking techniques including simmering, sautéing, and frying; you can even use the bottom of a standard cast-iron skillet as a pizza pan or to bake flatbread. You'll certainly want to poach some items from your indoor and backyard kitchen, but don't forget that you'll also need plenty of things at camp that are more likely to come from your garage than your kitchen. Inevitably, you'll find you can't run an efficient camp kitchen without items like headlamps and tarps. The list below is just a guide; it may take you a few trips to get your camp kitchen system dialed in. Focus on must-have essentials first. And then, after some trial and error, you can work on customizing your kit to suit your needs.

CAR CAMPING KITCHEN KIT LIST

Plastic totes. For cooking gear and food storage, you'll need at least a couple of totes. I like those in the 25- to 30-gallon size range for general use. Stay away from the generic cheapies made out of thin, transparent plastic. For function and durability, you can't go wrong with Action Packers and Brutes from Rubbermaid.

Cooler(s). Keeping perishables cold is critical on camping trips. The size and number of coolers you'll need depends on how long you'll be camping and the amount of food and beverages you bring. At a minimum, you'll want a hard-bodied cooler in the 75-quart range for perishable food and a 20- to 40-quart soft-sided cooler for drinks. The Yeti Tundra, Flips, and Hopper coolers will last you a lifetime. There are plenty of less expensive options, but the cheapest coolers have a way of ending up in the landfill after just one or two uses.

Ice and/or ice packs. Bags of ice cubes, block ice, frozen jugs of water, and reusable hard-sided ice packs all have their pros and cons. Ice cubes are great for chilling fresh-caught fish and making cocktails. However, they melt quickly in hot weather, which can result in soggy ingredients. For a longer-lasting option that won't ruin the contents of your cooler, freeze tap water in recycled two-liter soda bottles. After the ice melts, you can drink the water or cook with it.

Water jugs. If you're boondocking where there's no potable water available, you'll either need to bring your own water or else treat water from a natural source by boiling or filtering it. Natural water sources are often silty or muddy, and finding water close to camp is never a guarantee. So, for car camping, I prefer to bring way more water than I think I'll need inside 5- or 6-gallon water jugs.

A 5-gallon bucket. You'll find a multitude of uses for a bucket. On the same camping trip you might use it

as a camp stool, as a trash can, or as a receptacle for foraged foods like wild mushrooms or razor clams.

Camp table. You'll want a sturdy camp table that packs down into a lightweight package. The Camp Time Roll-a-Table and the Camp Chef Mesa are two of the best.

Large lightweight tarp. It's no fun to cook or eat in the rain or under a blazing hot sun, so pack a lightweight tarp that can serve as a cooking and eating shelter. Don't forget to bring some paracord and extra tent stakes for rigging your shelter.

Large tools. A shovel and a hatchet are required car-camping tools, but you may also need a maul, or even a chainsaw, for cutting and splitting firewood.

Small tools. Always carry a small basic tool kit, a folding EDC (everyday carry) knife, and a multi-tool for quick fixes around camp. These will come in handy when fashioning wood skewers or grill grates that might be missing from your cooking kit.

Headlamps, lanterns, and flashlights. If you're cooking before the sun comes up or after it sets, you can't get by without artificial lighting.

Utility lighters. Keep a couple of utility lighters in your kit. Their long nozzle makes lighting propane grills and campfires much easier.

Heavy-duty gloves. Standard leather work gloves are handy for all kinds of camp chores, but heat-resistant leather fireplace or welding gloves are even better for working around campfires and hot pots and pans.

Cooking fuel. Bring enough propane (and tinder, kindling, and fuel wood, if necessary) to last for your entire camping trip.

Pots, pans, and other cookware. Bring what you need based on what you'll be cooking. At a minimum, you'll want a large frying pan, a large pot, and a water kettle. Fair warning—food burns easily in cheap, thin aluminum cookware, and plastic handles have a nasty habit of melting. Cast-iron Dutch ovens, skillets, and griddles have long been considered the best option for campfire cooking, and they work great on stoves, too. But if you're looking to save on weight without giving up performance, carbon-steel pots and pans are more durable than stainless steel or aluminum. Carbon steel can also handle high temperatures very well. Other items to consider are metal skewers, steamer baskets, and iron-pie makers (see page 151).

Cooking utensils. Plastic measuring cups and spoons are fine for camping, but avoid plastic cooking utensils. Long-handled metal ladles, spatulas, and tongs won't melt on a hot skillet or if they're left too close to open flames. A full set of kitchen knives isn't necessary. Instead, you'll want at least one sharp chef's knife for chopping veggies and cutting meat. I always have a fillet knife around camp, too, in case there's a nearby opportunity for fishing. Thin, flexible plastic cutting boards are ideal for camping. Lightweight nylon boards are a good choice as well.

Plates, bowls, cups, and silverware. For all their time-saving convenience, single-use plastic silverware and paper plates create a lot of trash. You can get a nice durable set of metal camping dinnerware and silverware for not much more than you'd pay for the disposable stuff. For beverages, standard travel mugs make for excellent camp cups. And of course, you'll need a dishwashing bin, dish soap, and a couple of scrub pads. If you've got the money, collapsible silicone cups and bowls are the best option. They are lightweight, take up minimal space, and are very easy to clean.

Basic cooking ingredients. Keep a handful of basic cooking ingredients on your car-camping packing list. At a minimum, pack a bottle of oil and some salt and pepper. Other useful items include eggs, flour, milk, sugar, honey or maple syrup, butter, hot sauce, soy sauce, and all-purpose spice blends such as Cajun or Greek seasonings.

The standard kitchen kit used by backcountry hunters, anglers, and backpackers is designed for one primary purpose: boiling water for instant oatmeal and freeze-dried meals. But that type of food gets old in a hurry. Fortunately, if you add just a few extras to your pack, it is possible to cook some surprisingly delicious food on backcountry trips. With nothing more than a backpacking stove, a small nonstick pot, and a miniature bottle of cooking oil, you can fry chunks of elk meat and simmer up a huckleberry sauce to drizzle on that elk meat. A piece of aluminum foil, some seasoned salt, a small lemon, and a campfire are all you need to transform a freshly caught trout and some wild mushrooms into a meal you'll remember forever.

BACKCOUNTRY KITCHEN KIT LIST

- BIC cigarette lighter(s)
- Fire-starting aids like cotton balls slathered in Vaseline
- Small, lightweight backpacking pot like MSR Trail Lite
- Large, folded piece of aluminum foil
- Sea to Summit long-handled titanium spork
- EDC knife for carving skewers and forks
- Small bottle of cooking oil
- Small bottle of seasoned salt, hot sauce, or any of the rubs in this book (see pages 347 and 355)

COOKING OVER FIRE

A cooking fire has a life cycle comprising three stages: youth, middle age, and old age. A young fire is flashy, with lots of flames dancing about and not much in the way of history—meaning that the base of the fire is lacking a bed of embers and charcoal. A young fire might look like it's kicking ass, but looks can be deceiving. The structure of the ignited wood could tip over, a heavy wind might blow through, or a bit of rain may fall and the fire dies. It has no real staying power. Young fires are only good for a fine point of intense heat located near the flame. It's okay for blackening a hot dog, but that's about it. On the other hand, an old fire at the end of its life cycle is nothing but fading embers; the last of the fuel has been consumed and now the fire is shedding its heat. Even if you toss new wood on an old fire, it might be too late to make a difference unless you stir up the coals and blow some air on it. Otherwise, the new log will do nothing but smolder and smoke. It has some use for warming foods, but that usefulness is waning.

That leaves a middle-aged fire, which is the fire you want. It's been burning for an hour or so and has a rich bed of coals and ash. Hold your hand a few inches over the bed of coals—you shouldn't be able to leave it more than a few seconds. A fresh log thrown on this charcoal bed will combust in short order, so it's possible to keep a fire like this going for as long as you care to feed it. It gives you a lot of options. You can pile the coals together in order to throw some intense heat on a steak for a good sear, or you can spread the coals out and get some nice, slow heat that'll penetrate a turkey breast without incinerating the outside. Or, you can do a bunch of things all at once: You've got a hot place for meat grilling, a bed of embers to brew a pot of coffee, and a few scoops of charcoal to place on top of a Dutch oven full of biscuits.

Of course, building a great cooking fire is easier said (and written) than done. It shouldn't be surprising that the people who are best at cooking over fires are the people who've been doing it the longest. There are all kinds of idiosyncrasies around wood qualities and climatic conditions that will complicate your efforts. Over time, you learn how to deal with them and make the appropriate adjustments. The information you'll find below, and sprinkled throughout the book, will hopefully shorten your journey to mastering the cooking fire by many years. Take it all in and start practicing. But make sure to remember the most important thing: Let that damn thing burn for a while!

STARTING A FIRE

Matches are about as antiquated as bow drills when it comes to starting fires. They get ruined when wet, and the strike pads are equally vulnerable to moisture and overuse. The most effective tool for getting fires started is an electric or propane grill torch. I don't personally have one of these, but I'd be excited if I found one in my Christmas stocking. Till then, I remain a devoted fan of the reliable, inexpensive BIC Classic lighter.

The tinder you use will depend a lot on where you're building your fire and the current weather conditions. If it's dry, you should be fine with a handful of paper or lightweight cardboard. Natural tinder supplies abound. You can make wood shavings with a pocket knife, or use an old bird nest or dry grass. A while back, my buddy Cal stumbled across an old dried-out pine stump that was caked in resin. He packed out enough of that fat wood to supply several of his friends with a lifetime supply of highly flammable, naturally waterproof tinder.

In rainy or windy conditions, your tinder might need a little booster. Lighter fluid is a standard option for many folks, but I don't use it very often, because it creates black soot and has an unpleasant odor. I'd rather use just a bean-sized hunk of Coghlan's Fire Paste. You'll find it in most sporting goods and hardware stores; a little goes a long way, so a tube should last you months or even years. For backpacking trips, I like a chewing tobacco tin filled with cotton balls slathered in petroleum jelly, aka Vaseline. These burn great, even when wet, and the Vaseline can also treat chapped lips, prevent chafing, and act as a lubricant on everything from tent zippers to the locking mechanisms on pocket knives.

Kindling is mid-sized fuel that comes between tinder and firewood. In other words, tinder ignites kindling and kindling ignites your primary pieces of firewood. The most common mistake I see from rookie fire builders is that they transition too aggressively from tinder to big pieces of wood. They think they've got a good fire going, but as soon as the tinder is exhausted, there's nothing to show for their efforts besides a little smoke. A dozen pieces of kindling, ranging from the thickness of a pencil to the diameter of your finger, will generally do the trick. You can split these pieces off larger blocks of firewood with a hatchet, or just search around for dry sticks.

If you're building a campfire for the ambience or to stay warm, you can burn pretty much any dry wood. For a cooking fire, the type of wood you burn is a more important consideration. We'll discuss cooking with different woods in a bit. For now, suffice it to say that your firewood needs to be thoroughly dry, or seasoned. If wet wood burns at all, it'll be smoky and weak. My fish shack in southeastern Alaska sits in one of the rainiest environments on the planet. You could walk around for days without finding a piece of wood on the ground that's dry enough to burn. The yellow cedar we cut and stack for our wood stove has to be seasoned for at least a year before we can even think about getting it burning, and even then it's not always easy. Ideally, it has dried in a covered place for two years. This place is an extreme anomaly, but I'm mentioning it to illustrate the lengths I'll go to in order to have dry wood at my disposal.

1. A hatchet can be used to split large, dry pieces of firewood into kindling, tinder, and small pieces of fuelwood.

2. Used in conjunction with a loose ball of natural tinder like dry grass and small twigs, artificial fire starters like the ones pictured here can come in handy in the backcountry during inclement weather.

AN IMPORTANT NOTE ON SAFETY AND WEATHER CONDITIONS

Let's say you've got plenty of dry wood on hand and you're ready to build a fire. Before you flick that lighter, you'll need to consider the weather conditions. Rainy days will make it challenging to get the fire started. Once you've got it cranking, though, a light drizzle won't have any impact at all; you can even keep a fire burning through a steady downpour, though it's a good idea to keep your wood under a tarp or other overhead cover. (A pro tip is to use your fire to dry out the wood that you'll be burning next.) Likewise, high winds can disperse the heat from your fire enough to make cooking difficult. A stiff wind can even extinguish small campfires. But these are problems that can be overcome with a little ingenuity: Place your fire in the lee of a natural windbreak or build a windbreak with a stack of rocks. A much larger concern with fires and high winds is one of safety, especially when those winds are coupled with hot, dry conditions.

Unfortunately, we are experiencing this type of weather pattern more than ever before in many areas of the country. Wildfire seasons have grown longer, and the number of fires per season has increased. Many of these wildfires are caused by people who are being careless. Others are caused by people who blatantly disregard rules. When handling fires and other cooking setups, you have to pay attention to what you're doing, and you need to obey fire restrictions. Otherwise, you not only risk shutting down millions of acres of public land to other uses, but you also risk killing innocent people and damaging invaluable ecological resources. There's not a burger in the world worth that.

Of course, a campfire can turn into a wildfire even without hot, dry winds. All it takes is for you to walk away from a fire that isn't properly extinguished. You'd be shocked by how well a smoldering fire can travel underground by following tree roots or other organic matter in the soil. I've personally seen fires pop out of the ground and start burning twenty feet away from my fire pit. That's one of the reasons I've started using metal fire pits such as Breeo stoves when I'm camping in the arid West. Wherever you make your fire, thoroughly douse it with water in order to put it out. Make sure to stir the water around so it reaches the buried coals. If possible, shovel a few scoops of dirt or sand over the fire as a final safety measure.

COOKING WITH DIFFERENT TYPES OF WOOD

The type of firewood you select will impact how hot your fire burns, how long the coals will last, and what flavors your food will absorb from the smoke. Hardcore barbecue fanatics are as picky about the species of the wood they cook over as they are about the quality of their meat, and experts like the Argentine chef Francis Mallmann and the American grilling aficionado Steven Raichlen have devoted many pages into the minutiae of the subject. While I have a great deal of respect for folks who pour that level of dedication into their craft, this isn't that kind of book. I appreciate the smoky flavor of a pizza cooked in an oak-fired oven and subtle sweetness of a trout smoked over applewood, but I've also cooked countless backcountry meals over plain old spruce or willow coals when there wasn't an oak or apple tree within hundreds of miles. While spruce and willow are generally regarded as poor choices for cooking, they've produced some of the best and most memorable meals that I've ever eaten.

The type of firewood we have access to is generally dictated by where we live. In the Northeast and Midwest, hardwoods like hickory, maple, and oak are readily available. In much of the South, pecan is a favorite. Mesquite is synonymous with Texas barbecue. Up in Alaska, alder is the wood of choice for smoking salmon, though cottonwood is commonly used if alder can't be found. Hardwood fruit trees like apple and cherry are available throughout much of the country, but in the Rockies you're often stuck with softwoods like aspen, pine, and spruce.

The flavor profiles different woods lend to your food are best approached in general terms. If you're planning on cooking over a pine or spruce fire, wait until the smoke dies down and you've got nothing but red-hot coals. (The resin in coniferous treewood produces a bitter smoke so don't use it in your smoker.) Alder, maple, and hardwood fruit trees are all known for their mild and sweet smoke that complements fish and fowl. On the other end of the spectrum, mesquite and hickory are often used in conjunction with meats that can handle a more powerful smoky flavor like venison, beef, and pork. Species like oak and pecan fall directly in the middle ground, with smoke that's described as nutty.

Of course, there's more to a cooking fire than the flavors it might produce. If you're making a stew in a Dutch oven, you'll need wood that creates hot coals that will smolder for a long time. A lot of research has gone into what happens when different types of wood are burned, including how fast or slow they burn and how much heat they produce. In terms of energy output, this information is expressed as a fuelwood's Btu (British thermal unit) value; one Btu is the amount of energy required to raise the temperature of one pound of water by a single degree Fahrenheit. The Btu value of firewood is measured by the amount of Btus (in millions) produced by one cord of seasoned (dry) wood. Fortunately, it's unnecessary to have an advanced degree in physics and chemistry to understand which types of wood have the best thermal qualities.

Regardless of the type of wood, moisture content plays a major role in heat output. Dry wood burns hot. When unseasoned wood is burned, much of its potential energy is wasted heating and vaporizing the water trapped inside. Next, in very basic terms, high-density hardwoods burn hotter and longer than low-density softwoods. The Btu value of black locust, for instance, is almost 28 million per cord, while red cedar measures in at just 13 million. If well-aged, hickory, oak, sugar maple, and apple all produce hot fires that burn for a long time. But don't get too hung up on Btu values. Even if all you have is a lower quality firewood like cottonwood that doesn't kick out as much heat, you can still produce a great meal.

COOKING-FIRE BUILDS

In the course of making this book, we refined lifetimes of outdoor cooking experience in order to serve you the best information on fire building. What we found was that the specific type of fire you build isn't nearly as important as how you maintain that fire. After all, you can't always control what types of wood you have access to, but you can control how you arrange it when constructing a fire. At home, you might have the time and resources to pull off an all-day fire in order to roast a whole hog for thirty guests. But on a remote backpacking trip, you might have to scrounge around for twenty minutes to find enough dry twigs to keep a small campfire burning long enough to cook yourself a single trout. On a car-camping trip, a cooking fire could fall anywhere in between these two spectrums. With that said, you'll find a lot of strong opinions out there on the best way to construct a cooking fire. A quick internet search will result in several build styles specific to over-the-fire cooking, a couple of which we describe in the following pages. But in the end, pretty much any basic fire-building strategy will work as long as you're familiar with a couple of different ways to manipulate the fire and the heat it produces for different cooking purposes.

A typical campfire is burned inside a ring of stones. The stones help prevent the fire from spreading, they absorb and contain heat, and they can mitigate the effects of wind gusts. Your fire ring doesn't have to be large; smaller fires are easier to manage. A three-foot-diameter ring is about right for a family meal, but you may need a larger one for big groups, and a smaller one will work just fine for one or two people. A selection of grapefruit- to volleyball-sized rocks are about right for making a fire ring from scratch. Just make sure to gather dry rocks; wet river rocks, especially those with hairline cracks that can trap moisture, will often split apart when exposed to high temperatures. Sometimes, they crack rather violently and send out showers of heated rock that can cut or burn.

TEEPEE FIRE

Just about every wilderness skills book out there, including my own, will tell you that building a teepee fire is the simplest and most efficient way to get a fire burning. Teepee fires are also ideal for getting bigger, longer-burning fires going. As the teepee burns down, slowly add larger pieces of fuelwood to create the coals you'll need for cooking.

1. First, place an artificial fire starter between two large pieces of kindling.

2. Place a layer of small kindling over the artificial fire starter.

3. Form a loose bundle of kindling over the tinder ball and ignite it. Blow on the flame lightly to encourage the kindling to burn.

4. When the kindling is burning steadily, begin forming a teepee frame with small pieces of fuelwood. Gradually add larger pieces of fuelwood to the teepee frame as needed.

LOG CABIN AKA HASHTAG FIRE

Rather than tending a teepee fire until it produces coals, you can speed up the process by building the frame for a "log cabin" fire around your teepee fire before you light it. The log cabin fire's stacked hashtag design creates plenty of airflow, which efficiently burns larger pieces of firewood from the inside out.

1. Build a tinder ball between two thick pieces of fuel-wood.

2. Stack layers of kindling over the tinder ball in a hashtag pattern.

3. Stack layers of larger fuelwood on top of the kindling in a hashtag pattern and ignite the tinder ball.

4. Add more fuelwood as necessary.

STUMP STOVE

Stump stoves, also known as Swedish fire logs, are one worthwhile exception to the rule of keeping your fire builds simple. Frankly, before I tried one out, I was skeptical of their efficacy. You'll have to be handy with a chainsaw to build a stump stove, but out of all the fires we built, this one burned the hottest and for the longest period of time. The fact that you need only a single log for a fire that'll burn at least a couple hours is reason enough to give it a try, but they have other distinct advantages as well. For starters, stump stoves are a super-efficient cooking system because the chainsaw cuts used to create them are made to draw air upward, like a chimney, instead of outward in all directions. In fact, there's not a better way to get a big pot of water boiling over a fire. They also make for a stable cooking platform; you can throw a big, heavy cast-iron skillet full of food directly on top of a stump stove without worrying about everything tipping over. It's worth cutting a few logs for stump stoves in advance of needing them, so you'll always have one around for the backyard or camp.

 To begin, you'll need a log from which you can cut several rounds between 18 and 24 inches long and about 10 to 12 inches in diameter.

1. First, cut a 4- to 6-inch square through the top that extends two-thirds the depth of the log.

2. Make two additional cuts inside the square. Next, make four cuts across the top of the log, dividing it into eight wedges that extend two-thirds of the way downward.

3. Here's what the log will look like at this point.

4. Create a vent by cutting a notch all the way through the side of the log, near the bottom.

5. Hollow out the cut at the top of the stove, removing as much wood as possible to create an open chimney.

6. Add some fire-starting gel, tinder, and kindling to the chimney and ignite it. Let the fire burn for a while, then use the top of the log as a cooking platform.

REFLECTOR FIRES

Reflector fires, which use rocks arranged to direct a fire's heat in a specific direction, are a very efficient way to keep warm when it's cold and windy. The rock wind barriers also act almost like an oven, so reflector fires excel in cooking situations, especially if you're working with a small fire that isn't producing a lot of hot coals. Build your fire right in front of a big boulder or prop up as many slabs of rock around the fire as you need to make a wall that contains and reflects heat. You can also arrange stones against the reflector wall to serve as a convenient cooking platform.

1. A reflector fire built against a stone slab to preheat the rocks.

2. The stone slab protects the cooking fire from wind and elements, while adding radiant heat to the pan.

KEYHOLE FIRES FOR COOKING

A keyhole fire is one the best setups for cooking over hot coals while maintaining an active fire at the same time. The fire (and the stone ring that surrounds it) is shaped like, you guessed it, a skeleton keyhole. The main body of the fire goes in the round part of the hole with the thin arm of the keyhole (lined with rocks) extending outward from there. It's here, away from the active flames, that you'll do your cooking. By using a shovel, coal rake, or stick, you can drag hot coals out of the main fire into the keyhole's slot. Depending on the width of the arm, you can balance a Dutch oven or grill grate directly over the narrow part. Otherwise you'll need to locate a stone slab big enough to create a platform that spans the gap.

01 OVER THE FLAMES

n 2009, I was given an ambitious assignment by *Outside* magazine to find the best steak in Argentina. This was one of the most exciting assignments I'd ever gotten. The Argentineans are regarded as masters of open-flame cooking. Here was a chance to get paid while studying their techniques.

First off, the beef in Argentina is outstanding. Their cattle eat a free-range diet of grass throughout their entire life instead of spending their final months confined to a pad of concrete while they slurp up prodigious volumes of corn. The meat is a little bit chewier than typical USDA Prime beef, but it has a more robust flavor. It's prepared simply but fastidiously: a bit of salt, then careful monitoring above an open flame.

What I liked even better than Argentinean beef was the grilling contraptions upon which it was cooked. Someone who is unfamiliar with outdoor grilling might mistake an Argentinean grill, or parrilla, for one of those medieval torture devices used to stretch people out. It features a chain and sprocket system with a big wheel that can be turned by hand to make micro adjustments to the height of the welded metal

grill. The fire table is at the height of a countertop, so the grill man, or asador, is looking pretty much eye to eye with the meat. The asador keeps a fire of hardwood burning at the edge of the fire table and uses a small shovel and a set of tongs to place embers and burning wood in strategic positions beneath the grill. No matter what, they don't ever let a flame make contact with the meat. To do so would be the moral equivalent of bestiality.

When I got back to America, I was dying to make one of these setups on my own back porch. I built a big table about as high as my belly button and stacked bricks on top of it to create a bunch of little shelves that would support my grill at whatever height I wanted it. For the floor of my fire table, I had a couple friends help me carry over a huge slab of landscaping slate that I'd pried up from the mud next to my garden.

The first time I used this grill was almost the last time I ever cooked anything. When that wet slate heated up beneath a burning mound of lump charcoal, the water trapped within the sedimentary layers of rock started to expand. At first I thought someone was shooting at me with a .22 rifle, but then I realized the slate was exploding with superheated rock fragments that were zipping all over the deck. Somehow I managed to escape unharmed. Later, when everything cooled off, I put what was left of that slate right back in the mud where I found it and replaced it with a piece of quarter-inch plate steel.

That jury-rigged Argentinean contraption was just one of a bazillion or so ways that I've grilled food over an open flame. I've cooked Dall sheep ribs and black bear loins on grills made of interwoven willow limbs supported by river cobbles. On a road trip down the entire length of Mexico's Baja peninsula, my buddies and I carried a wire shelf salvaged from a discarded refrigerator in the back of our rented minivan. At night we'd prop that thing on whatever was available, ranging from bricks to truck tires, and light a fire of

driftwood and coconut husks beneath it. Over the course of days, we grilled everything from onions to grouper to coconut meat on that thing. At the end of the trip, before leaving our last beach camp and heading to the airport, I hung that grill on a tree branch near our fire ring in hopes that someone else would find it and put it to good use.

Clearly, I've got as much love for grilling rigs as I do for grilled food. But if there's one thing I've learned from homemade grills, it's that store-bought grills are pretty damn nice. Turns out professional engineers know a thing or two about how to heat surfaces in a hurry with an efficient use of fuel and predictable results. My wife and I are currently raising three young kids, so this convenience means a lot to me these days. The kids often have after-school activities and we enforce bedtimes, so dinner needs to happen in an orderly and efficient fashion at night. In other words, I don't always have an hour to wander through the woods or rummage through a junk pile in search of some novelty that would hold a hunk of meat at an appropriate height above a flame. And since I'd never deny my kids or my wife and myself the pleasures and smells of outdoor grilling, we've slowly added conveniences such as a gas grill and an electric pellet grill to our outdoor cooking arsenal. It keeps us in the grilling game on a weekly basis, but without hot fragments of rock flying toward the kids' heads.

Of all the forms of outdoor cooking covered in this book, we're starting with the grilling chapter because grilling is a familiar and relatively easy way to produce great meals outside. From burgers to whole fish to spatchcocked fowl, you'll learn how to grill pretty much everything you can find from the top of the mountains to the bottom of the sea—including any grocery stores encountered along the way. Not only that, but we'll cover plenty of sauces and sides, along with strategies and recommended gear to keep you grilling great foods no matter where you might find yourself.

GRILLING: WHAT YOU NEED TO KNOW

In its simplest form, grilling is a cooking method that involves placing food on some sort of grate that sits over or near a dry heat source. Gas flames, wood fires, and charcoal briquettes can all be used as heat sources for grilling. Each will create a slightly different finished product (see page xxvi for more about this).

Cooking temperatures are typically high, often in excess of 500°F. The intense heat speeds up what's known as the Maillard reaction, which is a chemical process that breaks down proteins into amino acids that react with the sugars in your meat or veggies to produce a charred brown crust. The crust lends that complex and delicious umami flavor to grilled foods. The intense heat of a cooking grill also allows the outside of foods to be quickly seared without overcooking the inside. Although grilling is most often associated with the hot and fast cooking of foods like steaks, burgers, and fish fillets, you can also use a grill to slow roast foods such as whole birds, large cuts of meat, and even whole sheep, goats, or hogs. This is accomplished by using either a combination of direct and indirect heat or lower cooking temperatures.

When it comes to grilling (or any other method of cooking) wild game, I get asked over and over for recipes that pertain to specific species. My answer to those questions is always the same: Don't be concerned so much about the species as with the general characteristics of the flesh and the cut of meat you want to cook.

For hooved animals—including all species of deer, antelope, wild hogs, and even wild or feral sheep and goats—the cuts that work best for grilling are muscles without a lot of connective tissue. Backstraps, tenderloins, and roasts or steaks from the upper hind leg are best grilled hot and fast to medium-rare. Tough cuts like shanks and shoulders should be braised in liquid until nearly fork-tender before grilling. Another option is grinding tough cuts into burger or sausage with added beef or pork fat. A 1:10 fat-to-meat ratio works well for burger while a higher 2:10 ratio is ideal for sausage.

Much like big game animals, most upland game birds lack fat, and their legs can be tough and chewy. But the boneless breasts from just about any game bird are the equivalent of backstrap or tenderloin when it comes to grilling. It's fairly easy to get moist and tender results, especially if they've been brined or marinated in dairy first. The same goes for small whole plucked birds like quail and doves and like critters such as squirrels and rabbits. Large whole birds benefit from being spatchcocked before grilling (see page 75).

Grilling fish requires some special considerations, too. Thick chunks of firm-fleshed fish like tuna can be grilled with or without the skin, like a steak. Just be sure to oil both the grill grate and fillet to prevent sticking. When grilling more fragile fish, such as trout or bluefish, leaving the scaled skin on helps hold the fillet together. Grilling fish "on the half-shell" was popularized by Southern chefs working with unscaled, skin-on redfish fillets, but the technique works well with fish such as salmon that have sturdy skin and scales. Meanwhile, grilling whole fish without having the entire thing fall apart can be difficult. You can get around this by wrapping them in foil or banana leaves, but nothing beats a wire fish basket, especially for ultra-delicate fish such as flounder.

Direct Grilling

Direct grilling means the food is positioned directly over a heat source. When you're using a gas grill, direct heat means all of the burners are on, usually medium-high to high. For a charcoal grill or a grate over a wood fire, direct heat means the coals are spread evenly under the grate so that the food is positioned directly over the coals. With direct heat cooking, the entire area of the grill to be used for cooking is usually heated to the same approximate temperature.

Indirect Grilling

Indirect grilling involves creating two grill zones, one over medium-high or high heat, the other with no heat. This grilling setup gives you the most control over your grilling. It allows you to sear and char the outside of meats and vegetables over the direct heat and then move the food to continue cooking with indirect heat. (Think of the indirect portion of the grill like an oven—it's hot, but there's no concentrated or direct heat source below the food.) On a gas grill you can achieve this by turning off one of your burners. It can be the one in the middle on a three-burner setup, or on one side of the grill. On a charcoal grill, you can bank the hot coals off to one side or the other.

You can also set up your grill to create a single ambient grilling zone for long, slow cooks and for meat that drips a lot of fat, such as pork chops, duck, or beer-can chicken. Flare-ups from fat creates a lot of smoke and can impart nasty flavors. Ambient grilling solves this problem by allowing the fat to drip away from the heat source. It also helps to place a drip pan with an inch of water underneath the food to keep any dripping fat from running into the fire.

To set up on a gas grill, use one burner and place foods away from the heat source. On a charcoal grill, place coals to one side and offset the food to the other side; use the grill's lid to trap heat. With campfires, position your coals around the perimeter of the grill and place food in the center.

Cooking with Charcoal

The most useful accessory you can buy to simplify cooking on a charcoal grill is a charcoal chimney. In fact, we recommend getting the largest size you can find at your local home and garden store. Better yet, get two. A chimney expedites the process of getting coals hot enough for cooking, but it will still take a good 15 to 20 minutes before the coals are ready, so plan accordingly. Having plenty of coals on standby really helps when you're tackling a long grilling project or a large meal.

To light a chimney, follow these steps:

1. Fill the chimney with charcoal and set it on a heat-proof surface where you can safely light it.

2. Place a wad of newspaper or other tinder in the cavity at the bottom of the chimney reserved for tinder. Ignite the tinder.

3. The chimney is ready when the coals are smoldering, glowing orange, and showing some gray ash. This should take roughly 15 to 20 minutes.

4. Carefully pour the charcoal into the grill and arrange for direct or indirect heat.

5. Return the grate and close the lid to preheat the grill. Keep the vents open for oxygen flow.

With any grilling method, preheating is an important first step. Allow yourself adequate time to light a charcoal chimney, preheat a gas grill, or let a fire burn down to coals. When you take this step, the entire cooking process improves. A hot grill means you should be able to hold your hand a few inches from the grill for no longer than three to four seconds before having to pull it away. You'll also want to make sure your grates are very clean. Use a wire grill brush or a piece of wadded-up aluminum foil to scrape the grates.

After scraping, brush the hot grate with lightly oiled paper towels. If the food you're grilling already has oil or an oily marinade, you can skip the step of oiling the grate. The bottom line is that oil helps keep food from sticking to the grates. Just don't overdo it— if you use too much, you'll get flare-ups.

WHEN TO OIL GRILL GRATES

Should you oil your grill grates or rub down your meats and veggies? This topic is widely debated among grilling pros. But whether you oil your grates or load your grill with food that's already well greased, the bottom line is that oil helps keep food from sticking to the grates. If the food you're grilling already has oil or an oily marinade, you can skip the step of oiling the grate. If it doesn't and you're working with a steak with a dry rub or basting with a sticky glaze, oil the grate. Using tongs, brush the hot grate with lightly oiled paper towels. Don't overdo it—if you use too much oil, you'll get a flare-up.

BACKCOUNTRY GRATE

You might find yourself in a situation where you want to grill a bird, a fish, or a chunk of meat over a fire but don't have a metal grate. Fortunately, it's not all that difficult to make your own. In fact, this is something I do on a regular basis when I can carry only a limited amount of gear on backcountry hunts. Here's how to do it with just a knife or a hatchet and some green sticks:

1. Use a handsaw or hatchet to cut four sturdy green legs that end in a Y and are about 18 inches long. Arrange these legs in a square or rectangle 18 to 24 inches wide and pound them several inches into the ground.

2. Cut two more green support poles that span the gap between the leg poles. Rest them in the Ys of the legs.

3. Make a grilling grate with as many green sticks as needed.

4. Remove the sticks from the grate and light a fire. When the fire is hot, return the sticks to their position to form the grate. Add food and grill.

STICKY AND SWEET GRILLED FROG LEGS

SERVES 4 TO 6 AS AN APPETIZER

Bullfrogs are a popular food item in many rural areas of the American South, where gigging frogs at night is an age-old pastime. In many other parts of the country, the resource is hardly exploited. Where I grew up, in western Michigan, there are swamps that haven't seen a serious bullfrog hunter in decades. In terms of texture and flavor, frog legs bridge the gap between fish and fowl. The bulk of those harvested in the United States are breaded and fried, although the traditional French-style garlic-butter-and-lemon preparation is worth trying. This version is inspired in part by Chinese cuisine and delivers a sticky-sweet umami punch. It's the perfect appetizer to gnaw on while grilling up the rest of your dinner.

FOR THE SAUCE. In a small bowl, whisk together the honey, hoisin sauce, soy sauce, wine, sesame oil, five-spice powder, and garlic. Set aside.

FOR THE FROG LEGS. Prepare a medium-hot grill for direct and indirect grilling. Spread the coals in the center of the grill, allowing space around the edges for indirect grilling.

Rinse the frog legs and pat them dry with paper towels. Put them into a large bowl and drizzle with the oil. Sprinkle with the salt and pepper and toss to combine.

Arrange the frog legs on a well-oiled grill. Grill on one side for 4 to 5 minutes, brushing with the sauce several times. When the meat on the grill side becomes opaque, forms grill marks, and releases easily from the grill, it's time to flip. (If they stick, let them sit another minute.) Flip and move them away from the coals slightly, with the meatier sides closer to the heat. Cook, brushing occasionally with the sauce, until the legs are lacquered and cooked through, 5 to 6 more minutes. You'll know they are cooked through when the meat is fully opaque and loosens from the bone when pierced with a fork.

Serve immediately.

The sauce can be made well over a week ahead, but do not add the garlic until you're ready to use the sauce. Store in an airtight container at room temperature.

STICKY AND SWEET SAUCE

Yield ⅔ cup; serves 4 to 6 as an appetizer

3 tablespoons honey

2 tablespoons hoisin sauce

1 tablespoon soy sauce

1 tablespoon Shaoxing wine (see Cook's Note)

1 teaspoon toasted sesame oil

½ teaspoon five-spice powder

2 garlic cloves, grated

FROG LEGS

1¾ to 2 pounds bullfrog legs

1 tablespoon canola oil, plus more for grilling

2 teaspoons kosher salt

½ teaspoon ground white pepper

ALSO WORKS WITH. *The legs from common green frogs, though they're quite a bit smaller than the legs from bullfrogs. Plan on two or three times the quantity to get the same weight. This marinade works with parcooked rabbit or squirrel legs, as well as quail and other small game birds. It is also good for chicken wings and makes a good glaze for salmon or shrimp.*

COOK'S NOTE. *Shaoxing wine is a Chinese rice wine available online or at Asian grocers across the country. While Shaoxing does have a unique flavor, you can use Japanese rice wine or mirin as a substitute.*

STUFFIES

SERVES 8 AS AN APPETIZER

CLAMS

Kosher salt

12 topneck quahogs (about 3½ pounds), scrubbed clean

STUFFING

½ pound raw (soft) chorizo

Kosher salt

Olive oil for the pan, as needed

2 tablespoons unsalted butter

1 medium onion, finely chopped (about 1 cup)

1 celery rib, finely chopped (about ½ cup)

2 garlic cloves, minced

1 medium red bell pepper, cored and finely chopped

20 Ritz crackers, finely ground (about 1 cup)

1 cup fresh flat-leaf parsley leaves and tender stems, finely chopped

Lemon wedges and hot sauce, for serving

ALSO WORKS WITH. *Any large hard-shelled clam whose shell can be reused for stuffing—choose clams that can hold ¼ to ½ cup of filling.*

COOK'S NOTE. *Topneck clams are 3 to 4 inches in diameter and are the most widely available. If larger or smaller clams are used, adjust the yield of cooked meat; you will need ½ cup minced clam meat.*

These old-school appetizers hail from coastal New England—Rhode Island to be specific—where quahog clams are a regional favorite. Italian and Portuguese immigrants are said to have popularized this dish, but its true origins are unknown. You'll find recipes using a range of sausages that represent both of these southern European cultures. Traditionally these recipes used quahog clams, which have rich flesh and a strong briney flavor. But the recipe would work with pretty much any clam. For sausage, we're using a soft chorizo. You can use store-bought or homemade chorizo as well as Portuguese linguiça. The crackers that you use should be as basic as they come: oyster crackers, saltines, or a buttery cracker such as Ritz. (The latter option is my favorite.)

TO PURGE AND COOK THE CLAMS. Fill a large bowl with about 8 cups cold water. Add 3 tablespoons salt. Add the scrubbed clams; the water should cover them. Let sit at room temperature for 30 minutes to 1 hour to purge any sand or dirt. Remove the clams and rinse them in a colander. If the clams are exceptionally dirty or sandy, repeat the purging step.

Add 1 to 2 inches water to a saucepan and bring to a boil. Carefully add the clams, lower the heat to a simmer, and cover the pan. Cook for about 8 minutes, until all the clams open. Place the clams in a colander in the sink to drain, reserving the cooking liquid. When the clams are cool enough to handle, remove the meat. Mince the clam meat (you should have about ½ cup minced clams) and set aside. Rinse 8 of the whole clam shells and twist them apart. Lay the shells upside down on a baking sheet. Discard the remaining shells.

FOR THE STUFFING. Heat a large skillet over medium-high heat. Add the chorizo, sprinkle with ½ teaspoon salt, and break apart with a wooden spoon. If necessary, add a little olive oil to keep the chorizo from sticking to the pan. Continue to break into small pieces until cooked through, about 5 minutes, then transfer to a small bowl. Remove all but a thin layer of fat from the pan. Return the skillet to medium-high heat and melt the butter. Add the onion, celery, and garlic, stir together, and cook for 30 seconds. Add the bell pepper and ¼ teaspoon salt and cook until softened, about 8 minutes. Remove from the heat and stir in the minced clams, cracker crumbs, and parsley. Stir ¼ cup of the reserved clam broth into the stuffing. You want the stuffing to be moist and hold together. Add more broth if needed. You should have about 3 cups stuffing.

Prepare a grill for direct medium heat.

Fill each clam shell half with 3 tablespoons of the filling. Place the clams directly on the grill and cover for 2 minutes. Uncover the grill and continue to cook until the filling is bubbling and the tops are lightly crisped. Check after 5 minutes, although it could take as long as 10 minutes. If making these indoors in an oven, finish by browning the tops under a broiler.

Remove the stuffies to a platter and serve with lemon wedges, hot sauce, and a cold beer.

UNDERSTANDING QUAHOG VARIETIES

Quahogs are found on the East Coast from Canada to Florida. Most states require a license to harvest the clams, which are sold under names according to their size. Littlenecks (1½ to 2 inches) are the smallest and sweetest. Cherrystones (under 3 inches) are the second most desirable. These first two varieties are used in raw bars, steamed, and in pasta dishes. Topnecks (3 to 4 inches) are a medium-sized clam that can be sliced into strips and deep-fried or used in stuffie recipes like this one. Chowder clams (over 4 inches) are the largest and toughest of all. They're usually minced for chowders and stews.

Whether you're harvesting your own clams or buying them at a seafood market, there are plenty of suitable substitutes for the various quahog varieties. On the East Coast, Atlantic surf clams are widely available, and clam diggers on the West Coast have several options including razor clams, Pacific little-necks, Washington clams, and Manila clams.

BEAVER CONFIT TOASTS
WITH GRILLED FIGS AND BALSAMIC-HONEY GLAZE

MAKES ABOUT 24 TOASTS

CURE

1½ to 2 pounds bone-in beaver thigh or equivalent

¼ cup kosher salt

8 fresh thyme sprigs

2 fresh rosemary sprigs

2 garlic cloves, smashed

CONFIT

10 fresh thyme sprigs

4 fresh rosemary sprigs

2 garlic cloves, smashed

2 bay leaves

1 shallot, sliced

1 teaspoon freshly ground black peppercorns

Duck fat, bear grease, beef tallow, or olive oil (see Cook's Notes)

BALSAMIC-HONEY GLAZE

¼ cup balsamic vinegar

¼ cup honey

GRILLED FIGS

12 small fresh figs, stemmed and halved (see Cook's Notes)

1 tablespoon extra-virgin olive oil

¼ teaspoon kosher salt

TOASTS

1 baguette, cut on the bias into 24 slices

Reserved duck fat (optional)

I've read pretty much everything there is to read about the Rocky Mountain beaver trappers of the early nineteenth century. It's common knowledge that these fellas, otherwise known as mountain men, were big into eating beaver tails. When I first started cooking beaver tails in an effort to mimic their preparations, the results were so bad that I figured there must be some confusion about what exactly a beaver tail is. By "tail," maybe they meant the tail end, or rump of the beaver? While I eventually realized that they were in fact eating the black, scaly tails of beavers (they were after the fat inside), the experimentations led me to discover just how good the thighs are. I've been eating them for years in simple braised dishes. I also like to corn them, similar to how you'd fix corned beef for St. Paddy's Day. However, this preparation here is my all-time favorite. It came about when I substituted beaver thighs for goose thighs in a confit recipe. Here's a slightly modified and dressed-up version of that original preparation. It's probably the classiest thing you can do with a beaver thigh. And it's definitely the best.

FOR THE CURE. Put the beaver thigh in a resealable container and rub it all over with the salt. Scatter half of the thyme, rosemary, and garlic in the bottom of the container, then top with the beaver thigh and the remaining aromatics. Cover and refrigerate for 48 hours.

FOR THE CONFIT. Preheat the oven to 250°F. Thoroughly rinse the salt off the beaver thigh and pat dry. Place the thigh in a small, narrow baking vessel (like a loaf pan) set on top of a baking sheet. Scatter the thyme, rosemary, garlic, bay leaves, shallot, and peppercorns over the thigh in the loaf pan. Pour enough fat over the beaver to completely cover it. If you don't have enough fat to cover, add olive oil or avocado oil to top it off. Cover tightly with an oven-safe lid or aluminum foil. Cook until the beaver is very tender and shreds easily, 4 to 5 hours. Let the beaver cool in the fat. Discard the aromatics, cover, and refrigerate until ready to serve.

FOR THE GLAZE. In a small bowl, combine the balsamic vinegar and honey and whisk together until blended.

TO REHEAT. Prepare a grill for medium-high heat. Remove the beaver from the fat, then shred the meat (you should have about 2 cups). Heat a cast-iron pan or other heavy grill-safe pan on the grill. Add the beaver to the pan and heat gently until just warmed. If necessary, add more fat to keep it from sticking to the pan. Set aside.

FOR THE FIGS. In a bowl, toss the halved figs with oil and salt. Place them on the grill and cook until grill marks appear, about 2 minutes. Flip and lightly grill another 1 to 2 minutes, until they soften. Transfer to a cutting board. Cut each piece into halves. (See Cook's Notes for dried figs method.)

ASSEMBLE THE TOASTS. Dab the sliced bread with fat, if desired. Grill the bread on both sides until lightly toasted but still soft in the center. Top each toast with a generous tablespoon of the confit beaver and 2 fig quarters. Drizzle with the balsamic-honey glaze and serve.

COOK'S NOTES. *You'll need about 3½ cups duck/animal fat to cover the meat in oil if you're using a 10 × 5-inch loaf pan.*

To prepare when figs are out of season, use dried figs. Rehydrate them in warm water and add to a small saucepan with warm balsamic-honey glaze.

MAKE AHEAD. *The confit can be made up to 1 month in advance and stored in the fridge submerged under its fat. Or frozen up to 6 months. The glaze can be made up to 1 week in advance and stored in the fridge.*

CHEESEBURGER POPPERS

SERVES 10 TO 12 AS AN APPETIZER

Poppers are one of my favorite ways to use up smaller quantities of game meat. While I often use the breasts from quails or doves to make poppers, this version is ideal for using up the excess of ground game meat that every hunter seems to have in their freezer. This version is an ode to the cheeseburger, and boy does it nail it. It's fun for entertaining a group, and it can easily be doubled (or tripled) for a crowd. It makes a great appetizer for that first night of a car-camping trip. Whatever happens, don't skip the dipping sauce.

FOR THE FILLING. Heat the oil in a large skillet over medium-high heat. Add the onions and cook 3 to 4 minutes, stirring until softened. Push to the side of the pan, then add the ground elk and sprinkle with ¾ teaspoon salt and a few grinds of pepper. Break the meat up with a spoon and incorporate the onions into the meat. Cook the meat all the way through, 5 to 6 minutes. Stir in the tomatoes and relish and remove from the heat. Let cool.

Halve the jalapeños lengthwise and remove the seeds. Top each half with about 2 tablespoons of the meat filling. Arrange the filled jalapeños in flat layers in a storage container (use foil to separate the layers) and refrigerate until ready to grill.

FOR THE DIPPING SAUCE. In a small storage container, stir together the mayonnaise, ketchup, and onion powder. Refrigerate until ready to serve.

FOR THE POPPERS. Prepare a grill or wood fire with a grate for direct heat. Place the poppers on the grill and cook until the jalapeños are lightly charred, 7 to 10 minutes. Top each popper with half a slice of cheese. Cover the grill and cook for another minute, or until the cheese melts. Serve with the dipping sauce.

FILLING

1 tablespoon vegetable oil

½ red onion, diced (½ cup)

¾ pound ground game meat

Kosher salt and freshly ground black pepper

1 small plum tomato, diced (½ cup)

2 tablespoons pickle relish

12 large jalapeño peppers

12 American cheese slices, halved

DIPPING SAUCE

½ cup mayonnaise

1 tablespoon ketchup

¼ teaspoon onion powder

ALSO WORKS WITH. *All types of ground meat, wild or domestic. If using wild hog or bear, be sure to cook the meat to well done on the first step.*

MAKE AHEAD. *The filling can be made up to 1 week in advance or frozen for up to 2 months. The dipping sauce can be refrigerated for 2 weeks or kept in a cooler for up to 3 days.*

GRILLED TONGUE TARTINES
WITH ZUCCHINI, CORN, AND CILANTRO-LIME CREMA

Danielle Prewett

As a native Texan, I frequently eat foods that are heavily influenced by Tex-Mex cuisine. This culinary tradition really shines through with this tartine recipe. If you're new to tartines, it's just a fancy word for an open-faced sandwich. This one is layered with grilled zucchini, romaine, and sweet corn. The chile rub on the tongue adds the perfect amount of heat and vibrant red color to an otherwise unattractive piece of meat. A quick sear on the grill adds caramelization and incredible flavor. The texture reminds me of lamb shawarma from Middle Eastern cuisine, the kind that's been shaved off a vertical rotisserie. It's very tender and very delicious!

SERVES 6 TO 8 AS AN APPETIZER OR 4 AS A MAIN

CHILE RUB

2 teaspoons coarse sea salt

1½ teaspoons ancho chile powder

1 teaspoon brown sugar

½ teaspoon dried oregano

¼ teaspoon ground cumin

¼ teaspoon cayenne pepper

GARNISH

Cilantro-Lime Crema (recipe follows)

Quick Pickled Red Onion (recipe follows)

Chopped fresh cilantro leaves

TARTINES

1 elk tongue or 2 deer tongues
(about 12 ounces total)

1 garlic head, halved but unpeeled

2 bay leaves

½ bunch fresh cilantro, sprigs and
stems separated

Neutral-flavored oil (such as avocado
or grapeseed oil)

2 medium zucchini

Kosher salt and freshly ground black pepper

2 ears of corn with husks

8 slices sourdough bread

1 cup shredded romaine lettuce

½ cup cotija cheese

FOR THE CHILE RUB. Stir together the sea salt, chile powder, brown sugar, oregano, cumin, and cayenne in a small bowl and set aside.

FOR THE TARTINES. Start by cooking the tongue in a large pot with water to cover. Add the halved garlic head, bay leaves, and cilantro stems. Bring to a boil, skim off any scum that rises to the surface, and reduce to a low simmer. Cook for about 4 hours, or until the tongue is tender when pierced with a fork. Keep in mind that tongues from older animals may take longer to braise.

Remove the tongue from the water and let it cool enough to handle. While still warm, use a knife or your fingers to peel away the outer skin. (This step can be done up to a day in advance.) Transfer the peeled tongue to a refrigerator or freezer for 15 to 20 minutes to firm up; this makes it easier to slice. Slice the chilled tongue into thin ⅛-inch pieces at a 45-degree angle to create wider pieces of meat and place it in a bowl.

Drizzle enough oil over the meat to fully coat it and season generously with the chile rub.

Using a mandoline or sharp knife, slice the zucchini lengthwise into ⅛-inch-thick pieces. Brush both sides with oil and season with kosher salt and black pepper. Set aside until ready to grill.

Recipe continues

Prepare and preheat a grill. If using propane or charcoal, make a small foil packet with wood chips to infuse a smoke flavor. Grill the whole corn, husks intact, over medium-high heat with the lid closed for 15 minutes. Remove and shuck the corn when it's cool enough to handle. Brush the corn with oil and season with kosher salt and black pepper. Increase the heat of the grill to high heat. Return the corn and lightly char it on all sides. Remove and cool to room temperature, then use a sharp knife to cut the kernels off the cob. Set aside.

Oil the grill grates. Working in batches, grill the zucchini strips over high heat for 1 to 2 minutes on each side, just until you see char marks. Don't overcook it or it will turn to mush. Remove when ready and continue with the remaining zucchini. The zucchini will soften into beautiful ribbons when it cools.

Finally, brush the sliced bread lightly with oil. Place the bread and the sliced tongue on the grill. Grill the bread on both sides until toasted. Grill the tongue for a couple minutes on each side until lightly seared. (You can also prepare this recipe in a cast-iron skillet over a campfire.)

Assemble each tartine by layering the toasted bread with tongue, romaine, zucchini, and corn. Top with crema and garnish with a spoonful of cotija cheese, some pickled onions, and cilantro.

CILANTRO-LIME CREMA

1 cup Mexican crema or sour cream

1½ limes, zested and juiced

½ jalapeno, chopped

½ bunch of cilantro, chopped

1 clove of garlic

Combine all of the ingredients for the crema together in a small food processor. Pulse until you reach a smooth consistency. Store in an airtight container in the refrigerator until ready to serve.

QUICK PICKLED RED ONION

1 red onion, sliced with the grain

1 cup white vinegar, apple cider vinegar, or lime juice

1 cup water

2 tablespoons sugar

2 teaspoons coarse sea salt

Place the sliced onion in a mason jar. Heat the vinegar, water, sugar, and salt in a small saucepan over high heat. Once it boils, remove from heat and stir to combine. Pour the hot vinegar over the onions. Once the vinegar has cooled completely, place a lid on top and store in the refrigerator. This is best done in advance and served cold.

STUFFED VENISON BURGERS, THREE WAYS

MAKES 4 BURGERS

1½ pounds ground venison, with an 80/20 ratio of meat to added fat

Neutral oil for grill

Kosher salt

Freshly ground black pepper

4 hamburger buns

Condiments and toppings of your choice

ALSO WORKS WITH. *Beef burger, or any ground big game meat mixed with added fat. If using wild hog or bear meat, bring the internal temperature of your burger to 160°F for safety.*

ADDITIONAL FLAVOR COMBINATIONS

Kalamata olives, feta, and capers

Cheddar, diced apple, and smoked ham

Shredded mozzarella, marinara, and breadcrumbs

Pimiento cheese and chopped pickle

Manchego cheese and membrillo (quince paste)

Sauerkraut, Russian dressing, and shredded Swiss cheese

Because game meat is inherently lean, it takes a bit of skill to grill a juicy game burger. Adding beef fat or pork fat certainly helps, but it's still way easier to mess up a game burger than a standard beef burger. This recipe, for stuffed burgers, is perhaps the most surefire way to grill the game burger of your dreams. The filling combos are endless, but I've outlined three of them here, along with some additional options in the sidebar below. Whatever you choose as a stuffing, the process is the same. This can be a fun project with kids, so get them involved. These recipes can also be doubled or quadrupled, depending on the crowd you're feeding.

If you're making these for car camping, fully assemble and chill the burgers overnight before transporting them to the campground. Grill and serve them on the first or second night of camp for best results.

CHILLING AND GRILLING. Form the ground venison into eight (3-ounce) balls. Then gently pat out to 3½ inches wide and ¼ inch thick. Assemble and stuff the burgers according to the specific filling recipe of your choice. Cover and chill the patties for at least an hour before grilling. This helps them hold together.

TO GRILL. Prepare a charcoal, propane, or wood fire grill for high-heat direct grilling. Grease the grill grate.

Sprinkle both sides of the patties with salt and pepper. Place on the grill and cook until the bottoms form a light brown crust, about 5 minutes. Flip the patties. Grill a few more minutes, until the other side browns and the internal temperature of the meat is 130°F to 135°F for a medium-rare burger. (If you're making the Green Chili Cheeseburger, add cheese and cover with the lid for a minute to help the cheese melt.) Remove the burgers from the grill to a platter.

Put a burger on each hamburger bun and serve with your favorite condiments and toppings.

1. Form the ground venison into eight 3-ounce balls. Then gently pat each out to measure 3½ inches wide and ¼ inch thick.

2. Spread a heaping tablespoon of your filling (see recipes on following page) into the center of four of the patties.

3. Place plain patties on top of the filling-topped patties and press edges together to seal.

BACON JAM AND BLUE CHEESE FILLING

MAKES ABOUT ½ CUP

FOR THE BACON JAM. Add the bacon to a medium skillet and cook over medium heat, flipping occasionally, for about 10 minutes. Add the onions and cook, stirring occasionally, until they are softened, about 10 more minutes. Add the vinegar, 2 tablespoons water, and the brown sugar and, when it starts to simmer, turn the heat to low and cook until the onions are very soft and jammy and little liquid remains, about 10 more minutes. This mixture can be made up to 1 week in advance and stored in the refrigerator.

TO ASSEMBLE. Gently smoosh a heaping teaspoon of the blue cheese in the center of 4 of the patties. Next, add 2 teaspoons of the bacon jam per patty. Place the remaining 4 patties on top and press the edges to seal. Follow the burger chilling and grilling instructions.

4 slices thick-cut bacon (4 ounces), chopped

1 medium onion, thinly sliced with the grain (about 2 cups)

2 tablespoons balsamic vinegar

1 tablespoon light brown sugar

2 ounces blue cheese, crumbled

BOURBON-GINGER MUSHROOMS WITH GRUYÈRE FILLING

MAKES A HEAPING ⅓ CUP

FOR THE MUSHROOM MIXTURE. Heat a large skillet over medium-high heat. Add the butter to melt and then add the mushrooms. Cook and stir for 5 to 6 minutes, until soft. Add the ginger, ¼ teaspoon salt, and a few grinds of pepper. Stir and cook until fragrant, about 30 seconds. Remove from the heat and add the bourbon. Return to the heat and cook until the liquid is incorporated. Set aside to cool. This mixture can be made a week in advance and stored in the refrigerator.

TO ASSEMBLE. Evenly divide the bourbon-ginger mushrooms among 4 patties (about 1 tablespoon per patty). Top with a quarter of the shredded Gruyère. Place the remaining 4 patties on top and press the edges to seal. Follow burger chilling and grilling instructions.

2 tablespoons unsalted butter

4 ounces cremini mushrooms, finely chopped

1 (1-inch) piece ginger, peeled and grated (1½ teaspoons)

Kosher salt and freshly ground black pepper

2 tablespoons bourbon

1 ounce Gruyère, shredded (about ¼ cup)

GREEN CHILE CHEESEBURGER FILLING

TO ASSEMBLE. Pile 1 tablespoon of the chiles in the center of 4 patties. Place the remaining 4 patties on top and press the edges to seal. Follow the burger chilling and grilling instructions. Add a slice of Monterey Jack cheese on top of each burger during the last minute of grilling.

4 tablespoons diced green Hatch chiles

4 slices Monterey Jack cheese

A FEW FANCY WAYS TO DRESS UP YOUR HOT DOGS

SERVES 4 TO 6

Hot dogs and bratwurst are plenty tasty with just a squirt of mustard, but the magic really happens when they're paired with the right toppings. No matter how you cook your dogs—on a grill, on a griddle, or over a fire—these tried-and-true toppings add layers of flavor and texture that turn simple dogs into a masterpiece. Use any of your favorite hot dogs, brats, or other sausages, or make the Camp Sausage recipe on page 36. All of these toppings can be made in advance of a camping trip or on-site.

Choose a topping combination; each topping makes enough for up to 6 dogs.

4 to 6 cooked hot dogs or Camp Sausages (page 36)

4 to 6 hot dog buns or long Italian rolls

KIMCHI SLAW

MAKES 1½ CUPS

Stir the mayonnaise, kimchi juice, lime juice, sesame oil, and salt together in a medium bowl. Add the cabbage, kimchi, cilantro, and scallions. Toss to coat.

Put a hot dog in a bun. Spoon some kimchi slaw over top. Serve immediately.

COOK'S NOTE. *We've made this with napa cabbage, which is tender and has a flavor that is mild and sweet. You can swap with a sturdier savoy cabbage or a green cabbage if that's all that is available.*

MAKE AHEAD. *Although this slaw can be prepped ahead of time, it shouldn't be assembled until ready to serve as it gets soggy quickly. Combine the dressing ingredients, store them in a resealable container, and refrigerate; prep the slaw components, omitting the kimchi, and refrigerate. When ready to serve, combine the slaw with the dressing and kimchi.*

DRESSING

1 tablespoon mayonnaise

2 teaspoons kimchi juice

1 teaspoon fresh lime juice

1 teaspoon toasted sesame oil

¼ teaspoon kosher salt

SLAW

⅛ head napa cabbage, finely chopped (about 1 cup or ¼ pound; see Cook's Note)

½ cup kimchi, chopped

½ cup packed fresh cilantro, chopped

2 scallions, white and green parts, thinly sliced

CHICAGO-STYLE RELISH

MAKES 1¼ CUPS

5 teaspoons sweet relish

¼ medium white onion, chopped (⅓ cup)

1 medium plum tomato, chopped (heaping ½ cup)

1 whole jarred kosher dill pickle, chopped

4 sport peppers, pickled serrano peppers, or peperoncini, finely chopped

¼ teaspoon celery salt

¼ teaspoon poppy seeds (optional)

Yellow mustard, for serving

In a small bowl, stir together the relish, onions, tomatoes, dill pickles, peppers, celery salt, and poppy seeds (if using).

Put a hot dog in a bun. Squiggle yellow mustard on top and generously spoon about 3 tablespoons of the Chicago-style relish over the top.

PEPERONATA-STYLE

MAKES 2 CUPS

2 tablespoons olive oil

2 medium red bell peppers, sliced into strips ½ inch thick

1 medium yellow bell pepper, sliced into strips ½ inch thick

1 jalapeño pepper, seeded and sliced into strips ¼ inch thick

1 medium yellow onion, halved, sliced ½ inch thick with the grain

2 garlic cloves, minced

1 teaspoon dried oregano or 1 fresh thyme sprig

1½ teaspoons kosher salt

1 tablespoon red wine vinegar

4 to 6 slices provolone cheese (roughly ¼ pound)

Hot sauce, for serving

Heat the oil in a 4-quart saucepan over medium-high heat. Add the peppers, onions, garlic, oregano, and salt. Cook, stirring occasionally, until the onions start to stick to the bottom, about 10 minutes. Splash in ½ cup of water, then reduce the heat to medium-low. Cover with a lid and continue to cook for 10 minutes, stirring occasionally, adding a little water as needed if the onions stick. Cook until the peppers are very soft. Remove the lid and raise the heat to medium-high to evaporate any excess liquid. When the mixture is stewlike and very soft, about 30 minutes total, turn off the heat. Remove from the heat. Stir in the vinegar.

Place a slice of provolone in each bun. Add a hot dog and top with peperonata. Serve with hot sauce.

CAMP SAUSAGE

MAKES 10 POUNDS LINKED OR BULK SAUSAGE

8 pounds lean game meat, cut into 1-inch cubes

2 pounds pork fatback, cut into 1-inch cubes

20 feet of natural hog casings (32 to 35 millimeters in diameter; optional)

4¼ tablespoons kosher salt

2 tablespoons ground white pepper

1 tablespoon fresh thyme leaves

1½ teaspoons caraway seeds

1½ teaspoons ground nutmeg

1½ teaspoons ground allspice

1½ teaspoons ground ginger

1½ tablespoons crushed red pepper flakes

3 tablespoons minced garlic

¾ cup white wine vinegar or champagne vinegar, chilled

½ cup ice water

SPECIAL EQUIPMENT

Meat grinder

I used to mess around with a buddy of mine trying to make traditional hot dogs from wild game. The process is a pain in the ass, and I was never entirely happy with the results. Instead, I now prefer to make a basic camp sausage that can stand in for hot dogs and still be used for a variety of other purposes. You can braise them just like a bratwurst in a mixture of beer, butter, herbs, and onion. After braising, you can grill them to finish. Or poach them in water with a splash of wine, then grill; this helps prevent them from bursting open on the grill. You can also hot-smoke these sausages if you'd like; see the Cook's Notes for instructions.

This sausage is based on an 80/20 mixture of lean game meat and pork fatback. You can raise the fat level to 70/30 for a juicier sausage that's not overly greasy. Alternatively, you can sub a pound or three of lean game meat for something like pork butt if you desire, but the 80 percent wild game version is just fine. Use natural hog casings with diameters between 32 and 35 millimeters.

TO GET STARTED. Place the cubed meat and fat in a bowl in the freezer to chill and harden, but don't freeze them all the way through. Meanwhile, set up your meat grinder according to the manufacturer's instructions and soak the natural hog casings (if using) in lukewarm water. Once the casings are pliable, change the water and soak them another 20 to 30 minutes. Then fit one end of each casing over the kitchen faucet and run a cup or two of water into the casing. Push the water all the way through to rinse the inside of the casing. Set aside in clean water until ready to use.

TO GRIND THE SAUSAGE. Combine the chilled cubed meat and pork fat with the salt, white pepper, thyme, caraway seeds, nutmeg, allspice, ginger, and red pepper flakes in a large bowl and mix well to coat evenly. Cover and marinate in the refrigerator for 24 hours for the best flavor.

Fill a tub with ice and place the bowl of chilled meat inside the tub to keep it cool. Using a medium die, grind the sausage mixture into another bowl that's also set in a tub filled with ice. Using a rubber spatula, fold in the garlic and vinegar, distributing them evenly. While it's not necessary, it wouldn't hurt to further combine the mixture in a stand mixer with the paddle attachment for a smoother consistency, or you could run it one more time through the medium die (it will still make a great sausage if you skip this extra step). The mixture should be like a wet paste. If it does not seem moist, add up to ½ cup ice water as needed. Cover and refrigerate while you set up your sausage stuffer to either case the meat in the soaked hog casings or divide it into 1-pound poly bags as bulk sausage.

STUFF THE SAUSAGES. Fill the hopper of your sausage stuffer with the sausage mixture. Crank the handle to clear all the air out of the stuffer tube and fit the tube with a clean casing. Tie a simple granny knot in the end of the casing. Working slowly, stuff the sausage into the casing. Be careful not to overstuff, and expel any large air bubbles inside the casing by pricking it multiple times with a sewing needle. When filled, tie off the casing with another granny knot.

TO CREATE LINKS. With the end of the casing tied off in a granny knot, make two creases in the casing, one 5 inches from the end and another at 10 inches from the end. Twist the sausage at these two creases about eight times. Now you have two links. Make two more creases at 5-inch intervals and spin these. Continue down the length of the casing. To separate the individual links, gently pull the links apart and snip the middle of the "twist" with a pair of scissors or knife.

COOK'S NOTES. *To hot-smoke your sausage, heat a pellet or vertical smoker to 200°F. Smoke the sausages with a mild fruitwood until the internal temperature of the meat reaches 145°F (or 160°F for bear or wild hog). You can eat them immediately or save for later and warm them up on a hot grill.*

When freezing your cased sausages in vacuum-sealed bags, make sure to orient the sausages vertically rather than horizontally. Horizontally placed sausages can form a dam in the bag that prevents the sealer from removing all of the air. I generally freeze my bulk sausage in poly burger bags, though it can also be frozen in a thin layer inside standard vacuum bags. In a hurry, you can toss a vacuum-sealed bag of sausage into a tub of cold water, and it'll thaw pretty quickly. This comes in handy when you're trying to prepare a meal in a rush, and you didn't thaw anything out beforehand.

ALSO WORKS WITH. *This sausage can be made with all kinds of big game, and it would also work with beavers or geese. Sausages made from bears, wild pigs, and javelinas should be cooked to an internal temperature of 160°F.*

BULGOGI LETTUCE WRAPS

SERVES 6

MARINADE

Makes 2 cups

6 tablespoons soy sauce

¼ cup packed dark brown sugar

2 tablespoons mirin

2 tablespoons toasted sesame oil

¼ teaspoon freshly ground black pepper

1 pear or sweet apple, or ½ Asian pear, peeled, cored, and cut into chunks

8 garlic cloves

1 small onion, cut into chunks

4 scallions, cut into 2-inch batons

1 tablespoon toasted sesame seeds

2 pounds elk backstrap, sliced ⅛ inch thick; partially frozen

SSAMJANG

Makes ⅓ cup

¼ cup miso or doenjang (see Cook's Note)

2 tablespoons seasoned gochujang sauce (see Cook's Note)

1 tablespoon honey or granulated sugar

1 teaspoon toasted sesame seeds

1 teaspoon toasted sesame oil

1 garlic clove, grated or minced

Neutral oil for grilling

FOR SERVING

Red or green leaf-lettuce leaves

Kimchi, cut into bite-sized pieces

Steamed white rice

Sliced scallions (optional)

Bulgogi is a traditional Korean dish made of thinly sliced marinated beef or pork that is grilled over fire. Its origins go back thousands of years. It's now one of the most popular Korean dishes served in the United States, and it can be scaled up to serve a crowd. The key to good bulgogi is having thinly sliced meat that's been perfectly marinated. The pear used in this recipe will release enzymes that tenderize the meat, so don't skip it. The ingredients for the Ssamjang, the dipping sauce served alongside the meat, are available in most grocery stores across the country; if not, you can find them in Korean markets or online. You can vac-seal and freeze the bulgogi sauce alone or with the meat in the marinade to use at a later date.

FOR THE MARINADE. Add the soy sauce, brown sugar, mirin, sesame oil, pepper, and pear to a food processor. Pulse until chunky. Add the garlic and onion and blend until smooth. Transfer to a large bowl and stir in the scallion batons and sesame seeds.

Add the meat to the marinade and stir to coat well. Cover and refrigerate for at least 2 hours or up to overnight.

FOR THE SSAMJANG. Combine the miso, gochujang sauce, honey, sesame seeds, toasted sesame oil, and garlic. Cover and set aside until ready to serve.

TO GRILL. Prepare a hot grill for direct grilling. Oil the grill grate. Working in batches, cook the meat for 1 minute, until lightly charred, and flip. Cook for another minute. Transfer to a platter when done. Clean the grill as necessary between batches. Repeat until all of the meat is grilled.

FOR SERVING. Cut the meat into bite-sized pieces with kitchen shears and serve with the ssamjang, lettuce leaves, kimchi, rice, and (if using) perilla leaves, garlic, and scallions to make lettuce wraps.

COOK'S NOTES. *Doenjang is a Korean fermented bean paste.*

Gochujang Sauce is a Korean condiment made from a fermented red chili paste thinned out with soy and vinegar.

ALSO WORKS WITH. *A whole muscle roast or a backstrap from any hooved big game or a wild hog, or domestic beef or pork.*

HOW TO COOK A WILD GAME STEAK

Grilling a great steak ain't as easy as you might think, and it can be especially tricky when you're dealing with wild game steaks. Here we break down the process, from butchering and seasoning to grilling and serving.

Butchering

The best steaks on big game animals come from either the backstrap or the large muscles on the upper hind leg. When I'm butchering an animal, I like to freeze these cuts as 2- to 3-pound whole muscle pieces. This gives me the option to cook an entire piece or slice it into steaks after it's thawed. You can also precut the steaks and freeze them that way, if you know that's how you're gonna use them. When you're cutting a lean wild game roast into steaks, don't skimp on the thickness; you're much more likely to overcook a thin one. A thicker steak is more forgiving on the grill and yields a juicer, tastier product. Steaks that are about 1½ to 2 inches thick are ideal. They can tolerate a hard sear on the outside and remain tender and rare to medium-rare on the inside.

Marinating

After butchering, the next step is imparting flavor with rubs or marinades. It's important to understand the role of acidity in a marinade: The acids in a marinade tenderize and flavor the steak by breaking down the long proteins in the meat. If you leave a steak in an acidic marinade for too long, however, it will begin to break down the proteins at the surface of the steak a bit too aggressively. This affects the texture, causing the meat to be mushy rather than tender. If your marinade includes wine, citrus juice, or even vinegar, it's best not to marinate it for more than 24 hours. Adding oil or some kind of insulating fat will help extend the marinating time.

A simple combination of olive oil, a few smashed garlic cloves, and some torn rosemary works great on wild game steaks. To up the ante a bit, try a splash of soy sauce, balsamic vinegar, and toasted sesame oil or sliced ginger, a bit of neutral oil, and a squeeze of lime. There are more flavor-packed marinades in this chapter and in the back of the book (page 346).

Dry Rubs

Dry rubs and dry brines are another simple way to impart flavor. You can add a rub right before cooking, but they season steaks all the way through if they're left on for 12 to 24 hours. The best ones maintain a balance of flavors with salt, sugar, something spicy, and something earthy, for example, kosher salt, a pinch of light brown sugar, a good dash of smoked paprika, and some ground cumin. Or try kosher salt, brown sugar, crushed red pepper flakes, and mushroom powder. Once the steak is seasoned, place it on a rack over a baking sheet and set the rubbed steak in the refrigerator for the desired amount of time. A bit of air circulation is good here to aid in drying out the surface of the meat, but you can also store pre-rubbed steaks in a plastic bag if you're transporting them to camp. Rubs and dry brines can also be made ahead of time and stored in an airtight container. (See a list of rubs and dry brines on pages 345 and 347.)

Grilling Steaks

1. PREHEAT the grill with the cover closed in order to make sure the grate is hot. Charcoal grills or wood fires need plenty of time to develop hot coals. The old hold-your-hand-four-inches-above-your-grill test holds true. If you can hold it there for longer than 4 seconds, it's not hot enough.

2. BRING MEAT TO ROOM TEMP. For steaks 1½ inches thick or thicker, pull it out of the refrigerator about 30 minutes before cooking. For thin steaks, you can skip this step. The colder center will help prevent overcooking.

3. DRY THE STEAK on all sides with paper towels. Moisture is the enemy when searing a steak, so you want to remove as much of it as possible.

4. SEASON THE STEAK with kosher salt and black pepper. You can skip this step if you have dry rubbed your steak, but a last-minute sprinkling of salt is not a bad thing. If you are starting with a naked steak, season with gusto.

5. DRY YOUR MEAT AGAIN. It can't be too dry.

6. DRIZZLE THE STEAK WITH A BIT OF NEUTRAL OIL. There is much debate as to whether you should oil the meat or oil the grill. To play it safe, lightly oil both. You don't want the oil to pool on the meat, just lightly coat it. If you are using a pan, a good drizzle in the pan is all you need.

7. GRILL. If your steak is very thick, it is beneficial to prepare a section of the grill for indirect heat, in case it needs to cook a bit longer (see page 8 for details).

When the heat is right and your steak is ready, wipe the grates of the grill with lightly oiled paper towels. Add your lightly oiled meat to the hot grill and cook undisturbed for 3 to 4 minutes with the cover on. Don't try to move the meat, don't press it down. It will release from the grates on its own when it is properly seared. Using tongs, flip the steak to a clean area of the grill. This ensures that the grates will be oiled and perfectly heated to sear the second side of the steak. Cook covered for another 3 to 4 minutes, or until the desired temperature is reached. I prefer to cook big game steaks rare to medium-rare. That's 125°F to 135°F on an instant-read thermometer. If you go much past that point, the meat gets dry and tough. Once the steak hits the bottom of that temperature range, remove it to a plate and allow it to rest for 10 minutes. At this point, it is beneficial to squeeze a bit of lemon juice over the steak. The juice adds a bit of fresh brightness to the richness of the steak. If served with an acidic, herby condiment like chimichurri, there's no need to add the lemon. Slice, season with a bit of coarse salt, and serve after the steak has rested.

Cooking Steaks in a Skillet

Just like grilling, the key here is to get your pan nice and hot before adding anything to it. You'll need a pan made of stainless or carbon steel or cast iron that can withstand the heat of the grill. Once hot, add a tablespoon or so of neutral oil or lard to the pan and swirl it to coat the bottom. Add the steak to the pan and let it sear for 3 to 4 minutes. It will release itself from the pan when it is ready. When a brown crust has formed on the steak, use tongs to flip it and continue to cook for about another 3 minutes, or until the internal temperature reaches 120°F to 125°F. At this point, it is nice to add a few pats of unsalted butter, a few cloves of smashed garlic, and perhaps some herbs. Toss all of those into the pan and tilt the pan toward you to allow the fatty, flavorful butter to pool near the handle. Now push the steak to the other side of the pan. Use a large spoon to baste the steak with the butter. After a minute of basting, remove the steak to a plate and pour on all of the aromatics and butter. Rest for 10 minutes before serving.

WEEKNIGHT BUTTERFLIED STEAK

SERVES 4 TO 6

This is a favorite recipe due to its simplicity and approachability. Anyone who loves a good steak is gonna love this preparation, so it's a safe bet for folks who might not be entirely adventurous eaters. This marinade is great for any steak, but we're talking here about a butterflied cut of meat; it's a technique where you can take a sizable chunk of meat, open it up with a knife, and then flatten it into a steak of uniform thickness. It's an easy way to get a delicious, healthy meal on the table in a hurry.

TO BUTTERFLY THE STEAK. The goal of butterflying a roast is to turn a thick chunk of backstrap or roast into one big flat steak. (Following the illustrations on page 46, make a horizontal cut across the roast through the middle, stopping short of cutting all the way through. Lay the two halves open like the wings of a butterfly. Pound to tenderize and flatten if necessary to ¾ to 1¼ inches thick.

FOR THE MARINADE. Combine the garlic, olive oil, soy sauce, Worcestershire, vinegar, lemon juice, Dijon mustard, and thyme (if using) in a baking dish. Coat both sides of the steak in the marinade and put it in a large baking dish. Let it sit at room temperature for up to 30 minutes. Flip the steak halfway through the marinating time.

TO GRILL. Prepare a grill for a hot fire with both direct and indirect heat. Remove the steak from the marinade to a plate. Pat the steak dry and season with the salt and pepper. Strain the marinade into a small pot.

Oil the grill grate and place the steak over direct heat for 4 to 5 minutes. If the fire seems too hot, move the steak to the indirect side, then back to the direct side as needed. Flip the steak after 4 minutes and cook on the second side for about 3 minutes. Using a meat thermometer, check the internal temperature of the steak. When it reaches 125°F to 130°F, remove the steak from the grill to rest.

Meanwhile, boil the marinade on the grill for at least 5 minutes. Remove from heat and set aside.

Use the boiled marinade as a sauce for the steak and for grilled vegetables (see page 272). Serve with bread and a side salad (see page 300).

1 (2- to 3½-pound) piece of big game top round roast or large, thick backstrap

Neutral oil, for the grill

MARINADE

Makes 2¾ cups

4 garlic cloves, grated on a rasp

1 cup extra-virgin olive oil

¾ cup soy sauce

½ cup Worcestershire sauce

¼ cup balsamic vinegar

Juice of 1 lemon (about ¼ cup)

2 tablespoons Dijon mustard

2 fresh thyme sprigs, leaves stripped, or 1 teaspoon dried (optional)

½ teaspoon kosher salt

½ teaspoon freshly ground black pepper

ALSO WORKS WITH. *Beefsteak. Also backstrap from bison, elk, or moose, and top round or other tender hindquarter roasts from deer-sized animals. You can do this with a goose breast as well.*

MAKE AHEAD. *For car camping, make the marinade ahead of time, store it separately from the steak in a sealable container, and bring it with you in a cooler. Marinate the steak in a resealable bag.*

BUTTERFLYING A ROAST

1. Lay the roast on a cutting board and place one hand on top of the roast to keep it in place.

2. Use a chef's knife to make a lengthwise cut with the grain that divides the roast horizontally into an upper and lower half. Stop about 1 inch short of cutting all the way through.

3. Lay the two connected halves out flat on the cutting board as if you were opening a book.

4. Pound the whole steak to tenderize and ensure it is an even thickness of roughly ¾ to 1 inch throughout. If necessary, even out any thick spots by scoring the steak a few times with your knife (being careful not to go all the way through the steak) and pound again.

VENISON CHOPS SCOTTADITO-STYLE

SERVES 4 AS A MAIN OR 8 AS AN APPETIZER

A favorite grilled meat from the days of the Roman Empire was called *abbacchio a scottadito,* or "young lamb in the scottadito style." According to writers from the time, the dish was sold by vendors in the Roman Forum. *Scottadito* roughly translates to "scalds finger," which means these are meant to be eaten hot and with your hands—no knives and forks necessary. *Abbacchio a scottadito* is still very popular today, and it may be served at Easter or anytime throughout the summer. The dish is certified as a protected recipe of the region, meaning that its preparation is an official piece of regional cultural heritage. Here, we are cheating tradition a bit by swapping young lamb for the rack of any kind of medium-sized big game from which you can easily remove chops. (To see the butchering process, turn to page 50.) The meat is pounded lightly and then marinated in rosemary, citrus, and garlic. It's then grilled quickly over high heat.

Trim the chops of any thick tallow and silverskin. Be careful not to overdo it or the meat may fall off the bone. Lay the chops in a baking dish or baking sheet. Combine the minced garlic and lemon zest. Sprinkle each chop with the lemon zest mixture and season with salt and pepper on both sides. Massage the seasonings into the chops. Lightly drizzle the chops with some of the oil to coat evenly. Divide the rosemary leaves among the chops (on both top and bottom) and set aside to marinate at room temperature for 30 minutes or in the refrigerator for up to 1 hour. Remove before grilling.

Preheat a grill to high heat for direct and indirect heat. When the grill is hot, add the chops, let the excess oil drip off, and grill the chops for 3 to 4 minutes per side, until well seared. Don't overcook them; you're aiming for rare to medium-rare with a caramelized crust on the outside. When done, remove the chops to a plate to rest. Drizzle with more olive oil, add a squeeze of lemon juice, and garnish with the lemon wedges and additional rosemary sprigs. Eat while they're hot enough to burn your fingers, just as the Romans did.

8 to 10 rib chops from a mule deer rack, cut a rib's width wide

2 garlic cloves, minced

1 lemon, zested and cut into wedges

Kosher salt and freshly ground black pepper to taste

¼ cup extra-virgin olive oil

2 large rosemary sprigs, leaves stripped, plus more sprigs for garnish

ALSO WORKS WITH. *Rib racks from all hooved game animals, as well as lamb.*

HOW TO CUT CHOPS FROM A MULE DEER RACK

1. The chops are located in the middle, or "saddle," portion between the shoulder and the hip. Using a bone saw, make one cut through the rib cage a few inches below the backstrap and another through the rib cage between the backstrap and the spine.

2. Use a knife to free the entire bone-in section of backstrap.

3. Cut this section into individual bone-in chops by making a slice through the meat between each rib bone. Trim any large chunks of fat, silverskin, or gristle.

HOW TO GRILL FISH FILLETS

There is nothing more frustrating than putting all of the time, care, and attention into catching and cleaning a fish only to ruin it when you cook it. Using the following techniques, you'll enjoy eating your fish as much as you did catching it.

1. MARINATE IT. This a great way to bump up the flavor of otherwise mild fish. When you think about a marinade, always consider the thickness and fattiness of the fish. If it is a rich fish, such as salmon or bluefish, a touch of citrus or something bright like mustard is a smart addition. If it is a lean white fish, adding some fatty richness is a good idea; toasted sesame oil or coconut milk is a good option.

The great thing about fish is that you do not have to marinate it for long—30 minutes in a flavorful bath will give it just the lift you are looking for. Keep the sugar content low in marinades to avoid burning fish on the grill.

2. BASTE IT. Try basting fish with a glaze, flavorful sauce, or compound butter when they are just a moment from being done. Make these condiments ahead of time so you can put them on as soon as the fish is ready.

3. DRY RUB. When grilling fish it's best to keep rubs simple. A lemon pepper blend, or a mix of granulated garlic, paprika, celery seed, and cayenne pepper works well for all kinds of fish.

4. CONDIMENTS. Sometimes the simplest solution is to season the fish with kosher salt and freshly ground black pepper and pair it with a lively condiment. There are many options for these in the back of this book.

Grilling

Grilling fish doesn't take long, so have everything you need by your side before you start. This includes your basting sauce, seasonings, spatula, and a plate for the cooked fish. You'll also want a wire fish basket for grilling fillets of fish with delicate flesh. Otherwise, they'll fall apart.

1. Preheat your grill.

2. Remove fish from the refrigerator 30 minutes before cooking. This will allow for very even cooking.

3. If you are using skin-on fillets, score the skin crosswise in a few spots. This prevents the fillet from curling when cooking.

4. Dry your fish very well, even if it was marinated. You want to remove as much moisture as possible. Then season it with kosher salt and give it a good drizzle of neutral oil on all sides.

5. Get your fish on the grill. If using skin-on fillets, place the fish skin-side down on the hot grill. If you are using fillets without skin, place the side that did not originally have skin on it on the grill. This side

will be your "presentation" or "good" side. Allow the fish to cook, covered, until nicely browned and you can see that the flesh is beginning to turn opaque around the edges on the top side. This should only take a few minutes. The fish will naturally release from the hot grill when ready to flip.

6. If you're not using a fish basket, carefully flip the fillet with a fish spatula or a long rectangular grilling spatula. Don't use tongs; they will likely tear the fragile flesh. Move the spatula in the direction of the grates when you flip the fish in order to avoid tearing it. If possible, flip the fish onto a clean section of the hot grill. Cover once again.

7. Depending on the thickness of the fillet, the fish only needs to cook for a couple more minutes. If you are using a glaze, brush it on and allow it to cook on the fish during the final minute of cooking. A thick fish steak will probably need additional time over indirect heat.

8. Remove the fish to a plate to rest. If you are using a compound butter, add it now so it melts and coats the fish. Serve immediately.

GRILLED MACKEREL
WITH PANCETTA-ONION JAM

SERVES 4

The various mackerel species are among those fishes that are often criticized for being too fishy. The complaint of excessive fishiness is hard for a lover of fish to argue against, because it's used in the same haphazard fashion as the complaint of "too gamey." A coho salmon that isn't particularly fresh might be described as "too fishy" by one person, while a totally fresh but improperly cleaned lemon shark might be described as "too fishy" by the next. (The white flesh on a lemon shark is good; the reddish flesh and fat that lies against the skin is admittedly heinous.) Countering claims of "too fishy" usually comes down to educating the complainer. But when it comes to arguing about the fishiness of mackerel, there's not a lot you can do. Folks who say it's too fishy are probably referring to the robust flavor of the oily flesh, to which you can only say that they're missing the point. The robust flavor of a mackerel's oily flesh is what makes it so damn good. Mackerel is especially suitable for grilling because that oil makes it a bit more forgiving. A mackerel can withstand a moment or two of neglect on the grill. And thanks to the robust flavor of the fish, you can dress it up with the Pancetta-Onion Jam in this recipe without risk of overpowering it. Go ahead and try it with bluefish or salmon as well. You're gonna love it. Just don't come complaining about fishiness.

FOR THE ONION JAM. In a medium saucepan, cook the pancetta over medium heat, stirring occasionally, for about 15 minutes, until most of the fat renders out and the pancetta is lightly browned. Add the butter and let it melt. Add the brown sugar, salt, pepper, thyme, onions, and bay leaf (if using) and toss to coat the onions evenly. Cook for 5 minutes then lower the heat to medium-low and cook, partially covered, for 20 to 25 minutes, stirring occasionally until the onions cook down and are very soft. Stir in the vinegar and continue to cook, stirring occasionally, until thick and jammy. Discard the thyme sprigs and bay leaf. Transfer the onions to an airtight container and let cool. The onion jam can be stored in the refrigerator for up to 10 days.

FOR THE FISH. Remove any pin bones with tweezers; this can be done with freshly caught fish, but it is easier if the fillets have been frozen and thawed. Season the fillets with the salt and pepper. Let sit for 20 minutes.

While you're waiting, prepare a medium-high grill. Pat the fish dry and brush with the oil. Place the fish skin-side down on a well-oiled grill and cook for about 3 minutes, until the skin is browned and blistered in spots. Carefully flip the fish over and cook for another 1 to 2 minutes. Transfer the fish to plates, skin-side up, and spread the onion jam on top of the fillets. Serve with lemon wedges and remaining onion jam.

PANCETTA-ONION JAM

Makes 1⅓ cups

4 ounces pancetta, diced (about ¾ cup)

2 tablespoons unsalted butter

3 tablespoons packed dark brown sugar

1 teaspoon kosher salt

⅛ teaspoon ground black pepper

6 fresh thyme sprigs

3 large red onions, thinly sliced (about 5½ cups)

1 bay leaf (optional)

2 tablespoons sherry vinegar

---

4 whole or portions of mackerel fillets (6 to 8 ounces each)

2 teaspoons kosher salt

¼ teaspoon freshly ground black pepper

1 teaspoon avocado or canola oil, plus more for the grill

Lemon wedges, for serving

ALSO WORKS WITH. *Atlantic, Spanish, cero, or king mackerel as well as bluefish, salmon, and trout. Cut large fish into steaks and fillets into serving-sized portions.*

COOK'S NOTE. *Onion jam can be used on basically anything—grilled meats, fish, pizzas, sandwiches, eggs, and even a piece of toast. The longer you cook it, the jammier it gets. It's worth making a double batch to keep in the fridge for other uses.*

GRILLED WHOLE FISH IN FOIL
WITH GRILLED SCALLIONS

SERVES 2

1 (2-pound) whole fish, gutted, scaled, fins trimmed off

2 teaspoons kosher salt

¼ teaspoon freshly ground black pepper

1 garlic clove, thinly sliced

1 small serrano or Fresno chile, with seeds, thinly sliced into rounds

5 thin orange wheels

5 thin lemon wheels

9 large fresh marjoram or oregano sprigs

1 large shallot, thinly sliced into rounds

1 large fennel bulb, thinly sliced crosswise

3 tablespoons extra-virgin olive oil

1 tablespoon drained capers

4 scallions, white and green parts, ends trimmed

ALSO WORKS WITH. *Various species of snappers and Pacific rockfish, striped bass, surf perch, Spanish mackerel, and speckled trout. You could also try this with smallmouth bass, large crappie, and even tilapia.*

The Atlantic black sea bass pictured in the photo opposite this recipe is counted among the dozens of species of fish that have been undeservedly regarded as "trash fish" by anglers. If you have ever heard someone say that about black sea bass, bonk them on the head for me. This species is one of the most flavorful and interesting fish that are readily available to fishermen along the Atlantic Seaboard. The fish has delicate flesh that is sweet and firm, and it's usually harvested in the 1- to 3-pound range, which is ideal for cooking whole. But you can use any 1 to 3 pound whole fish in this recipe, which essentially steams the fish over high heat inside its packaging of foil, large leaves, or even a salt crust. The filling can easily be simplified for the backcountry or adjusted with foraged ingredients such as wild garlic, ramps, or mushrooms.

Prepare a medium-hot grill for direct grilling.

Rinse the fish inside and out and pat it dry. Set it on a cutting board and cut three or four parallel, angled slits on both sides of the fish, cutting into the fish until you hit the bone. Rub the fish, including inside the slits and cavity, with 1 teaspoon of the salt and ⅛ teaspoon of the black pepper. Stuff the slits with the garlic and chile slices. Halve one of the orange wheels and stuff it into the cavity, along with 1 of the lemon wheels, 1 of the marjoram sprigs, and a pinch of the shallots.

In a medium bowl, toss the remaining shallots with the sliced fennel, 1 tablespoon of the oil, ½ teaspoon of the salt, and the remaining ⅛ teaspoon black pepper. Set aside.

On a large 18 × 20-inch sheet of foil, drizzle 1 tablespoon of the oil in the center where the fish will lie. Layer 3 of the orange wheels and 2 of the lemon wheels, half of the fennel-shallot mixture, half of the capers, and 4 of the marjoram sprigs over the oil. Lay the fish on top and drizzle with 2 teaspoons of the oil. Layer the remaining marjoram, capers, fennel-shallot mixture, and lemon and orange wheels on top of the fish. Fold the sides and ends of the foil together tightly and seal to close.

Place the foil packet on the grill and cook for 5 to 6 minutes. While the fish is grilling, toss or brush the scallions with the remaining 1 teaspoon oil and ½ teaspoon salt. Grill the scallions for 3 minutes until slightly charred. Transfer to a plate.

Flip the fish and cook for another 5 to 6 minutes. Carefully open the foil to see if the fish is cooked through. The flesh should be opaque, not translucent. Reseal the foil and keep cooking if needed.

Serve the fish with the filling ingredients and the grilled scallions.

GRILLED WHOLE FLOUNDER
WITH SAUCE CHIEN BEURRE MONTÉ

SERVES 4

Butter sauces pair well with light-fleshed, nonoily fish like flounder. This one is an adaptation of the French West Indies' *sauce chien,* or dog sauce, a spicy, herby, garlicky sauce used for fish and meat. *Chien* actually refers to the knife that is used to chop the ingredients for the sauce. The dog knife, or *couteau chien,* was created in 1880. It's a steel knife with a watchdog carved in the hilt and is given out as a wedding gift in the French West Indies. My adaptation on the sauce utilizes the French technique of adding butter to emulsify the sauce and give it some additional richness (see Cook's Note). You can omit the butter and go with olive oil or vegetable oil for a lighter sauce. While sauce chien pairs perfectly with flounder, it would also be a nice addition to upland game birds.

FOR THE FLOUNDER. Scrub the flounder all over with 2 tablespoons of the salt. Rinse the fish, inside and out, and dry well with paper towels. Place the fish on a baking sheet or baking dish and chill in a cooler or refrigerator while you start the grill or prepare a campfire.

Prepare a grill or campfire with an area for direct and indirect heat. Just before grilling, gently brush the oil all over the fish and season with the remaining 1 tablespoon salt. Place in a lightly oiled fish basket. Place the basket on the hot side of the grill and cook, uncovered, until the fish chars in spots, about 4 minutes. Move the basket to indirect heat occasionally so the fish doesn't scorch.

Flip the basket and continue to grill for another 4 to 5 minutes, until the fish is cooked through at the thickest area toward the head. Use a small knife to check whether the flesh is flaky and opaque.

FOR THE SAUCE. Bring 2 tablespoons water to a boil in a small saucepan. Remove the pan from the heat and slowly whisk in the butter, 1 tablespoon at a time, until emulsified into a creamy sauce. Keep warm but do not let it boil. Stir in the lemon juice and (if using) zest, chives, parsley, thyme, garlic, habanero (if using), and shallots. Add salt and pepper and adjust the seasonings to taste.

Carefully transfer the fish to a platter. Pour half of the sauce over the fish and serve the remaining sauce on the side.

COOK'S NOTE. *Ideally, this sauce will remain in an emulsified state. Don't be too hard on yourself, however, if it breaks, especially when keeping it warm over a fire or grill outdoors. As you can see in the photo, we broke it, too. It still tasted great!*

FLOUNDER

1 whole flounder (about 2 pounds), gutted

3 tablespoons kosher salt

2 tablespoons neutral oil, plus more for the fish basket

SAUCE CHIEN

8 tablespoons (1 stick) unsalted butter, cut into tablespoons

2 tablespoons fresh lemon juice, plus (optional) zest from one lemon

2 tablespoons chopped fresh chives

1 tablespoon chopped fresh flat-leafed parsley

1 teaspoon fresh thyme leaves

1 garlic clove, chopped (about 1 teaspoon)

1 or 2 habanero or Scotch bonnet chiles, seeded (optional), finely chopped (about 2 teaspoons)

1 shallot, finely chopped (about 3 tablespoons)

½ teaspoon kosher salt, plus more as needed

⅛ teaspoon finely ground black pepper, plus more as needed

ALSO WORKS WITH. *Other flatfish such as sole and small halibut or any light-fleshed saltwater or freshwater fish. Also shrimp, lobster, quail, grouse, and pheasant.*

GRILLED LOBSTER

WITH KELP BUTTER AND FINGERLING POTATO SALAD

SERVES 4

KELP GODDESS DRESSING

Makes ½ cup

1 (⅛-ounce) piece dried kelp

¼ cup mayonnaise

1 tablespoon sour cream

1 teaspoon fresh lemon juice

1 teaspoon red wine vinegar

1 teaspoon anchovy paste

1 small garlic clove, minced

1 ounce fresh chives, chopped
(2 tablespoons)

KELP BUTTER

1 (⅛-ounce) piece dried kelp

6 tablespoons (¾ stick) unsalted butter

GRILLED FINGERLING
POTATO SALAD

2 pounds fingerling potatoes, halved if
large

Olive oil

Kosher salt and freshly ground black
pepper

1 celery rib, cut into ¼-inch half-moons

½ cup purslane, roughly chopped
(optional; see Cook's Note)

¼ cup Kelp Goddess Dressing

GRILLED LOBSTER

4 (1¼- to 1½-pound) lobsters

ALSO WORKS WITH. *Maine lobster,
spiny lobster, langoustines, prawns,
salmon, or clams and oysters on the
half shell.*

Perhaps you're familiar with the culinary saying "What grows together, goes together." There are notable exceptions to this, of course. I love oyster mushrooms, for instance, but I would never choose to pair them with insect larvae that you find proliferating in their bases near the season's end. Other pairings make more sense. American pronghorn and sage. Mule deer and juniper. Lobster and seaweed. This recipe is based on the latter. It uses kelp to make a butter topping for lobster (or pretty much any other seafood) that is served alongside a refreshing and lively grilled potato salad. The Kelp Goddess Dressing requires a food processor, so plan ahead if you want to make this at the beach with some fresh-caught seafood. Everything else can be done in the field. Dried kelp is becoming more available in grocery stores nationwide. It's also available online from small coastal farms.

FOR THE DRESSING. Cover the kelp with water in a small saucepan and bring to a boil over high heat. Reduce to a simmer and cook for about 20 minutes, until the kelp swells, softens, and turns a lighter green. (You may need to poke it from time to time to keep it submerged.) Drain and rinse under cool water. Squeeze and discard any water from the kelp and add the kelp to a food processor. Chop coarsely. Scrape down the sides of the food processor bowl and then add the mayonnaise, sour cream, lemon juice, vinegar, anchovy paste, garlic, and chives. Process until combined.

FOR THE KELP BUTTER. Toast the dry kelp in a small skillet over medium-high heat for 6 to 7 minutes, flipping occasionally, until it dries up and crisps. Remove from the skillet and let cool. In the same skillet over medium heat, melt the butter. Crumble the dried kelp with your fingers into the melted butter and let it infuse the butter for a minute. Remove from the heat.

FOR THE GRILLED POTATO SALAD. Prepare a grill or open fire for indirect medium-high heat. If you're using charcoal or a wood fire, bank the hot coals on one side. Toss the potatoes with oil, salt, and pepper. Arrange in a pan over indirect heat, cover the grill, and cook for 20 to 25 minutes, until the potatoes are soft and you can easily pierce them with a knife. Remove to a large bowl and toss with ¼ cup of the dressing, the celery, and purslane (if using).

FOR THE GRILLED LOBSTER. Hold the lobster firmly stomach-side down. Use a very sharp knife to pierce the head portion of the shell where it meets the abdomen. Push the knife down with the heel of your hand to

Recipe continues

MAKE AHEAD. *The Kelp Goddess Dressing requires the use of a food processor, but it can be stored in a sealed container inside a chilled cooler for up to 3 days and in a refrigerator for up to 1 week.*

separate the tail. Next, cleave the tail in half lengthwise. Remove the claws. Whack the claw with back of the knife to crack them. Repeat with the remaining lobsters.

Spread out the coals (adding more if needed to keep the heat going) and put the claws and tails (flesh-side up) on the grill. Spoon the kelp butter over the tail meat. Cover and cook until the meat is no longer translucent and the shells turn bright red. This should take 8 to 10 minutes for the tail sections and 10 to 12 minutes for the claws. Remove to a platter and serve with the fingerling potato salad.

COOK'S NOTE. *To clean purslane, submerge it in water and swish it around to get rid of the little black seeds and any other detritus. The seeds are edible, so it's okay if they don't all wash off. Trim any thick stems that look woody.*

GRILLED SEAFOOD PAELLA

SERVES 6

Paella is a dish that is meant to be cooked slowly over flames and coals in a shallow paella pan. In Valencia, Spain, the region that claims ownership of this dish, a true paella is made with rabbit, snails, and chicken over a fire of orange wood from the region. The rice is cooked until it becomes a shallow layer lacquered with stock and should adhere to the bottom of the pan. This sticky, crunchy layer of rice is called the socarrat—it's the sign of a well-made paella. By virtue of Spain's proximity to the ocean, seafood variations of paella are also popular. According to local traditions, however, seafood shouldn't mix with meat, so they never put chorizo in a seafood paella. This grilled seafood paella is a campfire classic. As an angler or a hunter, you can use this base recipe to make your own wild variations. Practice the patience it takes to rotate the pan methodically to achieve that crunchy, caramelized layer of rice. The results are well worth the effort.

For an open fire or fire pit, prepare a grate for direct and indirect grilling.

If using a charcoal grill, start a second chimney after the first is added to the grill. You'll need more coals when the first batch starts to die down.

Put a 14- to 15-inch paella pan on the grill grate. Add 4 tablespoons of the oil, the onions, ½ teaspoon of the salt, and ¼ teaspoon of the pepper. Cook and stir frequently until the onions soften, about 5 minutes, rotating the pan to the cooler part of the grill as necessary to avoid burning. Add the paprika and garlic and cook for 60 seconds, stirring constantly until fragrant. Add the tomatoes and use a spoon to smash and break them up. Cook and stir until the tomatoes have reduced into a paste, 5 to 8 minutes. Add the wine, cover, and cook until the liquid is mostly reduced, about 5 minutes.

Stir in the rice to coat it evenly. Add the saffron and the stock. Stir and spread the rice into an even layer. Let the paella simmer until most of the liquid has been absorbed, rotating the pan halfway through, 15 to 20 minutes. Taste a kernel of rice. If the rice is still partially raw and the liquid level is low, drizzle in more stock. Do not stir the rice.

Gently toss the shrimp, squid, and fish with the remaining 2 tablespoons oil, 1 teaspoon salt, and ¼ teaspoon pepper. Scatter the mussels and shrimp over the rice. Cover the pan (or close the grill lid) and continue to cook for about 5 minutes, or until the mussels just start to open up and

6 tablespoons extra-virgin olive oil

1 large onion, chopped (about 1½ cups)

1½ teaspoons kosher salt, plus more to finish

½ teaspoon freshly ground black pepper, plus more to finish

1 teaspoon smoked paprika

4 garlic cloves, grated or finely chopped

1 (15-ounce) can cherry tomatoes or whole peeled plum tomatoes in puree

1 cup dry white wine or dry sherry

2 cups short-grain Spanish rice, preferably Calasparra, Valencia, or Bomba

Pinch of saffron threads, crumbled

4 cups homemade or store-bought seafood stock or a combination of clam juice and water, plus more if needed

6 to 9 colossal (U10) head-on shrimp, peeled with heads and tails still attached, deveined (reserve shells for stock)

8 ounces cleaned squid bodies, sliced into ¾- to 1-inch-wide rings

8 ounces red snapper fillet, cut into 2- to 3-inch pieces

1¾ pounds mussels, scrubbed and beards removed

¼ cup fresh flat-leaf parsley, chopped

1 lemon, halved

Recipe continues

the shrimp are almost cooked through. Add the squid and fish, cover, and cook another 3 to 5 minutes, until everything is cooked through.

Remove the pan from the grill grate. Cover the pan with the lid or foil and let the paella steam for 5 minutes. Uncover and discard any mussels that haven't opened.

While the paella is resting, grill the lemon cut-side down over direct heat until charred, 2 to 3 minutes. Uncover the paella, sprinkle it with parsley, and squeeze lemon over it. Adjust seasonings and serve.

COOK'S NOTES. *You'll find fresh tomatoes in most traditional paella recipes. Here we use canned for convenience in outdoor settings. Feel free to substitute fresh tomatoes if they are in season.*

Never mind what makes a "true" paella, because it's a free country and you can do what you want! Here's a way to take the dish in wild directions. Try this when you're feeling adventurous and the freezer is full. The proportions are as follows: Give or take 2 rabbits; 1- to 2-pound upland bird, each broken down into quarters or eighths, 1 to 2 dozen live snails; ½ pound flat green beans, trimmed; a big pinch of pimenton (smoked paprika); and a sprig of fresh rosemary. Start by parboiling the rabbit and bird legs until tender (anywhere from 1 to 2 hours). Then, in a paella pan, brown the rabbit and bird parts well in olive oil, then stir in the onion and garlic. Add the tomatoes and cook them down to a paste. Add the green beans, pimenton, rosemary, saffron, snails, and a light game stock. Season with kosher salt and black pepper. Bring to a boil, then sprinkle in the rice. Without stirring, rotate the pan until the liquid has absorbed, roughly 15 to 20 minutes.

ALSO WORKS WITH. *Octopus, scallops, and other shellfish, plus any firm white-fleshed fish such as halibut, mahi mahi, redfish, and similar freshwater substitutes. (See Cook's Notes for information about rabbit, upland birds, and snails.)*

HOW TO CATCH AN OCTOPUS

Kimi Werner

I was eleven years old the first time I caught an octopus on my own. I had grown up tagging along with my dad as he would free dive and spearfish on the north shore of Maui. I was the bag girl, just observing him and putting in my orders for my favorite dinners as I helped him bag his harvests. But one day, he spotted an octopus in its hole in about fifteen feet of water. He encouraged me to hold my breath and swim down to the bottom to try to catch it. I had watched my dad do this many times and knew his rules—he never speared them in their home. He always used his three-prong pole spear to gently tickle them out of the hole. Then he'd grab them in his hand and dispatch them. He did this so he could make sure they were a good size to take—and also to ensure that he didn't end up fatally wounding an octopus that he wouldn't be able to recover. The theory made sense, but the actual practice was trickier than it looked. By the time I got to the octopus in its hole and started to "tickle" it, I'd be out of breath and have to return to the surface. My dad kept encouraging me to relax, which is key to staying down longer. I tried over and over again, and soon my tickles resulted in long, suction-cup-covered legs jetting out and wrapping around my spear. I'd rush to grab ahold of them and pull the octopus out, only to see it retreat immediately back into its hole. Finally, after a lot of coaching about patience from my dad, I let the octopus grab my spear with all of its legs and pulled it out completely. I remember the feelings of joy and victory as I brought it to the surface. That joy immediately collided with the most painful sensations I had ever experienced. Right when I broke the surface, a Portuguese man-of-war, an organism related to a jellyfish with an insanely powerful sting that feels like fire, wrapped around my neck. I screamed in agony and splashed at the surface, and my dad yelped, too, as he pulled it off and got stung himself. Our day pivoted immediately, with Dad rushing me out of the water as my neck and chest swelled up and taking me straight to a little mom-and-pop store, where he bought meat tenderizer and applied it to my throat to reduce the swelling. I felt horrible. But I never let go of my tako, or octopus. And I'm happy to say that octopus diving only got easier for me from there on out.

Hawaii is a place of connection. The plants and animals I harvest are the same ones I want to see forever thriving. I grew up with them. They've fed me and given me so much in life: a connection to the natural world that we are a part of, my greatest adventures, my fondest memories, my most excruciating challenges. They have taught me who I am and who I want to be. So whenever I cook a meal, there's a very special sacredness I feel simply by acknowledging that I am putting nature into my body. Connecting to that idea makes me strive to turn those gifts from nature into dishes that are worthy of their components. This tako, or octopus, recipe was taught to me by my friend Justin Lee, who learned it from his friend Sam Myers. It's one of my go-to party-pleasers and is a hit every time. The dish is a vibrant celebration of the ingredients themselves!

OCTOPUS CHIMICHURRI
AN INSTANT POT METHOD

SERVES 4

1 (2-pound) octopus

3 tablespoons Hawaiian salt or coarse sea salt

Neutral oil, for grilling

CHIMICHURRI

Makes 2¼ cups

1 bunch cilantro, roughly chopped to yield 1 cup

1 medium bunch flat-leaf parsley, roughly chopped to yield 1 cup

2 fresh oregano sprigs, stems discarded, chopped fine

½ medium red onion, chopped fine

3 garlic cloves, minced

¾ teaspoon kosher salt

1 teaspoon crushed red pepper flakes or minced fresh red jalapeño

½ cup red wine vinegar

1 cup extra-virgin olive oil

FOR THE OCTOPUS. Gut the octopus by flipping the head inside out and pulling out the innards. Place the octopus in a large bowl and sprinkle it with the coarse salt. Massage it vigorously for 7 minutes, then rinse well to remove all the slime. Keep rinsing until the water runs clear and there are no more suds and bubbles. Add the cleaned octopus and 2 cups water to the Instant Pot. Pressure cook for 10 minutes. Once cooked, vent quickly using the steam release valve.

FOR THE CHIMICHURRI. Combine all the ingredients in a bowl and stir to combine. Set aside until ready to serve.

TO GRILL. Prepare a fire pit for direct heat. Remove the octopus from the Instant Pot and shake off the water. Slather it with oil and grill over high heat and open flames until charred. Smother the octopus in chimichurri sauce, cut it into bite-sized pieces, and serve.

Kimi Werner is a native Hawaiian, a steward for a sustainable global community, and one of the world's best free divers and spearfishers. She's also an avid cook with a lifetime of experience perfecting recipes that feature Hawaiian seafood. Kimi was born and raised on Maui and currently lives on Oahu with her family.

SPATCHCOCKING GAME BIRDS

One of my all-time favorite ways to handle birds such as grouse, quail, and chicken is to spatchcock them and throw 'em on a grill. Spatchcocking involves removing the backbone, snipping the breast bone, and flattening the bird into a more manageable shape that can be flipped on a grill and cooked evenly. (If you don't like the idea of tossing out the backbone, you can freeze it and save it for making game stock.) A bonus element of spatchcocking your birds is that the rib cage acts as a built-in roasting rack that protects the meat from the grill's direct heat; the crispy roasted skin on the other side helps to keep the meat moist.

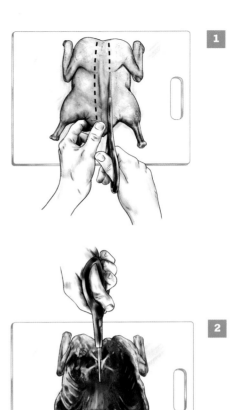

How to Spatchcock

1. Place the bird back-side up with the legs pointing toward you. Use kitchen shears to make a cut on each side of the hip, then continue the cuts along both sides of the spine until you can remove the hip, spine, and neck in one piece.

2. Starting on the other end of the bird, so that the legs are pointing away from you, use the shears to snip a notch in the thick upper part of the breastbone. Then use a knife to make a shallow slit on either side of the breastbone to disconnect the meat from the breastbone.

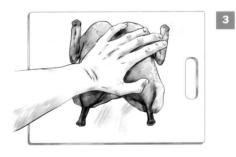

3. Flip the breast over and press gently in the center of the breast to flatten. You'll hear a little pop in the rib cage. Remove the wings and legs, if you wish to cook them separately. Save the backbone for stock.

MARINADES FOR SPATCHCOCKED BIRDS AND OTHER WILD GAME

The following three marinades are phenomenal with all kinds of birds, but they're also fantastic with big game, small game, and even vegetables. They can be made ahead of time for entertaining. Don't omit the side sauces where they appear. They're just as tasty as the marinades.

SHAWARMA-STYLE YOGURT MARINADE
(FOR SPATCHCOCKED BIRDS)

¾ cup plain full-fat Greek yogurt

¼ cup extra-virgin olive oil

3 garlic cloves, grated on a rasp

Juice of 1 lemon

1 teaspoon freshly ground black pepper

2 teaspoons kosher salt, plus more as needed

1½ teaspoons ground coriander

1½ teaspoons ground cumin

1 teaspoon ground allspice

1 teaspoon ground cinnamon

¾ teaspoon ground turmeric

ALSO WORKS WITH. *Upland birds, puddle ducks, and domestic chickens as well as hooved big game cuts like backstrap and roasts that have been cut into thin steaks.*

The tenderizing properties of this yogurt-based marinade are helpful when cooking with game. The recipe comes from the style of marinades frequently used for shawarma in the Middle East, where it's typically paired with lamb or chicken. It gets its name from the Arabic word for "turning"—referencing primarily the vertical rotating rotisserie on which marinated meats are roasted and then shaved for sandwiches, salads, and other dishes. A similar vertical roasting pit called the trompo is used in Mexico to make tacos al pastor (see our version of that dish on page 281). But interestingly, the trompo came to the region via the Syrian and Lebanese immigrants who brought their shawarma-style of vertical roasting spit to Mexico in the late nineteenth century.

It's best to let the marinade do its work on the meat for at least an hour before grilling or smoking. This marinade is traditionally used for skewers, but it's also a natural addition to a shawarma-style cook on a rotisserie.

The marinade will cover 1 medium game bird, such as a pheasant or large grouse, or 3 to 6 small game birds such as ducks or quail. Makes about 1¼ cups.

FOR THE MARINADE. In a bowl, combine all marinade ingredients and whisk to combine. Adjust salt to taste. Set aside.

TO MARINATE. Dry the meat well. Slather the marinade liberally all over the interior, exterior, and under the skin of the bird in a thick layer. Marinate for at least 1 hour. Remove most of the marinade from the surface of the meat before grilling. Any unused marinade that has not touched raw meat can be stored in an airtight container for up to 1 week in the refrigerator.

SOUR CREAM HERB MARINADE FOR GRILLED (OR SMOKED) GAME BIRDS

MAKES ABOUT 1¼ CUPS

Simple recipes like this one come down to the quality of your ingredients. It's worth it to source a decent sour cream (or a similar quality cultured dairy product like crème fraîche or Greek yogurt). If you have the time, the birds will benefit from marinating for a few hours or even overnight to let that lactic acidity do its thing and tenderize the meat. You can easily make this by hand and chop the garlic and herbs with a knife. You can also swap the specified herbs for any soft herb you have on hand. While dill and mint are fantastic, so are basil, parsley, cilantro, or a combination of them all.

Marinade will cover 1 medium game bird, such as a pheasant or large grouse, or 3 to 6 small game birds like ducks and quail.

FOR THE MARINADE. In a food processor with the motor running, drop the garlic cloves in one by one to mince them. Stop the machine and add the herbs, sour cream, salt, and pepper. Pulse until smooth (there will be visible pieces of herbs in the cream). Adjust seasonings to taste.

TO MARINATE. Dry the meat well. Slather the herb mixture all over the interior, exterior, and under the skin of the bird. Keep the marinade on while you grill. It will create a saucy, caramelized layer on the outside of the bird.

6 garlic cloves

1 cup mixed fresh soft herbs, like dill and mint, roughly chopped

1 cup sour cream

2 teaspoons kosher salt, plus more as needed

½ teaspoon freshly ground black pepper, plus more as needed

ALSO WORKS WITH. *Upland birds, small puddle ducks, wild turkey breasts, and domestic chickens as well as big game loins and tenderloins.*

COOK'S NOTE. *This marinade works for grilled, roasted, and smoked birds. It also makes an excellent dip for crudités. To make the dip, use only 3 garlic cloves and add 2 tablespoons mayonnaise and 1 tablespoon lemon juice.*

PERUVIAN-STYLE MARINADE FOR DUCK
WITH AJÍ VERDE (GREEN JALAPEÑO SAUCE)

MARINADE

Makes about ¾ cup

4 garlic cloves, smashed and roughly chopped

2 teaspoons kosher salt, plus more as needed

¼ cup vegetable oil, plus more for the grill

Juice from 2 large limes (about ¼ cup)

1 tablespoon red wine vinegar

1 teaspoon sugar

1 tablespoon ground cumin

2 tablespoons paprika

1 teaspoon freshly ground black pepper, plus more as needed

2 or 3 ducks (4 to 5 pounds), spatch-cocked with legs separated (see technique illustrated on page 75)

AJÍ SAUCE

Makes about 1½ cups

4 medium jalapeño peppers, roughly chopped (see Cook's Note)

1 garlic clove

1½ cups fresh cilantro leaves

½ cup sour cream

⅓ cup cotija cheese

2 teaspoons lime juice

2 tablespoons mayonnaise

1 teaspoon red wine vinegar

2 tablespoons olive oil

Kosher salt and freshly ground black pepper

COOK'S NOTE. *If you have access to Aji Amarillo paste, use 3 to 4 tablespoons in place of the fresh chiles.*

On any given day, Peruvians fire-roast millions of chickens that are paired with ají verde. Once you try it, you'll wish this dish was part of your own routine. The warm spices complement any kind of bird and hold up exceptionally well with waterfowl. The tangy, spicy ají sauce (Peruvian green chili sauce) works as well with roasted potatoes and French fries as it does with meat, so make extra in order to experiment a bit. Serves 4 to 6, depending on the size of the ducks.

FOR THE MARINADE. Make a garlic paste with the garlic and salt: On a cutting board, pile the salt on top of the chopped garlic and, using the side of your knife blade, press the garlic and salt together across the cutting board a few times to form a paste. In a medium bowl, mix the garlic paste with the vegetable oil, lime juice, vinegar, sugar, cumin, paprika, and black pepper.

Slather half of the marinade on the outside of the bird and underneath the skin. Season the inside of the cavity with salt and pepper. Place the bird into a resealable bag and pour the remaining marinade into the bag. Seal the bag and rub the bird with the marinade to coat. Refrigerate overnight. If car camping, bring it with you like this.

FOR THE AJÍ SAUCE. Add all ingredients into a blender except for the olive oil, salt, and black pepper. With the motor running, add the olive oil slowly through the top of the blender. When smooth, season to taste with salt. Refrigerate in an airtight container until ready to serve.

TO GRILL. The next day, bring the bird to room temperature in the bag. Meanwhile, prepare your grill or live fire with a grate for indirect heat. Oil the grill grates. Put the duck breast, skin-side up, close to the direct-heat side of the grill. Place the legs on the indirect heat side, flipping them occasionally. Flip the breast to sit over direct heat to render some of the fat and to brown the skin. Be careful not to scorch it. When it starts to brown and get crispy, flip it back over to continue cooking. Do the same with the wings and thighs, moving all of them to the indirect side after rendering and charring them a bit to finish cooking.

Cook the breast until it reads 135°F with an instant-read thermometer, then remove it from the grill to rest. Cook the legs and wings to 160°F. The whole process could take from 20 to 35 minutes depending on the heat of your fire and the ambient temperatures. Use the instant-read thermometer to let you know when it's done.

Serve with the ají sauce on the side and pair with coal-roasted potatoes and vegetables (see page 159).

WILD TURKEY AND MORTADELLA PINWHEELS

WITH SAGE BALSAMIC SAUCE

SERVES 6

SAGE BALSAMIC SAUCE

Makes 2 cups

½ cup sage leaves, stalks reserved

1 cup basil leaves

1 cup flat-leaf parsley leaves

1 medium shallot, halved

4 large garlic cloves

2 tablespoons balsamic vinegar

¼ cup freshly squeezed lemon juice
(from 1 large lemon)

¼ cup freshly squeezed orange juice

¾ teaspoon kosher salt

¼ teaspoon freshly ground black
pepper

1 teaspoon crushed red pepper flakes

¾ cup extra-virgin olive oil

PINWHEELS

1 skinless, boneless wild turkey breast
(roughly 3 to 4 pounds)

Kosher salt and freshly ground black
pepper

12 (¼-inch-thick) slices smoked
mozzarella or provolone

6 to 8 (⅛-inch-thick) slices mortadella
(about 5 ounces)

3 roasted red peppers (jarred)

Extra-virgin olive oil

3 fresh rosemary springs

8 tablespoons (1 stick) salted butter,
melted

SPECIAL EQUIPMENT

6 wooden skewers, cut down to
5 inches and soaked overnight

Butcher's twine

This is an elegant and fun way to serve up wild game in the backyard. It takes a bit of work to pull it off, but it's well worth it. It also makes a great appetizer. You'll see that the preparation involves hammering out a turkey breast into a thin sheet. This is a trick you should have up your sleeve whether you're making pinwheels or not, because you'll find that a big, thin sheet of turkey meat lends itself to all sorts of fun preparations. You can do these pinwheels with a lot of other types of meat as well, including goose and even venison, but I think turkey is the best. The key is to butterfly it and pound it to tenderize before filling, rolling, and slicing. The more tender you make it, the better it will be. (For more information on the butterflying technique, see page 46.)

FOR THE SAUCE. Place all ingredients in a blender and pulse ten to twelve times to help break down the herbs, shallot, and garlic. Once combined, let the blender run on a medium speed for 20 to 30 seconds, until evenly pureed. The sauce can be 1 day in advance and stored in an airtight container in the refrigerator.

FOR THE PINWHEELS. Trim any sinew or extra fat from the turkey breast. Flip the breast over so the interior is facing up and carefully spread out and butterfly the breast so you have a single piece that is somewhat even in thickness. Cover with a large piece of plastic wrap and pound flat until you reach a thickness of about ⅓ inch. You don't want to pound straight down; hit the turkey in the thicker spots and push to the side as you go to prevent the mallet from tearing through the meat.

Remove the plastic wrap and trim the sides of the turkey so that you're left with one nice large rectangle roughly 12 × 8 inches (this will vary depending on the size of the bird). Season the top side with salt and pepper and spread ¾ cup of the sage balsamic sauce evenly over the surface. Place the slices of cheese on the sauce, overlapping them slightly as you go. Try to leave about 1 inch of meat uncovered on one of the long sides of the rectangle. This will be the side that tucks in and seals the roulade once it's rolled. Next, lay the mortadella on top and then the roasted red pepper, keeping the layers flat and uniform.

TO ROLL THE ROULADE. Starting with the long side of the rectangle with the fillings up to the edge and using both hands, tightly tuck and roll the turkey onto itself until you are left with one long roll. Slide skewers through the roulade every 2 inches down the entire length to secure it.

Be sure the skewers catch the end flap of meat that has no filling. Rub olive oil all over the outside and season with salt and pepper. (At this point you can roll the roulade tightly in plastic wrap and stash in the refrigerator to cook later.)

TO GRILL. Set up your grill for indirect cooking. If using charcoal, light two chimneys of coals. When hot, bank the coals on one side of the grill. Cut the turkey roulade in between each skewer so you have 6 pinwheels (see illustration). Oil the grill grates. Dry the pinwheels and drizzle olive oil onto one side of each pinwheel. Flip the pinwheels and pour 1 tablespoon of sage balsamic sauce onto each pinwheel.

Tie the sage and rosemary together in a bundle with the butcher twine. Place the melted butter in a small pot, add the herb bundle, and keep it warm on the cooler side of the grill.

Grill the pinwheels over the hottest part of the fire for 2 to 3 minutes per side, until grill marks appear, rotating often to prevent charring. Use the herb bundle to brush each side of the pinwheels with herb butter as they cook. Move the pinwheels to the cooler side of the grill and cover with a lid. Continue to cook, flipping and brushing with herb butter occasionally, for 20 to 25 minutes, until the turkey reaches an internal temperature of 160°F. Remove from the grill, transfer to a platter, and allow to rest for 3 to 5 minutes.

Remove the skewers and pour the remaining sage balsamic sauce over the pinwheels. Serve while hot.

ALSO WORKS WITH. *Goose breast, big game, and wild hog roasts (be sure to cook the wild hog roast to 160°F to kill off any trichinosis)*

Slice the rolled turkey breast between each skewer.

02 INTO THE SMOKE

round 2010, I spent a couple of weeks on a river trip in Guyana with a Macushi friend of mine named Rovin. Macushi territory straddles the borderlands of Guyana, Brazil, and Venezuela. Rovin and his family use rivers to access scattered garden plots of cassava and chiles that are fertilized by the annual flood cycles. Along the way, they collect fish with handlines and nets, and hunt a variety of birds and mammals with archery equipment that is made with natural materials found in the jungle—right down to arrow fletching made from the wing feathers of black curassow. As a child, Rovin's primary mode of transportation was a dugout canoe. Even today, aluminum boats are a fairly novel concept. I don't care what kind of backwoods badass you are, Rovin has you (and me) beat.

Guyana's southern border sits just north of the equator. Average daytime highs are in the mid-eighties. It's so humid that when you reach into your duffel bag to get a clean T-shirt, it feels like you're pulling a wet load of laundry out of the washing machine. Food spoils almost immediately in this climate. Bunches of picked bananas will stay green for days, but their yellow phase seems to last about as long as the yellow light at a traffic stop. Meat is worse. Lay a fish on the riverbank and in a few hours you'll have a stinking mess coated with flies and bees. Typically a person would solve such a problem by burying the fish in a cooler of ice or wrapping it in plastic wrap and placing it on a shelf in the fridge. But these methods have zero relevance to a river trip in the jungles of Guyana, where there's nowhere to plug in a fridge and ice has

the same life expectancy as a wounded fish tossed into a school of piranhas.

Instead, the Makushi have a method for preserving their fish and game that is magical in its simplicity and effectiveness. Every time that we moved upriver and established a new camp, Rovin walked into the jungle with a machete and cut four wooden posts that were each about 4 feet long. The posts terminated at the top end in a Y shape. He set each of these posts vertically into an elbow-deep hole in the sand that he dug by using his machete as a trowel. Rovin then spanned each pair of vertical posts with a long horizontal pole laid into the crotch of the Ys and overlaid these poles with tightly spaced limbs that were just an inch or two in diameter. When it was all said and done, he had a grill-like structure that sat about 30 inches off the ground and covered about 25 square feet of space. Above the setup, Rovin constructed a canopy of palm fronds to help trap the smoke and shield the fire from afternoon rain showers. Beneath it we kindled a slow-burning fire that would be kept alive twenty-four hours a day for as long as we stayed in that one particular camp.

Over the course of our time together, we laid an astonishing array of protein on that wooden rack to bask in the smoke of the smoldering fire: turtles, curassows, guans, catfishes, piranhas, peacock bass, and paca (a semi-aquatic, herbivorous rodent weighing about twenty pounds). Each of these critters was processed in its own particular way before getting a light coating of salt. Large catfish were gutted and chunked up with a machete, the heads split in two lengthwise; curassows and guans were plucked and spatchcocked; the bone-in legs and neck of the turtle were parboiled in a pot made from the turtle's own shell; piranhas and peacock bass were split in half down the spine with the two halves held together by a strip of belly flesh.

From the Makushi in South America to many native Alaskan cultures, the process of preserving food with woodsmoke is still widely used around the world, either because refrigeration isn't an option or because, despite access to modern conveniences, those cultures haven't turned away from traditional preservation methods and cultural foodways that have been practiced for millennia. But even though most of us store the bulk of our meat and fish in the freezer, we cer-

tainly haven't lost our taste for smoked food. And it's easy to imagine how it all began: Some long-ago human notices that the flies aren't nearly as annoying when she stands in the smoke of the fire. At some point she hangs strips of meat there in order to keep the maggots at bay. At first, it's not so much that the smoke tastes good; it's just the flavorful by-product of a novel technique. Soon, the flavor has such positive connotations that it starts to taste pretty damn good all on its own. Someone eventually couples that smoke with another natural preservative, salt. Thousands of years go by, and you can now drive down to your local grocery store and buy a 3.5-ounce bottle of a product called liquid smoke. That's right, get that great smoky flavor without the hassle of flames!

You won't find liquid smoke in any of the smoked foods recipes in this chapter. But please don't think I'm disparaging the stuff. It's described in technical lingo as a natural aqueous condensate of woodsmoke, meaning it really is what the bottle says it is: liquid smoke. The reason that we don't typically use liquid smoke is because we prefer the real stuff. However, we're not terribly picky about how that real smoke gets made. We like pellet grills, we like foil packs full of wood chips, we like good old-fashioned firewood. Nor are we terribly picky about what we put in the smoker. Here you'll find proven and honest recipes for smoking salmon, eels, all kinds of birds, venison, wild hogs, and even eggs and moose nose. With the right strategies and preparations, you'll be surprised what you can get away with. And I've got some good news for you: The more you smoke fish and game, the more skilled you'll get. So keep at it and let these recipes be a stepping stone for you.

SMOKING: WHAT YOU NEED TO KNOW

This chapter explores a range of game and fish recipes that employ different smoking techniques and equipment. Since smoking is a very broadly defined category of outdoor cooking, the ingredients, techniques, and equipment used will have a big influence on how your finished product turns out. For example, there's no reason you can't smoke catfish—just don't expect it to turn out like salmon. On a similar note, brining wild game meat and then smoking it at lower temperatures than you'd use with fatty domestic meat ensures it won't dry out. Likewise, tough cuts need to be braised before smoking. Equipment matters, too, no matter what the provenance of your meat. For example, a hog ham smoked in a pellet grill will not be the same as one smoked in a charcoal grill. I've found that I get the best results by hot-smoking fish and eels in a big propane chamber smoker. And you'll see that I don't cover cold-smoking fish at all since it relies on air-drying fish in ambient temperatures rather than the application of heat, which means it falls outside the scope of the smoking techniques used in this book. Remember, too, that smoking is never an exact science; things won't always turn out perfectly, so make it a point to learn from your successes and your failures. And as with any kind of cooking, once you have a good understanding of the basics, then you should feel free to experiment. There's always room for substitutions and innovations. With those goals in mind, here are the primary smoking methods and the equipment used in this book.

Domestic pork and beef are generally smoked at fairly low temperatures for long periods of time, with a nearly constant stream of smoke. As we've mentioned, wild game hams and fatty sausages can be smoked for longer periods, but other types of lean game meat can present a challenge using this technique. Fortunately, lean game roasts, waterfowl and upland bird breasts, and fish that cook fairly quickly can be smoked directly on grills. It is important to note that if you've got your heart set on smoking tough, sinewy cuts like shanks or shoulders, you'll need to braise or confit them before smoking on a grill.

It's very simple to turn your grill into a smoker. On a charcoal grill, you can add a smokebox full of wood chips or just toss some chips on top of smoldering briquettes. Keep the lid on to trap the smoke that's produced. Some gas grills have an offset chamber that's specifically designed for adding wood chips, but if yours doesn't, all you need is some aluminum foil. Place a fistful of wood chips and woody herbs like rosemary in a store-bought foil tray (see the illustration on page 92). Place the tray over a burner and close the grill lid. Pretty soon the chips will start releasing smoke. If you don't have a foil tray, wrap the chips in a foil packet and poke a few holes in the top of the bundle; the smoke will release through the holes in the foil. The flavor you achieve will depend on what combinations of wood chips, herbs, and spices you use. You can also experiment with aromatic teas.

Lastly, keep in mind that the temperature of propane grills is easily adjustable with the turn of a knob. It is more difficult to maintain a steady, low smoking temperature on a charcoal grill, although barbecue-focused websites like Meathead Goldwyn's Amazing Ribs have excellent tips on how to do it. In addition to a quality meat probe thermometer, it's worth investing in a digital oven thermometer to keep track of the temperature inside your grill.

SMOKING METHODS

Smoking over a Wood Fire

The most basic and purest form of smoking happens over or adjacent to a fire. A smoky fire transmits smoky flavor into game or fish, though you'll generally have more control with other methods of smoking.

Smoking with Foil Trays

A simple foil tray or packet filled with wood chips can be used to add smoky flavor to grilled foods, especially with a propane or charcoal grill. For more unique flavors, you can add dried spices, teas, and hardy fresh herbs such as rosemary, lemongrass, or thyme.

Smoking over a Charcoal Fire

Charcoal smoking can be done in a run-of-the-mill kettle grill, a Japanese kamado-style grill like the Green Egg, or a charcoal chamber or offset smoker. It's a good idea to supplement smoldering lump charcoal with a few blocks of hardwood or soaked hardwood chips for longer smokes.

Chamber Smokers

Charcoal, electric, and propane chamber smokers come in a lot of sizes and configurations, but I prefer the tall vertical propane models for long wild game and fish smokes. They can be easily adjusted and held at a wide range of temperatures. They're also great for turning out big batches of food. One knock against them is that during long smokes, you need to keep adding wood chips to the tray. This can be partially mitigated by soaking the chips in water for 20 to 30 minutes before smoking, or using larger pieces of wood that will smoke longer.

Pellet Grills

The ease and simplicity of smoking with electric pellet grills can't be overstated. All you need to do is pour your preferred flavor of wood pellets into the hopper, set the temperature and timer, and you're off to the races. The pellets are fed automatically and continually into the grill for a steady supply of smoke. They do require regular maintenance and cleanup to keep them functioning properly.

From big offset oil-drum charcoal smokers and vertical charcoal smokers to small electric models and all the various iterations of homemade smoking contraptions in between, there are, of course, more options than what's listed above. If they're not covered in this book, don't take it to mean that we think they're in some way inferior. We feel it's only fair to focus on the methods and equipment we know well and that apply to the recipes in this book. You may already have, or will develop, a preference for a completely different kind of smoker setup. That's great—the recipes in this chapter will still work for you.

MAKE SURE TO PACK YOUR SMOKER FULL OF GOOD STUFF

If you have a large-capacity chamber smoker, it seems only logical to fill the thing up rather than use just a single shelf. For efficiency's sake, I'm a big fan of smoking multiple things at once, including nonmeat items. Mushrooms, apples, pears, butter, cheeses, and hard-boiled eggs (see recipe for Smoked and Deviled Eggs on page 117) can all benefit from a stint in the smoker. Try soaking shiitake mushrooms or pears in ponzu, soy sauce, or Worcestershire with or without a pinch of crushed red pepper flakes. The umami flavors become more intense as the food dehydrates in the smoker. The finished product can be added to soups and salads, served with goat cheese as an appetizer, or used to garnish seared steaks or duck breasts.

A NOTE ON BARBECUE

These days, it seems like there's a barbecue joint around every corner selling smoked brisket, ribs, and chicken wings. There are also hundreds of wildly popular barbecue cooking competitions held all over the country that draw thousands of hungry spectators with imposing rigs of wood-fired offset smokers. And, of course, backyard barbecuing has long been a national pastime. There's a good reason for that: There's just something uniquely appealing about the bold aromas, dripping fat, tender meat, and intense flavors of smoked foods slathered in flavorful rubs and sauces.

Obviously, smoking is an integral part of the barbecuing process. But traditional barbecue-style smoking that we associate with the American South involves long hours of smoking fatty, marbled cuts that self-baste and become fall-apart tender when they're done. With the exception of hams and sausages, it's difficult to truly "smoke" big game cuts in that tradition because of their lack of fat. As such, this is not a barbecue smoking chapter in the traditional sense. This is a chapter about using smoke for flavor and preservation.

COLA ANCHO JERKY

MAKES 1 POUND DRIED JERKY

This jerky recipe is reliable and tasty, with just a hint of heat. It's not full of ghost peppers or other gimmicks that will turn kids off or make it hard to enjoy more than a bite or two. If you do want more heat, ramp up the cayenne. Take note that this recipe uses pink curing salt, which in combination with the smoke makes this jerky extremely resistant to spoilage. If you're planning on eating the jerky pretty quickly and have concerns about the nitrates and nitrites in the curing salt, substitute with ½ cup of kosher salt.

FOR THE MEAT. Move the meat from the freezer to the refrigerator for 3 to 6 hours, until it's just beginning to thaw. Slice while partially frozen into thin pieces, about ¼ inch thick *with* the grain. (If you slice across or against the grain, the jerky will be crumbly rather than having the ideal chew factor.) Transfer the meat to a baking sheet.

FOR THE CURING MARINADE. In a flat nonreactive baking dish, combine the cola, vinegar, soy sauce, brown sugar, hot sauce, cloves, and pink curing salt.

Submerge the meat into the marinade, toss to coat. Seal tightly. Refrigerate for at least 12 hours.

FOR THE JERKY. The next day, remove from the marinade and pat it dry between layers of paper towels. Combine the ancho chile, garlic powder, and cayenne in a small bowl. Prepare a baking sheet with several layers of freezer paper. Dust the meat lightly with the mixture on both sides and lay it out on layers of freezer paper on the baking sheet.

Set up your smoker. For wood chips, fruitwoods produce the mildest flavor, but oak will work as well.

Preheat the smoker to 165°F. Transfer the meat from the freezer paper to a rack in the smoker, being sure to leave room between the slices of meat. It's important to maintain a temperature between 165°F and 200°F when dehydrating or smoking the jerky. After 2 hours, check the texture. The goal is to smoke the jerky until the meat is pliable and leathery, but not overly dry and brittle. It should crack and bend a little but not break easily into small pieces. Continue checking the texture every 15 to 30 minutes, pulling any thinner pieces that might have finished before the thicker ones. The whole process can take up to 4 hours depending on ambient humidity, the consistency of your smoker temp, and how thinly you cut your meat. Remove finished pieces to cool and store them in a resealable or vac-sealed bag.

If you used the Prague powder, the jerky can be stored at room temperature. If you didn't, store in the refrigerator for 6 to 8 weeks or in the freezer for up to 1 year.

JERKY

4 pounds frozen venison bottom round roast

2 cups cola

½ cup apple cider vinegar

½ cup soy sauce

⅓ cup brown sugar

2 tablespoons hot sauce

¼ teaspoon ground cloves

1 teaspoon pink curing salt #1 or Prague powder #1 (optional)

ANCHO DUST

2 tablespoons ground ancho chile

2 tablespoons garlic powder

1 teaspoon cayenne pepper

COOK'S NOTE. *Pink curing salt #1 or Prague powder #1 should not be confused with pink Himalayan salt. Pink salt #1 is a curing salt that is used in curing hard and semisoft sausages, bacon, ham, pastrami, and corned beef. It inhibits harmful bacteria growth and adds a pink appearance to cured meats.*

ALSO WORKS WITH. *I prefer the grain of a bottom round roast for jerky, but a top round, sirloin, or eye of round roast from any red meat big game animal also works great. Goose breasts are ideal for this recipe, too. There are cuts from the front shoulder of big game animals, like the flatiron steak, that make decent jerky as well, though they tend to yield a much chewier end product.*

SUMMER SAUSAGE

MAKES 10 POUNDS

8 pounds meat, cut into 1-inch cubes

2 pounds pork fatback

6 tablespoons kosher salt

¼ cup dextrose (see Cook's Notes)

2 teaspoons pink salt #1 or Prague powder #1 (see Cook's Notes, page 101)

1½ tablespoons mustard seeds

1 tablespoon dry mustard powder

2 teaspoons garlic powder

2 teaspoons freshly ground black pepper

2 teaspoons ground ginger

1 cup Fermento (see Cook's Notes)

4 (2½ x 18-inch) collagen casings

SPECIAL EQUIPMENT

Meat grinder

I've been making this summer sausage recipe for most of my adult life. I initially shared it in the first volume of *The Complete Guide to Hunting, Butchering, and Cooking Wild Game*. I'm sharing it again here because it's stood the test of time so well that I haven't found a reason to change anything. It's perfect for everything from a backpacking trip to a holiday appetizer. You can mess with the flavor profiles if you wish by swapping spices, but this version is a proven winner. This recipe makes a 10-pound batch. You can halve or even double it if you like. I recommend a 2-day ferment, so be sure you plan appropriately.

TO GRIND/PREPARE THE SAUSAGE MIXTURE. Keep everything ice cold (following the chilling instructions for Camp Sausage on page 36). Combine the game meat, pork fat, and all of the other ingredients except for the Fermento and casings in a large bowl. Mix to combine with your hands. Work in small batches and keep the meat cold by returning it to the fridge or freezer as needed. Using the ¼-inch (medium) plate on your grinder, grind the meat mixture into the bowl set over ice. Change to the ³⁄₁₆-inch (small) grinder plate and pass the mixture through the grinder again.

Meanwhile, in a bowl, dissolve the Fermento in 1 cup of water and stir with a spoon. Add to the ground meat mixture and again mix well with your hands until it's all incorporated. (You can also use a standing mixer and incorporate the Fermento and water on low speed.)

Firmly press a piece of plastic wrap over the surface of the meat, making sure there are no air bubbles. Cover the bowl with a second layer of plastic wrap and set it in the refrigerator to ferment for 2 days.

After about 48 hours of fermenting, make a test patty and cook it in a sauté pan to be sure your seasoning is what you'd like it to be. Adjust the seasonings if needed.

TO STUFF THE SAUSAGE. Using a sausage stuffer, stuff the sausage into the casings. Let the stuffed casings rest in the fridge, uncovered, for 1 to 2 hours to dry out.

PREPARE THE SMOKER. Soak a pan full of applewood chips for 20 minutes. (Alternatively, choose applewood pellets if using a pellet grill smoker.) Preheat a smoker to between 112°F and 130°F; this is lower than most pellet smokers will go, so go to the lowest setting your smoker allows if that is the case. Drain the wood chips and add them to the smoker. Throughout the smoking process, keep the applewood-chip pan full. When the temperature is between 112°F and 130°F, lay or hang the sausages in the smoker. Smoke for about 1 hour at this temperature, then raise the temperature to 180°F. Smoke until the internal temperature of the sausage reaches 150°F, which will probably take 2 to 3 hours, depending on your particular smoker and the ambient temperature outside. Refill the wood chips as needed if they get low.

When the sausages are done, let them hang at room temperature for 1 hour to cool, then wrap well or vac-seal and refrigerate. They will last 4 months in the fridge and can be frozen for 6 to 12 months.

Serve with crackers and/or cheese or simply eat with a hunting knife while taking a break on a hike.

COOK'S NOTES. *Fermento is a fermentation starter made from cultured whey protein and skim milk. It's commonly used in summer sausage and other semidry sausages. It expedites the fermentation process, eliminating longer curing times. You can find it online, at specialty butcher shops, or in sporting goods stores with a well-stocked assortment of game processing supplies.*

Dextrose powder is a sugar used in sausage making. It is a nutrient that feeds the lactic organisms and aids in the fermentation process.

ALSO WORKS WITH. *Any ground meat, ranging from whitetail deer to beef.*

BROWN SUGAR WILD HOG HAM

Kevin Gillespie

Smoking a ham that has been slathered in something sweet isn't a new idea, but sometimes it's better to refine rather than reinvent. This particular version came about as a way to stop my mom from showing up to every holiday function with a precooked honey baked ham that she ordered through the mail. To me they taste overly processed and bring zero sense of nostalgia to the table. I wanted a ham that reminded me of what my late grandmother would serve every Christmas and Easter. Something with a perfect balance of sweet, salt, and smoke that left a lasting impression. I prefer to make this preparation with feral hogs because I like smaller-sized hams, but it works just as well with domestic hogs.

SERVES 4 TO 6

CURING BRINE

1¼ cups packed light brown sugar

1 cup kosher salt

1 pound onions, peeled and quartered

½ cup garlic cloves

1 tablespoon whole cloves

1 cinnamon stick

Pink curing salt #1 or Prague powder #1

2 quarts ice cubes

1 (5- to 7-pound) bone-in ham from a feral or farm-raised pig

SUGAR COATING

1 pound light brown sugar

2 teaspoons ground cloves

2 teaspoons ground cinnamon

1 teaspoon freshly ground black pepper

FOR THE BRINE. Combine the brown sugar, salt, onions, garlic, whole cloves, cinnamon stick, and 2 quarts water in a large pot and bring to a boil over high heat. Remove from the heat and stir in the curing salt. Immediately add the ice cubes, stirring till they melt and the brine is cooled completely.

Trim all discolored pieces from the outside of the ham, paying close attention to any spongy glands or membranes, as they may cause spoilage. Cut off the meat 1 inch from the shank end of the ham, exposing the bone. Trim any meat around the hip bone as well in order to expose the bone. This will allow the brine to penetrate the meat evenly.

Place the meat in a large resealable storage bag, and pour as much brine into the bag as possible. The meat needs to be fully submerged in the brine. Force any excess air from the bag and place it into a large bowl to collect any potential leakage. Place this in the fridge to cure for 7 days, making sure to flip or rotate the bag daily to ensure even curing.

On the seventh day, remove the ham from the brine and discard the liquid. Place the ham on a rack over a sheet pan and return it, uncovered, to the refrigerator for 1 more day so the exterior can dry. Alternatively, you can dry the exterior thoroughly with paper towels and place it near a fan for an hour before moving on to the next step.

Preheat your smoker to its lowest temperature and highest smoke setting. This will vary depending on the smoker you choose to use, but the goal is to create maximum smoke without cooking the ham. This step creates flavor while also providing an extra level of preservation in the final product. Smoke the ham for 2 hours.

FOR THE COATING. While the ham is smoking, mix together all the ingredients for the sugary coating and set aside. Place three pieces of heavy-duty foil, overlapping, on a sheet tray and set aside.

Preheat the oven to 350°F.

Remove the ham from the smoker and place it on top of the foil with the fat side facing up. Pack the contents of the sugar coating on top, making sure to use the entire amount. Wrap the ham in the foil, leaving room for steam to collect; ensure that all the seams are facing up so none of the juices escape during cooking.

Bake the wrapped ham for approximately 15 minutes per pound, or until the center reaches a temperature of 155°F. (The temperature will continue to rise above 160°F after the ham is removed from the oven, so don't worry about trichinosis.)

Remove the ham from the oven and allow the meat to rest for 1 hour before unwrapping and carving it. Pour the liquid contents of the package through a fine-mesh strainer into a measuring cup and skim away the fat that collects on the top. Carve the meat into slices and serve warm with the reserved juices. Alternatively, you can chill the ham overnight before carving.

COOK'S NOTE. *For larger hams in the 11- to 15-pound range, increase the brining time to 10 days.*

Kevin Gillespie is an Atlanta-based chef and restaurateur who is a seven-time James Beard Awards finalist and has appeared on Bravo's hit TV show Top Chef. *Kevin is also a lifelong hunter who has adapted many of his recipes for wild game.*

HOT-SMOKED TROUT
(OR WHATEVER OTHER FATTY FISH YOU'VE GOT)
Brody Henderson

During the spring and summer months, my family spends a lot of our free time fishing the chain of large reservoirs along Montana's Missouri River. My two sons absolutely love hauling limits of yellow perch and walleye into the boat, but often a large, chrome-bright rainbow trout ends up as a welcome bycatch when we're targeting those other species. Most of these trout are "stockers" that spend the first several months of their lives at a fish hatchery, swimming in cement raceways, where they're fed a steady diet of pellets that resemble dog food. At about 10 inches long, they take a ride in the stocking truck and get dumped into a lake. These smaller trout are very easy to catch but admittedly are not the best table fare. So, when we catch a little one, it gets released. After a few years, though, these fish transform into something more worthwhile. As they feed on aquatic insects, freshwater shrimp, and crayfish, they develop thick and meaty fillets that are a vivid orange color. If you didn't know better, you'd be forgiven for thinking you were looking at a piece of wild salmon.

I often tell my sons there are two kinds of fish. There's the fish you fry, like perch, and there's the fish you smoke, like trout. That's not strictly true, of course, but the boys have taken to calling rainbows "smokers." When we land a nice one—say 16 to 20 inches long—it gets bonked on the head, bled out, and tossed in the cooler right alongside those fish that are destined for the deep fryer. At home, the trout get filleted, and the fillets are vac-sealed and frozen until late summer or early fall. By then, we've usually built up a pretty good supply. I'll dry-brine a batch big enough to fill up my vertical propane chamber smoker. Glazing the trout with maple syrup or honey during the smoking process isn't a necessary step, but it does make the finished product more appealing to kids. Either way, it's perfect for making smoked fish dip, mixing with scrambled eggs, tossing in pasta, or on its own as an appetizer or snack. In fact, it's one of my go-to hunting snacks. Throughout the fall, I'll eat smoked trout out in the field as an alternative to jerky, so I like a product that's been dehydrated until it's a little harder and drier than the smoked salmon you'd typically find in a grocery store. That way, it won't get smashed into a mushy consistency when it's riding around in my backpack. If you prefer a softer, moister version of smoked fish, then cut down on your smoking time a bit. The great thing about this stuff is that once it's been preserved in salt, sugar, and smoke and tightly vac-sealed, it will keep for weeks in the fridge or months in the freezer without any drop-off in flavor or texture.

You'll need fillets from trout over 16 inches long or whole trout if smaller; brown sugar; kosher salt; and honey, for basting. For fish over 16 inches long, this method works best with fillets; for anything smaller, whole fish work well. For small whole fish, leave the head on so you can hang them in the smoker using the twine harness shown for hanging eels on page 113. Or smoke them lying horizontally on your smoker's rack, making sure to flip them occasionally. You can smoke just a single fish or a couple fillets, but it's better to have a pile of 6 to 12 fillets or several smaller whole fish so you can make a big batch and save a bunch for later.

FOR PREP. This step is not necessary, but I recommend it before brining: Run the tips of your fingers over the meatiest part of the fillet. You'll feel a line of pin bones that you can remove with tweezers or needle-nose pliers. This is easiest to do after the fish has been frozen and then thawed.

BRINING. A dry brine ratio of 2 cups brown sugar to 1 cup kosher salt is standard, but you can also do a 4:1 ratio for a less salty product. Make sure to brine your fish in a nonreactive container like a Pyrex casserole dish or a big plastic Tupperware container.

FOR FILLETS. Lay the fillets skin-side down in the brining container and generously coat only the flesh side of each fillet with the dry brine mixture. If necessary, you can stack fillets in layers. I don't usually brine longer than 8 hours, and you could do as few as 4 hours with small, thin fillets. If you go over 12 hours, you're going to end up with a super-salty product. You'll know the fish has been brining long enough when the fillets are swimming around in all the moisture that the brine has drawn out of the flesh.

FOR WHOLE FISH. Cover the fish inside and outside with the dry brine mixture. Aim to keep your brining time between 8 and 10 hours, but you might need more for fish with thick bodies.

CREATE A PELLICLE. Remove the fish from the brine, rinse it thoroughly, and pat it dry. Set it on a rack to dry for a couple hours in a cool spot or place it near a fan to dry. After 30 to 60 minutes, you should notice a glossy, sticky film on the surface of the flesh. This film, called the pellicle, traps minute smoke particles, which boosts the flavor of the final product.

SMOKE. Set your smoker to 160°F. Keep an eye on it throughout, and don't let the temperature get over 180°F. If you go hotter, you'll end up with a different end product, since you're cooking the fish quickly, not drying it out slowly. (And you'll also coax the white albumen from the flesh—nasty looking but harmless if it does happen.)

While smoking, baste the fish a couple times with honey so it becomes glossy and glazed.

For small whole fish, smoke just until the skin starts to become loose. Check after about 2 hours if you like your smoked fish soft and moist. Smoke up to 3 or 4 hours if you want it drier and more preserved.

STORAGE. Vac-seal the smoked fish and store it in the fridge for a few weeks or the freezer for a few months.

After a long guiding career in Colorado, Brody Henderson joined MeatEater as a wilderness production assistant. Now a senior editor on MeatEater's publishing team, he has collaborated with Steven Rinella on several books, including The MeatEater Fish and Game Cookbook, The MeatEater Guide to Wilderness Skills and Survival, *and this book.*

SALMON JERKY

MAKES ABOUT 2 QUARTS, PACKED LOOSELY

2 pounds coho salmon fillet, skin on

CURE

1 (2-pound) bag dark brown sugar (about 6 packed cups)

1 cup Diamond Crystal kosher salt (see Cook's Note)

SEASONING

4½ teaspoons coriander seed, toasted and coarsely ground

1½ teaspoons smoked paprika

1 tablespoon orange zest

⅛ teaspoon cayenne pepper

⅓ cup maple syrup

SPECIAL EQUIPMENT

Large, wide container with a tight-fitting lid

Rimmed baking sheet with a rack

These days there are so many names for hot-smoked salmon that you can't keep them all straight. You've got salmon candy, salmon jerky, kippered salmon, hard-smoked salmon, and on and on. I dig them all, even if I'm not totally sure what makes them all different. My brother Danny calls this version salmon jerky, and as he lives in Alaska and processes dozens of the fish every year, I'll defer to his judgment. The key to this recipe is that you keep your mixture at a 6:1 ratio of brown sugar to salt. The downside is that it uses a lot of brown sugar, which ain't free. The upside is that the brown sugar makes it impossible for the fish to get too salty. It's the perfect recipe for lazy or forgetful cooks, because you can leave the salmon in this cure mixture for a week and it still won't be too salty. Bag up the finished project with a vac sealer and you've got the perfect travel snack for just about any outdoor activity.

FOR THE SALMON. Cut the salmon lengthwise (from head to tail) into 5- or 6-inch-long strips about ½ inch thick. (If using small fillets, cut the strips as long as possible, even if it's crosswise.)

FOR THE CURE. In a large bowl, thoroughly combine the brown sugar and salt. Sprinkle a thin coat of the mixture over the bottom of a large, wide container with a tight-fitting lid. Arrange one layer of salmon on top of the cure. (Try to calculate how many more layers of salmon you will have and divide the cure amount so that you have enough to cover each layer.) Sprinkle more of the cure on top of the salmon. Continue to layer until all of the salmon and brine are used up. Cover and place in the refrigerator to cure for at least 8 hours or overnight.

The next day, fit a rack into a rimmed baking sheet and set it aside. Rinse the salmon well and pat dry.

FOR THE SEASONING. In a large bowl, mix the coriander, paprika, orange zest, and cayenne until well combined. Add the salmon to the spice mixture and toss until evenly coated. Arrange the salmon in a single layer on the rack. Place in the refrigerator, uncovered, to dry out for at least 8 hours or overnight.

TO SMOKE. Set the smoker to 160°F using the wood pellets of your choice. Transfer the salmon, still on the rack, onto the smoker grate. Close the lid and let the salmon smoke for 1 hour.

Brush the salmon with the maple syrup. Continue to smoke, brushing with the syrup every 15 minutes, until the salmon is dried and stiff but still pliable, 2½ to 3 hours total.

Transfer the rack to a baking sheet and let the jerky cool to room temperature. Once cool, transfer the jerky to a container with a tight-fitting lid and store in the refrigerator for up to a month. In a vac-sealed bag it should keep about 3 months in the fridge and 6 months in the freezer.

COOK'S NOTE. *We're using Diamond Crystal kosher salt in this recipe, which has 53 percent less sodium by volume than Morton's kosher salt, so it's important that you seek it out. If you choose to use Morton's kosher salt, it will be saltier in taste; you'll want to adjust the quantity.*

ALSO WORKS WITH. *Any species of salmon, char, or trout.*

SMOKED AMERICAN EEL

When I was writing my first book, *The Scavenger's Guide to Haute Cuisine*, I spent some time with an eel trapper named Ray who lived on the Delaware River and ran his own smokehouse. Ray had a lot of philosophies about life and how to live it. As he showed me around his facility, I was mostly focused on capturing all of his musings in my notebook. This caused me to miss what was perhaps the most important thing he told me all day, which was the exact brine recipe that he uses for his eels. I didn't know how much of a mistake I'd made until that night, when I finally sampled his wares and realized how damn good they were. Later, when reviewing my notes, I found just four simple things written down: salt, brown sugar, honey, water. I couldn't remember what other ingredients he might have listed, if in fact he listed any others at all. I had written nothing about quantities. Based on these admissions of mine, you might see how I'm torn about whether to say I stole this recipe from Ray the eel trapper. Maybe "inspired" is a better way to put it. When you make it, don't worry too much about the amount of eels you're using. This recipe will handle pretty much anywhere from one to ten if you've got an appropriately shaped container to brine these snakelike critters. But since it's not really worth firing up your smoker for just a single eel, let's say it's good for four to ten.

PREPARE THE EELS. If you have live eels, pour about an inch of salt in the bottom of a cooler and put the eels in there. This will kill them quickly and helps to remove their slime layer. Rinse the eels before making an incision on the underside of the body from the anal vent to the gills. Remove the guts and gills and rinse again thoroughly.

FOR THE BRINE. Combine all ingredients in a bowl or 3-quart dish large enough to hold the eels. Chill the brine. Add the rinsed eels and submerge them. If necessary, use a plate to keep the eels beneath the surface. Soak refrigerated for 24 hours.

SMOKE THE EELS. Truss the eels (see illustrations, opposite) so they're ready to hang in your smoker.

Prepare a vertical smoker for low heat—you want it to be 165°F to 175°F. Hang the eels from the top of the smoker. Add wet wood chips. Keep the smoker as cool as possible, adding more chips as needed.

The eel skins will take on a glossy golden hue when they're close to being ready. Similar to smoking trout, cook the eels until the skin begins to peel away and the meat becomes tender enough that you can easily break it apart. Remove the eels from the smoker and allow to cool for a few minutes before eating or storing in a vac-sealed bag for about 3 months in the fridge and 12 months in the freezer.

Serve over rice with a soy-based sauce like teriyaki.

4 to 10 American eels

Kosher salt

BRINE

1 cup kosher salt

1 cup brown sugar

¼ cup honey

8 cups lukewarm water

ALSO WORKS WITH. *Black cod (sablefish), mackerel, herring, eulachons (hooligans), bluefish, and any other oily white-fleshed flesh.*

TRUSSING EELS

1. Tie an 8- to 10-inch piece of kitchen twine into a loop.

2. Stick the eel's head through the loop and use a pair of hemostats or needle-nose pliers to feed the lower end of the loop into the gills/throat and out through the mouth.

HOT-SMOKED FISH SAUSAGES

CHORIZO-STYLE

MAKES ABOUT 5 SAUSAGE LINKS; SERVES 12 TO 16 AS AN APPETIZER OR 4 AS A MAIN COURSE

This recipe is great for when you've got a mixed collection of fish and seafood. It's really best not to skip the scallops, as they make the texture smoother and add a richness you won't get with just fish. This sausage is made by smoking it over indirect heat on a charcoal grill. It takes less than 20 minutes, so plan to have other vegetables or bread to grill on the hot side once it comes off. It's ideal for serving as an appetizer at a backyard dinner party, but you could also prepare the sausage in advance and make it for dinner while car camping.

If you're not into smoking this sausage, you can sear it on both sides in a pan and finish it on a grill or in the oven.

TO PREPARE TO GRIND. Soak the hog casings in fresh water for 30 minutes. Rinse a few times to remove the salt, then run water from the faucet through the casing to remove any excess salt inside it. Chill the grinder attachments in the freezer before getting started.

FOR THE SAUSAGE. Cut the white fish, salmon, and scallops into a medium dice and combine them in a bowl with the guanciale. Add the smoked paprika, salt, cayenne, granulated garlic, onion powder, oregano, dry mustard powder, and parsley to the bowl and mix well with your hands. Cover the bowl and refrigerate for 2 hours.

Remove the grinder attachments from the freezer and set up the grinder with a medium die. Take the fish mixture from the refrigerator. If you're making a large batch (double or more of this recipe), be sure to keep the fish mixture in a metal bowl over another bowl of ice to stay chilled while you work. In that instance, you may find that you'll need to return the mixture to the refrigerator occasionally to cool off if it loses its chill. Run the fish mixture through the grinder into a bowl.

Set up the sausage stuffer according to the manufacturer's instructions. Stuff the sausage loosely in a long, large link. Twist the sausage into links at about 5-inch intervals, the first one going clockwise, then counterclockwise, and alternating until you make it through the long link. You'll want to leave a little space between the links so they can be snipped later. You will be able to make about 5 links, give or take. Once the links are formed, examine the sausages for air bubbles and prick them with a pin or the tip of a knife to release the air. This will keep the sausages from popping when they're cooked. Refrigerate the links for at least 2 hours, uncovered, on a parchment-lined baking sheet to dry the skins out a little bit. (They can be vac-sealed and frozen for up to a year at this point.)

Recipe continues

FISH SAUSAGE

1½ pounds white fish fillets, such as perch, whiting, porgy, or halibut

1½ pounds salmon fillets

1½ pounds scallops

¼ cup diced guanciale (1¼ ounces)

2 tablespoons smoked paprika

1½ tablespoons kosher salt

1 teaspoon cayenne pepper

1 tablespoon granulated garlic

1 tablespoon onion powder

1 teaspoon dried oregano

1 teaspoon dry mustard powder

1 tablespoon chopped fresh flat-leaf parsley

RED PEPPER AIOLI

1 garlic clove

5 egg yolks

Pinch of kosher salt

2 roasted red bell peppers, seeded, or substitute 1½ cups drained jarred roasted peppers

2 tablespoons Dijon mustard

¾ cup neutral oil, such as canola

2 teaspoons lemon juice

Neutral oil for the grill

1 baguette, sliced into ¼-inch-thick rounds

Olive oil, for drizzling

SPECIAL EQUIPMENT

Hog casings

Sausage stuffer

Meat grinder

2 wooden skewers

ALSO WORKS WITH. *You'll want to keep the scallops, but otherwise feel free to substitute with any kind of fish, lobster, crayfish, shrimp, crab, or shellfish.*

FOR THE AIOLI. Drop the garlic down the food processor chute to mince it. (If you're using a blender, mince the garlic first before adding it.) Turn off the processor, add the egg yolks and a pinch of salt. Roughly chop the roasted peppers and add them and the mustard. Pulse to puree. With the motor running, add the oil to the pepper-egg mixture in a fine drizzle to make an emulsion. Continue to blend together for 30 to 60 seconds, until a thick aioli forms. Taste and add salt if needed and the lemon juice. Process for another 30 seconds to combine. Transfer the aioli to a serving dish or refrigerate in an airtight container. The aioli should be consumed within 24 hours, or it will begin to separate and break down.

TO SMOKE THE SAUSAGE AND GRILL THE BREAD. Soak 1 quart of cherrywood (or other fruitwood) chips in a bowl of water for 20 to 30 minutes. Set up a charcoal grill for indirect high heat. Light a chimney full of coals, and when ready, pour all of the coals on one side of the grill to make two heat zones. Sprinkle the drained cherrywood chips over the glowing coals. If using a propane grill, create two heat zones by turning off one or two rows of burners, depending on the size of your grill, and add your wood chips to a foil tray or a wood-chip smoking box.

Arrange the linked sausages in a spiral and insert two intersecting skewers to secure the spiral. When the grill is ready, lightly oil the sausages and the grill grates and place them on the indirect-heat side of the grill. Close the lid and hot-smoke for 10 to 12 minutes. Open the lid, flip the sausage, and cook for an additional 5 minutes. Check the internal temperature, which should be between 135°F and 145°F. Remove from the heat.

Lay the sliced bread out on a baking sheet. Lightly drizzle olive oil over the sliced bread on both sides. Place the oiled bread on the hot side of the grill, for about 2 minutes, flipping when it has deep brown grill marks. Cook for another minute and remove from the grill.

Slice the sausages on a bias, spread aioli on each piece of grilled bread, and top with a slice of sausage. Serve warm.

SMOKED AND DEVILED EGGS

MAKES 12 HALVES; SERVES 4 TO 6

Prepare a smoker to 225°F (this also works with a pellet grill, chamber smoker, and even a charcoal grill). Choose a mild-flavored wood, like pecan apple, or another fruitwood.

Lightly oil the grill grate. Place the eggs on the grate away from the smoke source so they are not touching the sides of the smoker or each other. Cover and smoke, maintaining the temperature as needed, for 30 to 40 minutes. The eggs will turn a streaky tawny brown when finished. Remove them from the smoker and let cool.

Cut the eggs in half lengthwise and scoop the yolks into a bowl. Mash with a fork until broken up. Mix in the mayonnaise, mustard, capers, dill, and red onion and continue to mash and stir until creamy and well combined. Use two spoons to fill each egg white with some of the filling (1 heaping tablespoon per half). Garnish with a small dill frond and pimenton (if using).

Neutral oil for the grill

6 large eggs, hard-boiled and peeled

5 tablespoons mayonnaise

2 tablespoons Dijon mustard

1 tablespoon capers, chopped

1 tablespoon dill fronds, chopped, plus more for garnish

1 tablespoon minced red onion

Pimenton or smoked paprika, for garnish (optional)

COOK'S NOTE. *The night before you hard-boil the eggs, lay them on their sides in the fridge. This will center the yolks.*

SMOKED VENISON SANDWICHES

SERVES 6 TO 8

ROAST

1 (2-pound) boneless venison roast, trimmed

Kosher salt

Neutral oil, for smoking

RUB

1¼ teaspoons dry mustard powder

1 teaspoon garlic powder

½ teaspoon onion powder

½ teaspoon paprika

½ teaspoon light brown sugar

¼ teaspoon freshly ground black pepper

¼ teaspoon kosher salt

⅛ teaspoon cayenne pepper

ANCHOVY MAYO

1 cup mayonnaise

1 tablespoon Worcestershire sauce

1 teaspoon anchovy paste

½ teaspoon fresh lemon juice

SANDWICHES

6 to 8 sandwich rolls

6 to 8 slices Swiss cheese

There's a lot of tension in my house around the subject of lunch meat. I like to run a strict wild game program in my kitchen, but my wife and kids are always complaining about not having deli sliced ham and beef for sandwiches. This recipe is a good compromise for us. Sure, you can eat the roast for dinner without confining it between slices of bread, but when paired with anchovy mayo, it makes a spectacular sandwich that'll beat anything you get from a deli counter. If anchovy mayo isn't your thing, go with a horseradish mayo or a sharp and spicy mustard.

FOR THE ROAST. Generously rub the roast all over with salt. Cover and refrigerate for 2 days, turning it once a day.

FOR THE RUB. Mix the dry mustard powder, garlic powder, onion powder, paprika, brown sugar, black pepper, salt, and cayenne in a small bowl.

TO SMOKE. The day of smoking, prepare a smoker to 225°F and maintain this approximate temperature throughout. Oil the grates. Remove the roast from the fridge but do not pat it dry. Massage the spice rub onto the meat. Smoke the roast until the internal temperature reaches 125°F (for medium-rare) to 130°F (for medium), about 3½ hours.

Remove the meat from the smoker and let it rest until the meat firms up in order to thinly slice, at least 1 hour.

FOR THE ANCHOVY MAYO. Whisk the mayonnaise, Worcestershire, anchovy paste, and lemon juice until smooth in a small bowl.

FOR THE SANDWICHES. Halve the sandwich rolls and spread each side with anchovy mayo. Put a slice of cheese on the bottom roll. Very thinly slice the meat against the grain and pile onto the rolls.

MAKE AHEAD. This is a roast you'll want to bring with you fully cooked in a cooler on a camping trip. It's great on its own, warmed up with a bit of pan gravy, and it's versatile. Use it in sandwiches like this one or the iron pies on page 170. For best flavor, keep the mayo in an airtight container in a cooler or refrigerator for up to 2 days.

GRILLED WILD BOAR RIBS WITH PEACH GLAZE

Jesse Griffiths

Feral hogs come in all shapes, sizes, and fat contents, and so do their ribs. Some are thick enough that they'll look like you bought them from a butcher. Others are so thin you can almost read a newspaper through them. Most ribs, however, fall somewhere in the middle, with a moderate amount of fat, a lot of connective tissue, and some delicious, lean meat. The dry heat of the smoker is only effective when there's enough insulating fat to keep the layers of meat underneath moist during the long cooking process, so an individual assessment of each hog—or any game animal—is imperative. To level the playing field, I like to "cheat" the leaner ribs by gently poaching them in a highly seasoned and spiced bath, then finish them on a smoky grill when it's convenient. This method works very well on other animals with meaty ribs, like mule deer and elk. By seasoning the ribs beforehand, you'll keep the broth from being too salty, and it can then be kept and used for other purposes, like cooking beans, lentils, or even rice. Here we are glazing them with a simple barbecue-esque sauce made from peach jam. Feel free to substitute most any other fruit jam to suit your preference, availability, sense of experimentation, or regional specialization. If you're feeding a family or a crowd, you might want to double this recipe.

SERVES 4 TO 6

1 single side of wild boar ribs, cut in half to make two racks	1 medium onion, peeled
Kosher salt	1 garlic head, halved crosswise
Freshly ground black pepper	1 cup peach or other fruit jam
1 teaspoon fennel seed	¾ cup apple cider vinegar
2 bay leaves	8 tablespoons (1 stick) unsalted butter
	Hot sauce to taste

Season the ribs with salt and pepper. Cover and refrigerate for 24 hours. Put the ribs, spices, onion, and garlic in a big pot and cover with cold water by about 6 inches. Bring to a simmer over medium-high heat and cook until tender but not falling apart, 2 to 4 hours, depending on the age of the animal. Add water as needed to keep the ribs submerged. Remove the ribs and cool them completely in the refrigerator. Strain the broth and reserve it for another use.

Soak a handful of pecan or mesquite wood chips for 30 minutes in water. Preheat a charcoal grill until you are able to hold your hand over it for no more than 4 seconds. When ready, toss the wood chips over the coals to add some smoky flavor.

Meanwhile, in a small pot over low heat, mix the jam, vinegar, butter, and hot sauce until melted.

Place the ribs on the grill and brush with the glaze. Repeat this basting process several times more, glazing the ribs well. Once nicely charred and falling apart, remove the ribs to a cutting board and cut between each rib. Serve immediately.

A frequent MeatEater collaborator, Jesse Griffiths is a hunter, fisherman, award-winning chef, and the author of the cookbooks Afield *and* The Hog Book. *He is the co-owner of Dai Due Butcher Shop and Supper Club in Austin, Texas, where he features fresh local ingredients, including wild game and fish.*

SMOKED BONE-IN HOG ROAST
WITH MOSTARDA (MUSTARD-APPLE COMPOTE)

SERVES 4 TO 6

1 bone-in wild boar loin roast
(2 to 3 pounds with 9 rib bones,
depending on the size of the hog)

DRY BRINE

2 teaspoons kosher salt

1 teaspoon freshly ground black pepper

1 tablespoon ground fennel seed

SAGE PASTE

4 garlic cloves, smashed and peeled

1 bunch fresh sage, leaves picked
(about 15 leaves)

2 teaspoons ground fennel

2 to 3 tablespoons olive oil

MAPLE-SAGE BUTTER

8 tablespoons (1 stick) unsalted butter

2 tablespoons maple syrup

4 fresh sage leaves

Pinch of kosher salt

1 recipe Mostarda (Mustard-Apple
Compote), see page 353

Pretty much any bone-in loin rack looks cool, but this one tastes as good as it looks. The wild hog loin is hit with a dry brine (you can use a wet brine if you prefer) and then paired with an apple compote that resembles mostarda, the Italian candied fruit that comes jarred in a mustard-flavored jelly. Because wild hog ribs generally have a small amount of meat on them compared to domestic pigs, limit the dry brining time to overnight. Any longer and you risk drying out the meat or making it too salty.

Truss the hog loin with twine for even cooking.

FOR THE BRINE. Combine the dry brine ingredients. Rub the dry brine all over the trussed roast. Place the roast on a baking sheet and loosely cover with plastic wrap—or better yet, leave it uncovered to air cure. Set in the refrigerator overnight.

FOR THE SAGE PASTE. The next day, pull the roast from the refrigerator and pat dry. Mince together the garlic and sage. Add the fennel seeds and olive oil to make an herby paste. Spread the paste over the hog loin on all sides and set aside for 30 minutes to come to room temperature while you set up your smoker and make the maple-sage butter and apple mostarda.

FOR THE MAPLE-SAGE BUTTER. Combine all of the ingredients in a small saucepan over medium-high heat and whisk to combine. Bring to a boil and reduce until thick, about 3 minutes. Set aside and keep warm so it doesn't congeal.

FOR THE SMOKER. Set your smoker for 225°F. Use any fruitwood chips you've got (I prefer applewood here). Add a drip tray with water to keep moisture circulating in your smoker. Place the roast in the smoker for 45 minutes, then check the internal temperature of the meat. Once it hits 100°F, raise the temperature of the smoker to 375°F or 400°F. Begin basting the roast with the maple-sage butter about every 15 minutes. Smoke the roast until the internal temperature is 160°F (as a precaution against trichinosis), 1½ to 2 hours. It could be ready earlier, so keep a close eye on it.

Serve warm with mostarda (see page 353).

BBQ-STYLE SQUIRREL
WITH THE SCHLITZ WHITTINGTON SMALL GAME BASTING SAUCE

Kevin Murphy

Schlitz Whittington was an insurance salesman on first shift and a cattle farmer on second shift. He obtained his people and veterinary skills working as a medic over Korea way along the 54th parallel. My friend Brooks and I worked on his farm when we were kids. He was lots of fun to work for, and we were eager to learn and not afraid to tackle a roll of woven wire fencing. We worked real cheap, too, and every day except Sunday. That's where I learned how to handle wild, exotic half-breed cattle and the concept of job responsibility. It's also how I learned about this basting sauce.

My friend and mentor loved to drink Schlitz beer, which he used to baste meats as well. He also taught me the recipe for this sauce, which was meant to keep your barbecue from drying out while cooking over wood coals. I never wrote the ingredients down, but the main components stuck with me—lard, butter, vinegar, hot sauce, and black pepper. Over time I adapted the sauce to work on wild game by adding extra lard, since most game has little fat.

The sauce has always been Schlitz's to me, but recently I found what appears to be the original recipe by way of fate. It came to me in a box of cookbooks I'd bought just last summer from Uncle Joe at Trade Day (our local flea market). This particular volume was called Kentucky Hospitality, *published by the Kentucky Federation of Women's Clubs in 1976. And lo and behold, what should I find but an "Authentic Barbecue Dip" from a BBQ stand in Old Eddyville that was owned by a Mr. Charlie Robinson around 1940! The place was behind a motel gas station in the town that Schlitz grew up in. Now it's all underwater, covered by Lake Barkley after the damming of the Cumberland River. But here was the origin of the Schlitz Whittington basting sauce!*

I have been mopping big ole fox squirrels with this sauce for forty-six years and counting. Just don't go too heavy or it will jump-start your fire and burn your squirrels.

To make the sauce, combine one gallon apple cider vinegar, one bottle of hot sauce, one pound of lard or butter, and a gob each of red and black pepper in a pot and heat to a low boil. Reserve and keep warm for basting.

Now about those squirrels. I am fortunate to live in Kaintuckie, where we are blessed with white oak and hickory in abundance. But feel free to use any hardwood that will reduce to red-hot glowing coals that create a superhot cooking surface. First build a roaring fire. After the fire has burned down, transfer the red-hot coals to your cooking area with a long-handled shovel. Place a metal cooking grate 18 inches or so above the coals using rocks or any kind of stable prop. You will need to add some coals as you cook, so be careful.

Spread 4 to 8 whole squirrels, washed, cleaned, and salted to taste on top of the grate. Baste with the Schlitz Whittington Small Game Basting Sauce real good over the top of each squirrel. Repeat this every 10 minutes. Turn the squirrel over after 20 to 30 minutes and start basting all over again every 10 minutes. After 50 minutes, start checking for doneness. I do this by sliding a fork into the thigh meat at its thickest part. When it slides through easy-peasy, it's done. If you can tear a rear leg off without much twisting at all, that's a sure sign, too! Over a hot hardwood charcoal fire it will take about an hour, maybe a little longer or a little less. At the end, you can add your favorite BBQ sauce and go to town.

Kevin Murphy is better known to MeatEater fans as the World's Best Small Game Hunter. Kevin lives in the Land Between the Lakes region of Kentucky, where he hunts, fishes, and cares for a kennel full of hounds and cur dogs that he uses to pursue his favorite game animals—rabbits and squirrels.

BRINED AND SMOKED TURKEY BREAST
WITH MAPLE-CHILE GLAZE

SERVES 6 TO 8

ENRICHED BRINE

½ cup kosher salt

½ cup packed light brown sugar

4 garlic cloves, smashed

10 black peppercorns

10 juniper berries

1 bay leaf

2 quarts ice (8 cups)

TURKEY BREAST

1 skin-on boneless turkey breast (2½ to 3 pounds), tendons removed from the tenderloin

1 teaspoon kosher salt

4 tablespoons (½ stick) unsalted butter, at room temperature and very soft

MAPLE-CHILE GLAZE

1 cup real maple syrup

1 tablespoon crushed red pepper flakes

MAKE AHEAD. *For camping trips, you can brine and smoke the breast ahead of time and then freeze it, sliced, in a vacuum-sealed bag. Add the meat to sandwiches and soups, iron pies, or just eat it as a snack. The glaze can be stored in an airtight container for up to 1 month.*

ALSO WORKS WITH. *Goose or duck breasts (skin on or off), domestic turkey and chicken breasts, and whole upland birds such as pheasant and grouse (remove the legs for another use, or cook them separately until tender).*

This recipe is tailored for pellet grills, because they make it a breeze to quickly smoke-roast meats at temperatures around 350°F. The Maple-Chili Glaze is ridiculously simple as well; it has just the right sweetness and heat to counter the smoke of the grill. You can use another kind of smoker, or any of the setups described on pages 92–93. Just bear in mind that you want to keep the heat fairly consistent and baste the meat often.

FOR THE BRINE. Add all brine ingredients and 6 quarts water to a pot, bring to a boil, and stir to dissolve. Remove from the heat to cool. Transfer the brine to a heatproof container and stir in the ice. This should cool the brine sufficiently enough so that you can add the meat; it should be cold to the touch, and ice cubes should still be floating.

FOR THE TURKEY. Brine the meat, covered and refrigerated, for 2 to 3 hours in a large container. The meat should be submerged under the brine. If it is not, weigh it down with a plate or pot lid.

After the meat has brined, remove it from the brine, rinse, and pat dry. Season the skin with salt. Slather the top of the turkey breast skin on top and under the skin with the butter. Tie the roast with cooking twine for even cooking (see illustrations on the next page).

TO SMOKE. Preheat a pellet smoker to between 365°F and 375°F. Choose a mild wood; apple or another fruitwood will work well. If using a portable grill to smoke, set the grill up for indirect heat (see the illustration on page 92).

FOR THE GLAZE. Meanwhile, combine the maple syrup and red pepper flakes in a saucepan and bring to a low boil. Boil for 3 minutes, reducing the heat slightly. Remove from the heat and allow the glaze to cool completely.

Place the breast in the center of the smoker with a drip tray slightly larger than your turkey and filled with water underneath. Don't skip this step; the butter will run off the bird and make a smoky mess if you do. Roast the bird with light smoke for about 1 hour and then begin basting it with the glaze. Keep basting every 20 minutes until the internal temperature is 155°F. (Start checking the temperature after 40 minutes. The cooking time could take about 2 hours, probably less.) The skin should be crisp and caramelized when finished. Remove the turkey from the pellet grill, glaze again, and let rest for 10 to 15 minutes before serving. Slice thinly, especially if you've got an old bird.

HOW TO TIE A TURKEY BREAST (OR ROAST)

1. Cut a length of kitchen twine about three times longer than your turkey breast or roast. Tie a basic knot around the end of the turkey breast and secure it with a second knot. Position the knot in the center of the skin-side-up turkey breast.

2. Lay the string along the top of the breast and hold it down with your forefinger about 1 inch from the first knot to form an L-shaped corner. Using the other hand, wrap the string around and under the breast to meet your forefinger, and tuck the long end of the string under the L-shaped corner to form a loose knot. Repeat this step for the length of the turkey breast, making as many loops as needed.

3. When you reach the end of the turkey breast roast, secure the last knot with an additional knot. You could end here, or continue on for a tighter version (especially if using a turkey or goose breast).

4. Flip the roast over. Weave the remaining length of the string under and then over the cross strings to bring a uniform shape to the underside of the roast. Repeat this under all of the strings.

5. After the last string on the underside, flip the roast skin-side up again. Pull the remaining loose string around the end of the roast to tie it with the original knot. You are ready to braise, roast, or smoke the turkey breast roast.

SMOKED DUCK
WITH HONEY, BALSAMIC, AND CHIPOTLE GLAZE

SERVES 2 TO 4

BRINE

½ cup kosher salt

½ cup packed light brown sugar

5 black peppercorns

5 juniper berries

1 bay leaf

2 quarts ice (8 cups)

---

4 wild ducks (roughly 1½ to 3 pounds each), plucked and gutted

Kosher salt

1 garlic head, halved crosswise

6 fresh thyme sprigs

HONEY, BALSAMIC, AND CHIPOTLE GLAZE

Makes about ¾ cup

1 cup honey

1 tablespoon chipotle chile flakes

2 fresh thyme sprigs, leaves removed

¼ cup balsamic vinegar

COOK'S NOTE. *Whenever I cook with a vertical smoker, I try to make use of any available upper racks that aren't filled with meat. It's a great opportunity to dehydrate, slow roast, or smoke mushrooms, tomatoes, and even fruit (see page 94).*

ALSO WORKS WITH. *Puddle ducks such as mallards, teal, and wood ducks; domestic ducks, or upland birds and chickens as well as wild hog roasts.*

In my opinion, duck breast is always best when it's cooked hot and eaten medium-rare. I can't say the same thing about duck thighs, which I tend to prefer when they're slow-cooked to the point that the meat is ready to fall off the bone. I'll sometimes separate the thighs and breasts on my ducks for this reason, so that each portion can be handled in its own particular way. For this recipe, though, go ahead and leave your ducks whole. You'll be smoking the bird to a decent middle point, where the breast is well done and the legs will be cooked through to satisfaction. The Honey, Balsamic, and Chipotle Glaze is what makes this dish truly special.

FOR THE BRINE. Add all brine ingredients (except the ice) plus 6 quarts water to a pot, bring to a boil, and stir to dissolve. Remove from the heat to cool. Transfer the brine to a heatproof container and stir in the ice. This should cool the brine sufficiently enough so that you can add the meat.

Add the duck to the brine for 2 to 3 hours.

FOR THE GLAZE. Meanwhile, combine the honey, chipotle chile flakes, and thyme leaves in a saucepan and bring to a low boil. Boil for 3 minutes, reducing the mixture slightly. Remove the glaze from the heat and allow it to cool completely, then stir in the balsamic vinegar. Transfer to an airtight container and store in the refrigerator for up to 2 weeks.

After the duck has brined, remove it and rinse and pat dry. Season the skin with salt. Prick the skin halfway through with a fork or paring knife, making slits in several places. This helps the fat to render evenly and the smoke to permeate the meat. Fill the cavity with the garlic halves and the thyme sprigs.

TO SMOKE. Set up your vertical smoker (or another kind of smoker) with wood chips. I prefer apple- or cherrywood for this smoke, but you can use whichever wood suits you. Preheat the vertical smoker to 250°F. With a vertical smoker, you control how much smoke you want to add to your food. I usually give the bird a stronger push of smoke in the beginning, and then let the heat of the smoker finish the cooking.

Be sure to add water to the drip tray. Place the duck above the drip tray and smoke, checking the internal temperature after 1 hour to see how fast it's going, then begin basting with the glaze. Check the temperature in 30 minutes and glaze again. You're looking for an internal temp of 150°F to 155°F, which will happen between 1½ and 2 hours. At this temperature, the breast will be well done, and the legs will be tender enough to slice and serve.

SMOKED MOOSE NOSE HASH

Jessee Lawyer

Growing up in the foothills of Vermont's Jay Peak, in the small border town of East Richford, I was no stranger to catching a glimpse of a moose. The sight always left me with a sense of awe. For my Abenaki ancestors, the animal was considered one of our most important relatives for both sustenance and daily life. My first taste of moose meat was equally inspiring. My Abenaki heritage comes from my father's side, but my grandfather and two uncles on my mother's side of the family were hunters who traced their lineage back to some of the earliest settlers in Quebec. My uncle Steve always shared his moose meat with us, and those meals are some of the most memorable of my life.

It wasn't until I met Jeff, who contributed the instructions that follow this recipe, that I was able to relive those memories. Despite growing up hunting, I didn't hunt large game with any success until later in life. And although I grew up with Abenaki culture and art, my family was missing a link to our traditional food systems. I've been cooking in professional kitchens for the last fourteen years, but it wasn't until six years ago that something clicked, and I became interested in our traditional foods. Diving deep into traditional foods means reconnecting with wild game and with sometimes faint memories of northeastern delicacies such as moose nose.

This recipe for moose nose hash is based on the first moose nose that Jeff and I cooked together with fiddleheads that he foraged. This was a great addition, but any foraged or farmed greens or herbs will do.

SERVES 4

8 tablespoons (1 stick) unsalted butter, cubed

1 medium onion, diced (about 1 cup)

3 large Yukon Gold potatoes, scrubbed and cut into medium dice (about 5 cups)

½ teaspoon paprika

½ teaspoon garlic powder

¼ teaspoon freshly ground black pepper

1½ tablespoons kosher salt

¾ cup smoked moose nose fat (see page 135)

3 garlic cloves, minced

1½ cups smoked moose nose meat (see page 135)

4 large eggs

Cholula Hot Sauce, for serving

Prepare a charcoal grill. When the briquettes are completely white, place a large cast iron skillet directly on the heat. (Or use a propane camp stove set at medium high heat.) Add 2 tablespoons of butter to the pan to melt. When butter is sizzling, throw in all of your onions.

When the onions begin to brown, stir in the potatoes until they are evenly distributed. Add 4 tablespoons of the butter, the paprika, garlic powder, black pepper, and salt. Cook until the potatoes begin to soften and brown on the edges.

Add the remaining 2 tablespoons butter and the garlic and stir for a minute or two. Add the moose nose fat first, and cook for 2 minutes, then add the nose meat and let it all brown together. It's finished when the potatoes get that beautiful hash crisp and the meat and fat are all heated through.

Remove from heat. In a separate skillet or saucepan, cook your eggs over easy; if you're classy or at home, poach the eggs. You can also cook the eggs right in the hash. Runny yolks are a must for a delicious sauce that brings the hash together. Serve with your desired amount of Cholula, and enjoy.

HOW TO SMOKE A MOOSE NOSE

Jeff Stewart

I grew up in a subsistence hunting household on the Penobscot reservation in Maine, where moose hunting is embedded in the culture and identity of our people. In our family, my father did the hunting, and he hunted only moose. But he didn't actually love moose hunting—it was a job, a duty. We were dependent on the meat, but I believe the drinking and camaraderie at moose camp was what kept him going year after year. He never took me or showed me how to hunt.

We ate moose several times a week growing up, but the meat wasn't treated like something special. It was ground meat and thin, overcooked steaks. It wasn't until I became a professional chef that I started to learn nose-to-tail concepts and eating the stuff most people threw in the garbage. But it took a while before I became a hunter.

After fifteen years as a chef, I left the kitchen and took a regular nine-to-five job. I had been wanting to get back to my roots and exercise my tribal sustenance hunting rights, and I now had the time to embrace the experience. One Saturday morning in 2013, I watched a show called MeatEater *for the first time. It had a profound effect on me. Here was a hunter who was demonstrating the ideology of my indigenous culture, in terms of honoring the entire animal by cooking things like hearts and tongues. Watching Steve inspired me to use my own culinary experience to respect every animal that I harvested. Now I treat wild game like any other protein I'd encounter in a professional kitchen. If it can be done with beef, then it can be done with moose is my attitude.*

Butchering. There are a couple ways to remove the nose from an unskinned moose head. With a reciprocating saw, cut straight down all the way through the nose where bone meets the cartilage. This method gives you some bony structure to hold things together while you're cooking. Or you can use an extremely sharp boning knife with a 7- to 8-inch blade to carve the nose off. Where the bone meets cartilage on top of the nose, cut down and out along the bone to remove the nose. If you have experience with butchering animals, this part will feel intuitive, and you could also try it with a bison or bull elk. To avoid spoilage, remove the nose while field dressing or not more than 24 hours after death. Wash the nose with cold water and coarse salt to remove blood, paying special attention to rinsing the nostrils until clean.

Boiling. In a large stockpot, add the nose and a couple tablespoons of salt and cover with water. Bring to a boil over high heat, cover the pot, and reduce the heat to medium. A slow rolling boil is ideal. Cook for approximately 4 hours. If needed, add water throughout the process to make sure the nose is always submerged. Periodically skim away any floating hair, dirt, and other loose bits. To check your nose for doneness, try peeling off a small piece of the hide. If it comes off easily, the meat is ready. Remove the nose from the pot and shock it with cold water.

Peeling. It's best to peel when the nose is still warm, so don't let it sit in the cold water for more than 3 minutes. Start at the bridge of the nose and peel the thick parts first. Be careful not to get hair on the peeled parts as you're working; the fat is very tacky and makes getting hair off difficult. Use a cloth hand towel to grip the skin and help keep hair off the fat. Peeling can be a real pain in the ass, but resist the urge to put the whole thing back in the water and cook it longer. This will ruin the top layer of fat. The most difficult parts to peel will be in and around the nostrils. Use a sharp paring knife for those areas. The age of the moose is a major factor in the peeling process. The easiest nose I've ever peeled was from a young bull, and the hardest was from a very old cow.

Smoking. Get your smoking going at 225 to 250 while you're peeling the nose. I prefer to smoke with apple or maple, which are plentiful in Maine. Smoke for one hour. The cartilage in a moose nose is a maze, so removing it without wasting edible parts can be difficult. While the nose is still warm, I cut the nose in half the long way and slowly pull out the cartilage. This part, like peeling, requires some patience. A paring knife will come in handy.

Once the cartilage has been removed, you can portion out the meat. There will be some very marbled, meaty bits as well as some white fatty bits. I like to separate the meaty parts from the fatty ones. The fatty parts are incredible and can be eaten as is, but I like to cook them like bacon in a pan with some butter or bear fat. Some of the nose fat will caramelize and get crispy and other parts will melt. The meat is wonderful in sandwiches, tacos, stew, and in the hash recipe on page 133.

1. Moose noses removed by a reciprocating saw. They can also be removed with a boning knife.

2. Moose nose, post boil—peeling skin in preparation for smoker.

3. Fully cooked moose nose cut in half the long way. The cartilage is maze-like and very hard to remove once the nose has cooled.

4. Broken-down fully cooked and smoked nose.

5. Fatty bits separated from meaty bits.

Jessee Lawyer and Jeff Stewart are friends, hunting partners, and chefs. Jessee is a member of the Abenaki Nation in Vermont, and Jeff is a member of the Penobscot Nation in Maine. They have made it their mission to teach other hunters about the virtues of butchering and cooking moose noses. They believe it's a worthy cut of meat to be honored and eaten rather than wasted.

BRAISED AND SMOKED WILD GAME BRISKET

RUB

1 tablespoon garlic powder

2 tablespoons ground black pepper

1 tablespoon paprika

BRAISE

1 large bison brisket (3 to 4 pounds), cleaned of sinew but keeping as much fat as possible

Kosher salt and freshly ground black pepper

½ cup pork lard, at room temperature

½ medium onion, sliced crosswise

1 (12-ounce) bottle light beer

ALSO WORKS WITH. *Moose, elk, or beef brisket. Or for you Texans, nilgai.*

When I go to one of those Texas BBQ joints where you get to pick your meat, I always go with beef brisket. One of the things I love about beef brisket is that it's so different from wild game. I can make an approximation of smoked ribs and sausages and even chicken with wild game, but brisket is a different story. The amount of fat and marbling in beef brisket makes it a hard thing to replicate with big game. What I've found, though, is that you can achieve the approximate results if you take an entirely different approach to get there. That approach is to braise the brisket until it's tender, and then finish the meat in a smoker. It's not the same process as Texas barbecue, nor is it the same greasy and succulent dining experience. But it is delicious nonetheless and introduces a whole new way to handle a cut of meat that usually just ends up in the grinder pile or, worse, the scrap heap. The brisket on whitetail and mule deer isn't big enough for this preparation, but bison, elk, and moose are all adequately sized. The braising liquid is a fat-laden mixture of beer and aromatics.

FOR THE RUB. In a small bowl, combine all ingredients. Set aside.

Preheat the oven to 325°F.

FOR THE BRAISE. Pat the brisket dry. Season liberally with salt and pepper on both sides. Sprinkle 1 tablespoon of the rub on the brisket, covering both sides. Slather the lard on the top of the brisket.

Measure two pieces of foil longer than a 9 x 13-inch baking dish by 6 inches on each side. Measure out a piece of parchment paper about the same length. Lay one piece of foil on the baking sheet lengthwise with the overhang even on the sides of the dish. Lay the other piece of foil perpendicular to the first piece in the middle, making a cross. Lay the parchment paper down lengthwise in the baking dish. Fold the sides of the foil up to form a loose bowl-like shape. Lay the onions down on the parchment. Add the brisket on top. Pour 8 to 12 ounces of beer into the foil—it should come halfway up the sides (make sure the foil holds in the liquid).

Carefully fold the parchment paper by joining the two short ends, then folding them over to make a somewhat airtight seal (like a tightly wrapped deli sandwich). Do the same with the two pieces of foil to enclose the meat, keeping the liquid inside the foil-parchment package.

Put the baking dish with the foil-wrapped packet into the preheated oven. Braise for 2 to 3 hours, or until tender, checking at 1½ hours. (To check, carefully open up the packet, use a knife to check tenderness, and wrap up again and return it to the oven if it's not ready.) When it is very tender with no resistance to the knife in multiple spots, remove it from the oven; the internal temperature will be over 170°F when it is ready.

Let the brisket rest at room temperature still wrapped in foil while you set up your smoker.

Remove the brisket from the foil packet, reserving the braising liquid for later use. Season with the remaining dry rub if a heavy pepper flavor is your preference.

Soak a large handful of wood chips in water, preferably a wood such as pecan or hickory. Preheat your smoker to 175°F to 200°F, and add the soaked wood chips when up to temperature. Smoke the meat aggressively for 20 to 30 minutes (the goal is to have a low cooking temperature and high smoke to impart flavor).

Slice and serve with your favorite barbecue sauce or the reserved braising liquid. Refrigerate any leftovers. To serve at a later date, reheat refrigerated slices in a sauté pan with the reserved braising liquid to warm through.

03 UNDER THE COALS

first moved to Montana in 1997, but it took me well over a decade to learn that the state picked up its "Big Sky Country" nickname from A. B. Guthrie, Jr.'s 1947 novel, *The Big Sky*. I'd known all along about the book, which is largely set in Montana, but I wrongly assumed that it took its title from the state's nickname rather than vice versa. As it turns out, the Montana State Highway Department secured permission from Guthrie to use his novel's title for an ad campaign. Starting in 1962, tourists were baited to Montana with the enticement to "Travel Montana, the Big Sky Country, Between Yellowstone and Glacier."

Guthrie's novel tells the story of a wild and hot-tempered boy from Kentucky named Boone Caudill.

In the early 1800s, Caudill flees home after nearly killing his abusive father by clocking him over the head with a piece of firewood. He winds up on a French keelboat full of traders headed up the Missouri River into what is now Montana. An ambush by Blackfoot warriors kills just about everyone on the boat. Caudill survives to become an accomplished and daring mountain man, but his hot temper never cools. Late in the novel, he puts a pistol ball through the chest of his own best friend. Alone and wayward, he's left to contemplate the death of the American West.

The novel's arc might seem like a rather gloomy foundation for a tourism ad campaign, and the treatment of Native American characters is pathetic, but

‹‹ "Panless" steaks cooked on an oiled rock

it's easy to see why the story has appealed to so many for so long. For one thing, it's an ode to outdoor cooking—not that the characters have any choice; there's no indoors available to them. You get a sense of the book's culinary sensibility early on when Caudill kills a rabbit after running away from home. He cuts it into small pieces and presses the pieces to a flat rock and then props the rock next to the fire. As an accompaniment to the rabbit, he uses creek water to moisten some cornmeal drawn from a small "poke" (that's a bag, for you folks who aren't hip to the old-timey vernacular) and rolls it into balls that he drops directly into the coals. Baked in such a way, he calls these johnnycakes. Over the course of the book, he eats a great many simple meals like this: dried corn and beans cooked with buffalo marrow, cubes of half-rotten buffalo bull meat cut with the grain to save "the blood and juice," and cubed meat boiled in a kettle with wild onions.

If Caudill has a signature dish, it's the head of a mule deer buried in the coals of a fire and left there to roast. Before reading the novel, I had experienced a similar dish in West Texas, just a few miles from the Mexico border. I was with some cowboys who shot one of their steers with a .22 rimfire and wrapped its head in chicken wire before burying it inside an underground brick oven. We used the meat to make tacos de cabeza. It was good, but not so memorable that I added it to my personal repertoire. That didn't happen until a few years later, when I was traveling with friends along the Missouri River just upstream from where Caudill first samples the deer-head-in-the-ground dish. We had the fresh head of a mule deer doe in our camp. After discussing the novel, we buried the head in the coals of a cottonwood fire and let it go for a few hours. The rich, greasy meat was textured similarly to braised

spare ribs and pulled away from the bone just about as easily. The recipe that was ultimately developed from that experience is covered in detail in one of my previous books, *The Complete Guide to Hunting, Butchering, and Cooking Wild Game, Volume 1: Big Game.*

This chapter is a massive expansion on that style of cooking. Here you'll find preparations that utilize ashes and coals to cook a wide variety of dishes: roasts, veggies, game stews made in Dutch ovens, gooey sandwiches made in iron pies, next-level foil packets, and even a venison shoulder cooked in a barrel. Of all the types of outdoor cooking explored in this book, cooking beneath and among the coals is perhaps the trickiest. A lot of the action is hidden from view; cooks who like to crack open the oven or grill in order to check on the progress of their dishes are likely to have their patience tested while attempting our Towel-Wrapped Roast Beneath the Coals recipe on page 172. I realize that this might scare you off. When most folks buy a cookbook, they're not looking for an experience in trial and error. They're looking for proven methods, with all the wrinkles ironed out. Admittedly, I can't totally guarantee that you won't have any surprises or disappointments when you're messing around with this chapter. Things might get a tad burned, or things might come out a little raw. But what I can guarantee is that you'll learn a ton. Cooking food nestled in the coals is not only a way to impart a smoky sweetness to foods like potatoes and squashes, which steam in their skins; it's an efficient way to utilize a campfire: You can be grilling steaks or a whole fish on a grate over the flames while steam-roasting potatoes adjacent to the flames in the coals. Stick with it and you'll have some amazing meals. And come to think of it, there's a second guarantee that I'll make. You'll enjoy cooking under the Big Sky, wherever you find it.

COOKING WITH COALS: WHAT YOU NEED TO KNOW

Just like all of the methods discussed in this book, cooking with wood coals or charcoal briquettes is never an exact science. Although there are well-researched formulas and guidelines for coal cooking (see the sidebar on page 152), you don't have the luxury of making adjustments with the simple turn of a knob as you do when working with propane grills, smokers, or campstoves. There's also a big difference between cooking over a fire that's crackling and blazing and cooking over (or under) a bed of slowly smoldering coals. For starters, coals do throw off a predictable and consistent level of heat, so they are easier to work with than active flames, which tend to fluctuate wildly. Keep in mind, however, that over time the heat output of wood coals slowly decreases. And since we're talking about outdoor cooking, the same uncontrollable environmental factors that can affect fires (wind speed, ambient temperatures, precipitation, etc.) can also impact coals, though usually to a lesser degree.

The type of wood or charcoal you're burning is another factor to consider. Pine and other softwood coals, for example, won't crank out heat nearly as long as dense hardwoods like oak. Likewise, manufactured briquettes and lump hardwood charcoal have varying heat outputs; compressed charcoals, such as binchotan, have even more. Still, wood coals can also be ma-nipulated in a manner that isn't possible with flames. Using shovels and coal rakes, coals can be moved around and placed precisely to allow for a variety of cooking methods ranging from searing steaks to roasting whole squash. Coals also have the staying power and high-heat output needed for all-day projects like cooking whole hogs in a caja china or drum-type roaster. The following chapter dives into several of our favorite coal cooking scenarios, along with the best equipment to use for each.

But first, it's important to understand that you're always playing the long game with coals. There are certainly times when a faster cooking method might be more practical. Even if a given recipe only takes a few minutes to cook, you'll need to plan for the additional time needed to produce coals. Charcoal chimneys and charcoal grills take a little while to heat up. It requires even more time for a fire to transform hunks of firewood into a bed of glowing orange coals. And you will need to maintain a fire or a series of charcoal chimneys in order to have a steady stream of active coals for longer cooking processes. In other words, cooking with wood coals isn't something that you can rush. In that way, it's a lot like hunting and fishing—you need to embrace the entire process, not just celebrate the end result. Approached this way, you'll get into a rhythm and get damn good at it, too.

Cooking Food Directly on Coals

Cooking food directly on coals is about as primal and basic as it gets. This can be done with lean hunks of venison, whole fish, and even sturdy hard-skinned vegetables like squash and yams. However, cooking really fatty stuff directly on coals will cause violent flare-ups. Even without fat, you're going to end up with a charred surface, but that's part of the appeal. If you want to cook something that is fatty or achieve a light sear rather than a hard char, then use a grate to suspend food away from the coals, as you would do with a charcoal grill.

Cooking in Foil Packs

The usefulness of heavy-duty aluminum foil in outdoor cooking can't be overstated. From steamed veggies to baked potatoes to roasted fish, you can season just about anything, wrap it in foil, toss the package on some hot coals, and the end result will turn out great—especially if you follow the guide on page 152. You can even turn out entire dinners packaged as individual servings this way. If you're looking for a way to keep prep and cleanup simple, foil-pack cooking is the way to go.

Dutch Ovens

Cast-iron Dutch ovens were invented for the purpose of cooking over fires and hot coals hundreds of years ago. The lids have a lip on the edge, which is meant to hold hot coals in place. Not much has changed about them since then, which ought to tell you it's worth having one around. There's really no limit to the range of cooking methods or types of recipes you can use with a Dutch oven that's hanging over, resting on, or covered up in coals. You can achieve controlled, steady temperatures that allow you to braise meat, fry fish, simmer stews, and bake desserts. (See sidebar on page 152 for Dutch oven coal ratios.)

It's hard to go wrong with a Lodge product, and when in doubt, bigger is usually better. Consider getting one with legs so you can easily shove hot coals underneath it. If yours doesn't have legs, get a pot stand, or you can make one with a few rocks. A tripod is another great accessory for hanging Dutch ovens over a fire or bed of coals.

Pie Irons

Pie irons are another cast-iron cooking implement that's designed for coal cooking. Basically a camping version of a panini press, pie irons are used to make sandwich-style dinners with multiple ingredients like ham, ground or shredded meat, onions, cheese, and/or vegetables. Whatever the ingredients, these sandwiches are regionally known as hobo pies, pudgy pies, mountain pies, or iron pies, as we like to call them. You can do a lot more with pie irons, too, from desserts to breakfast scrambles. And they're simple to use, so kids love cooking with them.

DUTCH OVENS
Counting Coals for Approximate Temperatures

The beauty of using a centuries-old cooking tool is that most of the kinks have been worked out. That's certainly the case with Dutch ovens, which have been in production since the 1700s. With a little research, you'll find plenty of charts showing how many charcoal briquettes to use around your Dutch oven in order to achieve your desired temperature. Campfire wood coals aren't an exact match to briquettes in terms of temperature, but they come close enough.

There are two common depths for Dutch ovens: a shallow or "baking oven" and a deeper Dutch oven. The baking oven's lid is closer to the food, so it can more easily brown the tops of biscuits and breads. The deeper oven is ideal for cooking large-volume stews and soups for a crowd. Whatever the size of your pot, the recipes in this book follow the coal-to-temperature guide below—if you're working with bigger or smaller pots, adjust as noted. These numbers come from the folks at Lodge Cast Iron.

We recommend starting out with these approximate quantities, knowing you may need to adjust on the fly. Learning when to add more coals is as much about gut instinct as it is following strict formulas—the more you do it, the more you will learn and feel comfortable riffing.

10-INCH-DIAMETER (4-QUART) *SHALLOW POT*
(USE 4 MORE COALS FOR A 5-QUART *DEEP POT*)

350°F—21 coals (7 underneath, 14 on top)   400°F—25 coals (8 underneath, 17 on top)

375°F—23 coals (7 underneath, 16 on top)   425°F—27 coals (9 underneath, 18 on top)

12-INCH-DIAMETER (6-QUART) *SHALLOW POT*
(USE 4 MORE COALS FOR AN 8-QUART *DEEP POT*)

350°F—25 coals (8 underneath, 17 on top)   400°F—29 coals (10 underneath, 19 on top)

375°F—27 coals (9 underneath, 18 on top)   425°F—31 coals (10 underneath, 21 on top)

COAL-ROASTED SMASHED POTATO BAR

SERVES 6

This is a fun dish to make with the family. It gives kids a nice primer on how to cook with fire using ancient techniques. Basically you're just wrapping potatoes in a protective coating—in this case, aluminum foil—and burying them in the coals until they have soft interiors and a smoky flavor from the fire. When done, you open up the foil and smash the cooked potato together with your choice of toppings. We're taking a pretty standard approach with this recipe, using sour cream, bacon, and chives. If you want some different options, check out the sidebar on this page.

Get some briquettes going in a charcoal grill or build a wood fire in a pit or campfire circle. If using a wood fire, wait until the wood burns down into coals, or crush some charred logs with a shovel to create hot coals.

Put each potato on a double layer of heavy-duty aluminum foil. Rub the skins with oil and sprinkle with salt and pepper. Enclose the potato in the foil. Use tongs to nestle the potatoes in the coals. Don't crowd them so they're touching each other. Cover the grill and cook, turning the potatoes occasionally so all sides are exposed to the coals. If cooking on a charcoal grill, you may need to add a second chimney of prepared coals to keep the temperature high. (If using a wood fire, just keep turning the potatoes every 5 to 10 minutes and add a log to the fire to keep the coals coming.) Cook until they are very tender, 45 minutes to 1 hour. Check for tenderness with a paring knife.

Unwrap the potatoes and place them on a cutting board or serving tray. Use the lid of a small pan, the bottom of a bottle, or a sturdy spatula to press down and smash the potatoes flat (about ¾ to 1 inch thick). Sprinkle with salt and pepper. Evenly top with the cheese. Then distribute the bacon, sour cream, chives, jalapeños, and tomatoes over the top or substitute a topping from the sidebar on this page. Serve warm.

ALSO WORKS WITH. *Sweet potatoes, yams, any color or kind of potato (red, purple, or russet).*

6 medium Yukon Gold potatoes

Olive oil or bacon fat, for rubbing the potatoes

Kosher salt and freshly ground black pepper

6 ounces sharp cheddar cheese, shredded

6 slices cooked bacon, crumbled

Sour cream

Chopped fresh chives

Chopped pickled jalapeños

Chopped tomato

MORE TOPPINGS

Feta, olives, chopped tomatoes

Peperonata (page 34) and mozzarella

Sausage, mushrooms, Gruyère cheese

Blue cheese, buffalo sauce, cooked game bird

Anchovy Mayo (page 118), cooked backstrap

Chili, cheddar cheese, sour cream

Arugula, prosciutto, mozzarella

MIX AND MATCH FOIL PACKS

You're not alone if the first meal that you ever cooked outdoors was a mixture of ground meat, potatoes, and onions wrapped up in a foil packet. Untold numbers of scout masters and camp counselors have trained several generations' worth of kids in this preparation. While foil packs remain a fun, simple way to make camp dinners, there's plenty that can be done to improve the experience. A shortcut to foil-pack perfection is to take a three-step mix-and-match philosophy that combines a protein, vegetable, and sauce into a hearty meal. You'll also find some more involved recipes that are worth the time and effort. For all of these recipes, we suggest using heavy-duty aluminum foil. For each serving, cut one 17 × 20-inch piece of foil.

STEP 1: CHOOSE YOUR AROMATICS AND PROTEIN

Aromatics are herbs and vegetables that add flavor and aroma to a dish. Many of the vegetables come from the allium (onion) family. You'll often see them mentioned when making stocks and stews or steaming recipes, for example, and because foil packets use a combination of steaming with a little searing against hot coals or grates, aromatics are a surefire way to add fast flavor to your meat and fish. Some of these are edible when cooked, others are too woody to eat.

Try chives and wild onions; garlic; leeks; thin slices of onion, shallots, carrots, parsnips, fennel or celery; scallions; ginger cut into coins (discard after cooking); spicy fresh chiles; bay leaves, rosemary or thyme (discard after cooking).

From a flavor perspective, the best proteins for foil packets are those that do well when poached or steamed. This brings fish and shellfish front and center, but big game and birds can be players, too. If using big game, choose ground meat or already tender cuts like backstrap, sliced thinly, and understand you may need a knife to cut them into bite-sized pieces. Whichever protein you choose, be sure to season it with kosher salt and freshly ground black pepper or a pinch of red pepper flakes before adding it to your packet.

Options include fish such as salmon or white flaky fish cut into 2- to 4-ounce pieces; small whole trout fillets; shellfish; large upland bird breasts, sliced thin and pounded, then cut into 2-ounce pieces; small whole upland bird breasts; ground game meat; thin strips of venison (this is not as palatable and my least favorite choice).

STEP 2: CHOOSE YOUR VEGETABLES

Just about any vegetable can make its way into a foil packet. Below are some of our top choices, but let your garden or the farmer's market be your guide. Heck, throw some foraged mushrooms or ramps in, too. Whatever is in season will shine when cooked this way. Keep in mind that most proteins will cook between 12 and 20 minutes, so the trick here is to cut large vegetables in a way that will allow them to cook within that time span. And remember, vegetables taste delicious with a little char. To achieve this, nestle one side of the foil packet against hot embers and flip every 5 to 10 minutes. It should also be said that vegetable-only packets are a worthwhile way to pull off a quick, healthy side while camping.

Try broccoli or cauliflower cut into ⅓ inch planks; thin strips of bell peppers, kale, bok choy, cabbage, or zucchini; green beans, wax beans, or snow peas cut lengthwise; spinach or mustard greens, potatoes or sweet potatoes cut into small rounds ¼-inch thick; cherry tomatoes.

STEP 3: CHOOSE YOUR SAUCE

Sauces for packets can be as simple as a ready-made sauce from a bottle, a drizzle of olive oil and a splash of wine, or a more elaborate concoction you make yourself. There are a few truths to keep in mind: First, fat carries flavor, so make sure you've got some in the form of olive oil, neutral oil, butter, or duck fat; second, too much acidity can burn a hole through your foil and reacts with foil in a way that creates an unpleasant taste. Insulate the acids with enough oil or other liquids. Additional flavorings like capers, olives, citrus zest, sun-dried tomatoes, wasabi, dry rubs, or seasonings can also add punch and brightness.

Great options for your sauces include citrus juice with zest; extra virgin olive oil; jarred sauces such as barbecue, Worcestershire, Thai peanut or Teriyaki; neutral oils; soy sauce; toasted sesame oil (a little goes a long way); any kind of vinegar; white or red wine—be sure to use the acidic sauces with oil so that the acidity doesn't pit the foil.

STEP 4: COOK YOUR PACKETS

Start by preparing a campfire (or charcoal or propane grill). For each foil packet: Cut your 17 × 20-inch pieces of foil. Lay your aromatics and proteins in the center of the foil and season with salt and pepper. Add your vegetables around or on top of the proteins. Add your sauce and any other additional flavorings.

Bring together the long sides of the foil up and over the food in the center. Fold the foil pieces over a few times, crimping them together securely. Seal the short sides of the foil by folding them over a few times toward the center mound.

The campfire is ready when there is a bed of glowing coals. With a coal rake or another tool, pull these coals out to the edge of the fire. Place the foil packets on and near the hot coals or on the grill grate. For fish fillets, cook about 15 minutes, flipping the packet halfway through. For other meats or all vegetable packets, cook for 20 minutes, flipping the packet halfway through. Allow the packets to rest for 5 minutes before opening and serving with a squeeze of lemon (if desired).

SOY-STEAMED GOOSE BREAST
WITH BABY BOK CHOY

Divide the scallion whites and garlic evenly between the two 17 × 20-inch pieces of aluminum foil. Drizzle each mound with 1 tablespoon of the olive oil and season evenly with ¼ teaspoon of the salt. Divide evenly and place the goose breast strips over the scallion whites and garlic and season the meat with the remaining ¼ teaspoon salt. Divide and arrange the bok choy evenly around the goose breasts. In a small bowl, stir together the soy sauce, mirin, rice vinegar, and sesame oil. Divide this mixture and pour over each portion of goose. Scatter the scallion greens on top. Seal and cook for 20 minutes. Serves 2.

ALSO WORKS WITH: *Duck or upland bird beasts, big game burgers, or thin strips of backstrap.*

COOK'S NOTE. *If you have the time, marinate the sliced goose breast for up to 4 hours in the mirin sauce mixture before placing it in the packets and steaming.*

VEGETABLE

4 small baby bok choy, halved lengthwise

AROMATICS AND PROTEIN

1 bunch scallions, white and green parts, cut into 1-inch pieces

2 garlic cloves, thinly sliced

2 tablespoons olive oil

½ teaspoon kosher salt

1 (10- to 12-ounce) goose breast, cut into ¾- to 1-inch slices (see Cook's Note)

SAUCE

1 tablespoon soy sauce or tamari

3 tablespoons mirin

1 teaspoon rice vinegar

1 teaspoon toasted sesame oil

Two 17 × 20-inch pieces of aluminum foil

MEDITERRANEAN RAINBOW TROUT

VEGETABLE

½ bunch Tuscan kale (about 5 large leaves), sliced into ribbons with thick stems removed

AROMATICS AND PROTEIN

½ red onion, thinly sliced

1 fennel bulb, trimmed and thinly sliced

1½ teaspoons kosher salt

3 tablespoons extra-virgin olive oil

4 (3-ounce) rainbow trout fillets

SAUCE

¼ cup drained and chopped sun-dried tomatoes in oil

¼ cup chopped pitted kalamata olives

½ teaspoon red wine vinegar

¼ teaspoon dried oregano

Two 17 × 20-inch pieces of foil

In a medium bowl, combine the kale, red onion, fennel, and ½ teaspoon of the salt. Drizzle with 2 tablespoons of the olive oil and toss well to coat. Divide the mixture evenly and place half in the center of each piece of foil. Score the skin of the fish fillets in three places. Season them evenly with the remaining salt. Top each mound of kale with 2 pieces of seasoned trout, skin-side down. In a separate bowl, combine the sun-dried tomatoes, olives, red wine vinegar, dried oregano, and the remaining 1 tablespoon olive oil. Stir to combine. Spoon half the mixture over the trout in each packet. Seal and cook for 15 minutes. Serves 2 (makes two packets).

COOK'S NOTE. *You can also make this recipe using a smallish whole cleaned rainbow trout wrapped in foil and use the topping as a stuffing. A whole fish usually takes a few minutes longer to cook.*

ALSO WORKS WITH. *Any fish, shrimp, or shellfish.*

SWEET CHILI-GLAZED SALMON
WITH BROCCOLINI

PROTEIN

2 tablespoons plus 2 teaspoons extra-virgin olive oil

2 (6-ounce) skinless wild salmon fillets

1 teaspoon kosher salt

VEGETABLE

1 small bunch broccolini, trimmed and cut into pieces

AROMATICS AND SAUCE

¼ cup sweet chili sauce

2 teaspoons sriracha

1 teaspoon toasted sesame oil

½ teaspoon grated fresh ginger

In this recipe, the aromatics are combined in the sauce.

Prepare a hot campfire (or charcoal grill or propane grill). Brush the inside of each foil pack with 1 teaspoon of the olive oil. Season the salmon fillets evenly with ½ teaspoon of the salt. Place a fillet in the center of each piece of foil. Divide the broccolini and place half in each packet. Drizzle each packet with another tablespoon of the olive oil. Season the packets evenly with ¼ teaspoon of the salt. In a small bowl, combine the sweet chili sauce, sriracha, sesame oil, grated ginger, and the remaining ¼ teaspoon salt. Stir until fully incorporated. Divide the sauce over the salmon and broccolini. Seal and cook for 15 minutes. Serves 2.

ALSO WORKS WITH. *Any fish, shrimp, or shellfish.*

IRON PIE SANDWICHES . . . OR WHATEVER YOU CALL THEM

We called them hobo pie makers when I was a kid growing up in Michigan, but that name has fallen out of fashion. You'll still get the right results when you type those words into a search engine, but you won't find the word *hobo* in the actual product description. Instead, you'll see terms like pudgy pie, mountain pie, campfire pie, or iron pie, which are all totally acceptable names for these classic cast-iron clamshells that can be used to make outstanding sandwiches and desserts with minimal preparation and cleanup. There aren't really any rules when it comes to iron pies—use what you've got and call them what you want.

MAKING IRON PIES

First, you've got to choose your bread. Soft, thick-cut square sandwich brioche bread is our favorite and the easiest to mold into the pie iron. Six-inch flour tortillas also work, although they require some finagling.

Next, you'll need to get some kind of grease involved. You can use softened unsalted butter, nonstick cooking spray, bear grease, duck fat, or other animal lard, or mayonnaise.

When it comes to fillings, adding meltable and oozy ingredients like cheese or peanut butter to pie iron sandwiches is our favorite way to go. These'll also help to hold the other fillings in place. Meat and cheese are an obvious pairing, but so are cooked vegetables and cheese. And don't sleep on heating up a peanut butter and jelly sandwich in a pie iron. The results are out of this world.

TO BUILD: Separate your pie iron into two pieces. Wipe out the inside of each side with a wet cloth and dry well. Liberally grease the insides of the pie iron. Or slather mayonnaise directly on both pieces of bread on the pie iron side.

Press a piece of bread snugly into each side of the pie iron as in the illustrations below. Pile your ingredients generously onto one piece of the bread. A fuller sandwich will make for a tighter press, allowing the bread to become golden brown and delicious. Place the second iron over the pile of ingredients to form a sandwich. Attach the two pieces of the pie iron and lock into place.

TO COOK: Prepare a campfire (or charcoal grill) for coal cooking. When you have a sufficient bed of coals, pull them out to the edge of the fire with a coal rake. Place the irons flat on the hot coals to evenly transfer the heat (if you're using a charcoal grill, bank the briquettes to one side so that you can lay the pie irons in the grill on top of the coals). A good starting point is to cook for a total of 2 to 4 minutes, then flip and cook for another 2 minutes. Pull the iron out, unlatch the handles, and carefully take a peek to see how browned it is (don't touch the actual irons—they're raging hot). If it needs more time, close it up and throw it back on the fire for a minute. If it looks good, lay the iron on a log or rock and remove the top half. Allow the sandwich to rest for a minute, then turn the iron over and deposit the sandwich onto a plate. The contents will be like molten lava, so warn any kiddos or unsuspecting adults to be careful of the hot, oozing filling when eating. Wipe out the pie iron, if necessary, add a little grease, and start your next sandwich or pie.

BIRD, CHEDDAR, AND FIG JAM SANDWICH

MAKES 1 SANDWICH

2 slices multigrain sandwich bread

1½ tablespoons softened butter

1 heaping tablespoon fig jam

3 to 4 ounces sliced cooked upland bird breast (smoked, roasted, or grilled)

4 small aged cheddar slices, or 2 precut slices (about 2 ounces)

Pinch of kosher salt

Freshly ground black pepper

Clean and dry the pie-iron interiors. Slather the insides of each pie iron with the softened butter. Press the bread slices into each half of the iron molds (see illustration on page 169). On one bread slice, spread the fig jam. Top the jam with slices of upland bird, overlapping to fill the space, then top the bird with cheese slices, also overlapping to fill the space. Sprinkle with salt and pepper. The sandwich should be piled high. If it's not, add more meat and cheese. Top with the second bread-lined pie iron and secure the fasteners to close the iron tightly.

Follow the cooking instructions on page 169.

TEN OF OUR FAVORITE IRON PIE COMBOS

We recommend using the style of breads suggested below, but feel free to experiment.

- Peanut butter and jelly or honey, country white bread
- Cooked ground-meat burger, diced onion, American cheese, ketchup, white sandwich bread or brioche
- Cooked ground burger or shredded game bird meat, taco seasoning, Mexican cheese blend, salsa, chopped onion, shredded lettuce, flour tortilla
- Sliced ham, pimiento cheese, pickles, sourdough or country white bread
- Cooked bacon or breakfast sausage, scrambled eggs, cheddar cheese, flour tortilla, brioche, or sourdough bread
- Smoked salmon or trout, cream cheese, dill, chives or pickled red onion, white or sourdough bread
- Cooked wild duck, Gorgonzola, Pancetta-Onion Jam (page 55), preserved amarena cherries, sourdough
- Peperonata (page 34), shredded mozzarella, sourdough
- Sautéed mushrooms, grilled zucchini, Gouda or cheddar, sourdough

TOWEL-WRAPPED ROAST BENEATH THE COALS

SERVES 4 TO 6

2½ pounds elk roast, exterior silverskin removed

2 pounds kosher salt (close to 2 cups)

1 dozen fresh herb sprigs (oregano, rosemary, thyme, and/or marjoram)

1 tablespoon orange zest (optional)

1 teaspoon chile-style rub, like chili powder, ancho powder, or chipotle powder (optional)

Chimichurri (see page 71), Chunky Pico de Gallo, Red Pepper Aioli (see page 115), and/or Garlic-Chipotle Faux Aioli (page 350), for serving (optional)

SPECIAL EQUIPMENT

Kitchen twine, 1 clean cotton kitchen towel, or 2 packages of cheesecloth approximately 12 x 21 inches (don't use synthetic towels). This towel will be ruined and charred in this process, so don't use the one you got for your wedding.

COOK'S NOTE. *This roast works great as a backyard recipe on a charcoal grill or fire pit and is equally simple to throw together at a campsite.*

ALSO WORKS WITH. *Deer, moose, elk, beef, and pretty much any big animal. You want a tender roast-sized hunk of meat, such as loin, tenderloin, sirloin, or round.*

This recipe uses the increasingly popular Colombian cooking technique for *lomo al trapo*, which translates to "beef tenderloin in a towel." The process is similar to baking a roast in a salt crust or a clay crust in coals, but you do it in a dampened cloth or towel instead. The result is a tasty, salt-seasoned roast that is tender and cooked to perfection. The unveiling of the meat brings a little drama and entertainment to a gathering. The traditional seasoning is salt and oregano, but, just like when you're baking with a salt crust, other aromatics work well, too. While testing this recipe, we tried it with herbs, orange zest, and even a chile-based dry rub. All were excellent.

Wet the kitchen towel or cheesecloth and wring it out so that it's dampened but not dripping wet. Lay the cloth flat on a work surface with one short side of the towel nearest to you, then follow the illustrations opposite to wrap the roast.

PREPARING AND MAINTAINING THE COALS AND FIRE. Prepare a medium fire inside a stone circle, with plenty of wood on standby. When the logs have burned and are turning into coals, use a shovel to arrange the smoldering wood around the perimeter of your fire circle (if you're using a fire pit, you'll want the logs on the edge of the pit). Move the hot coals into the opening in the center. Nestle your towel-wrapped roast on these coals (if you're cooking potatoes or other vegetables in coals also, place them on the coals now as well). You're using the direct heat of the coals and the ambient heat of the smoldering logs to cook the roast, so, if needed, add fresh logs to keep the fire going. Crush the spent logs with your shovel and toss the hot coals over the roast. Continue this process throughout the cooking time.

CHECKING FOR DONENESS. After about 20 minutes the salt on the bottom half of the roast will become hard. Do an internal temperature check with a meat thermometer through the towel. It should be around 100°F. Flip the roast at this point and add more coals under and around it. Your target internal temperature is about 130°F, so check the roast frequently, about every 10 minutes, until it reaches 100°F. It shouldn't take much longer than 30 minutes total, but keep in mind that it's nearly impossible to have perfectly even cooking from end to end, so don't be upset if there's a little variance.

Use tongs to remove the roast from the coals and let it rest for 5 to 10 minutes inside the cloth. Transfer to a serving platter, board, or baking sheet to reveal. Snip away the charred cloth and crack through the hard salt shell to reveal the roast in the interior. Slice and serve with your choice of condiments.

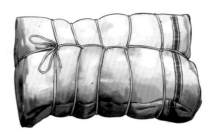

1. *Add the salt to the towel, starting 1 inch from the short edges of the towel, and 2 inches from the long sides. You should have a rectangular layer of salt that is about ½ inch thick. Maintain a salt-free border around the edge of the towel. Lay down the herbs on top of the salt. Lay the roast in the center of the salt and herbs, parallel to the short side of the towel.*

2. *Roll the roast up in the towel tightly like a burrito from the short side, tucking in the sides as you go. Next, truss the wrapped roast (see page 129) securely with kitchen twine.*

WHOLE VEGETABLES ROASTED IN COALS

SERVES 4 TO 6

If you've got some vegetarians running around, this is how you can introduce them to the joys of caveman cooking. In all seriousness, cooking whole vegetables in coals is a gorgeous preparation. When you dig out the finished product, it seems both elegant and ancestral. It's as though you're beholding some edible time capsule left over from humanity's earliest experiments with cooking. At home or when car camping you'll want a coal rake, long-handled tongs, and leather grilling gloves. In the backcountry, you'll have to do what our ancestors did thousands of years ago—use a stick.

PREPARING AND MAINTAINING THE COALS AND FIRE. Prepare a medium fire inside a stone circle, with plenty of wood on standby. When the logs have burned and are turning into coals, use a shovel to arrange the smoldering wood around the perimeter of your fire circle (if you're using a fire pit, you'll want the logs on the edge of the pit). Move the hot coals to the opening in the center. Nestle all the vegetables among these coals, and distribute some of the coals on top of the vegetables. You're using the direct heat from the coals and the ambient heat of the smoldering logs to cook the vegetables, so, if needed, replace the latter with fresh logs to keep the fire going. Using tongs or a coal shovel, rotate the vegetables—as one side becomes charred, rotate them so the non-charred side is toward the hottest coals. Flip and turn the vegetables in foil frequently, every 10 minutes. Crush the spent logs with your shovel and toss the resulting hot coals over the vegetables. Continue this process throughout the cooking time.

CHECKING FOR DONENESS. Use a paring knife or a hunting knife to check the doneness of the vegetables. The knife should be able to go through the foil and in and out with zero resistance. The vegetables cook at the following approximate rates: acorn and butternut squash, about 30 minutes; russet potatoes, sweet potatoes, and yams, about 35 minutes; beets, about 40 minutes. Times may vary.

When done, remove the vegetables to a baking sheet using tongs. With a damp cloth, carefully wipe the ash off the skins. Carefully use a sharp knife to cut open the vegetables without foil. Watch out—they'll be hot on the inside! For the squashes, slice open and scoop out the seeds and pulp using a spoon. Peel and slice the squashes, or spoon the cooked flesh out of the charred peel and transfer it to a bowl. At this point you can eat the vegetables or mash and chop them. For the vegetables wrapped in foil, carefully unwrap them; if the skins are charred, cut away the badly charred portions. Otherwise, cut them into wedges to serve. For all of the vegetables, season with salt and pepper, drizzle with olive oil, top with crumbled cheese or a sauce or dressing of your choice.

Approximate weights are listed to help adjust for cooking times. Any size will do, but if they are smaller or larger than below, it will take them less or more time, respectively, to cook.

1 butternut squash, whole and scrubbed (about 1 pound)

2 acorn squashes, whole and scrubbed (about 1 pound each)

4 beets, tops removed for another use, scrubbed well (about 2 to 4 ounces each)

2 garnet yams, scrubbed well (9 to 14 ounces each)

2 large potatoes, scrubbed well (2 pounds each)

PREPARE THE VEGETABLES: Wrap the beets and potatoes in foil. You can lightly oil the vegetables before wrapping them; the foil tends to release more easily and the skins become crisper. It also works without this step— do whatever is easiest.

ALSO WORKS WITH. *Any whole squash with firm skin, such as butternut, acorn, delicata, spaghetti, kabocha, sugar pumpkins, sweet dumpling, and red kuri; or root vegetables including sweet potatoes, yams, yucca, russet potatoes, beets of all sizes, carrots, and parsnips.*

COOK'S NOTE. *While campsites are the more common location for this technique, it also works great as a backyard recipe on a charcoal grill or fire pit.*

DEER SHOULDER IN A BARREL

SERVES 10 TO 15 WITH ACCOMPANIMENTS

1 small deer shoulder, roughly 6 to 8 pounds, sawed into 1-pound bone-in pieces, at room temperature.

1 cup bear grease, duck fat, beef tallow, pork lard, butter, extra-virgin olive oil, or other fat

4 potatoes, sweet potatoes, yuccas, or beets, cut in half

3 carrots, whole

2 large hard-skinned squashes, such as butternut, acorn, kabocha, halved, skin-on, seeds scooped out

2 bulbs fennel, tops removed and reserved, cut into 3 or 4 pieces

Kosher salt, freshly ground black pepper, or any dry rub for seasoning

3 shallots, peeled and halved, or a bunch of scallions, trimmed

2 heads garlic, cut in half horizontally and kept whole

3 unripe apples or pears (optional)

2 bunches cilantro, parsley, or other fragrant herb (optional)

Condiments from page 177 for serving

ALSO WORKS WITH. *Shoulders of sheep, goat, hog, or any big game animals including black bear. Remove the shank if the shoulder is too big for your barrel.*

Cultures all around the world celebrate special occasions by burying food beneath the ground in a bed of hot coals and rocks. In Hawaii, they have kalua pig. The Peruvians of the Andes have a traditional preparation known as pachamanca, where assortments of meat and vegetables (sometimes including guinea pig) are buried in an earthen oven and covered with heated rocks. There's a traditional Mayan preparation called cochinita pibil, in which a suckling pig is wrapped in leaves and cooked underground. In southern Chile, along the Chiloé Archipelago, they have a dish of shellfish, meat, and vegetables cooked in an earthen oven. And in North America, this grouping includes traditional in-ground barbecue pits popular across the southern United States, and clambakes, constructed in fires in the sand on the shores of New England. The communal quality of these meals is easily understood. The anticipation of unveiling the food is best shared with friends and loved ones, and the methods are conducive to cooking huge batches of food that can serve a crowd.

For this recipe, you don't necessarily need a place where you can dig a big hole in the ground. All you need is a large metal drum, barrel, or even an old metal wheelbarrow. In addition to a deer shoulder, we use a lot of vegetables. Go ahead and try any combination of squashes or pumpkins, root vegetables, onions, apples, pears, cauliflower, or fennel. The veggies and fruits will soften in the heat, and the resulting meat will be fall-off-the-bone tender. As for your cooking vessel, avoid any container that once held hazardous materials—even if you've cleaned it. This whole process will take you roughly 6 to 8 hours, so start early and plan your day around it.

TO BUILD THE FIRE. Add a couple of inches of soil to the bottom of the drum and arrange your rocks with even spacing on top of the soil. Kindle a fire on top of the rocks and let it rip. You want to burn as much wood as quickly as possible in the drum. (That's why smaller-diameter wood is better; it gets burning quicker.) Let the coals fill in around the rocks and keep adding wood. Periodically chop at the burning wood and coals with a shovel to create a dense layer of coals. You'll want a layer of 6 to 7 inches of live coals in the drum before you're done burning.

Meanwhile, wet the cloth and ring it out so it's damp but not soaking. Lay the cloth on a work surface. Season the meat and vegetables liberally with salt, pepper, or a seasoning rub. Slather the meat with the lard and arrange the shallots or scallions in the center of the cloth. Top with the fennel and then the meat. Surround the meat with the other vegetables and garlic, nestling them together. Add the apples or pears and herbs on top if using. Fold the cloth to make a packet enclosing the meat and vegetables. (Imagine you're folding up a burrito.)

When the coals are ready, cover them with a 2-inch layer of soil and pat it down. Lay the cloth packet containing the meat and vegetables on top of the soil, and then cover that up with more soil. Ideally, you'll fill the drum to within a couple of inches of the top. That'll give you plenty of insulation.

Kindle a small fire of coals or sticks on top of the soil. This may or may not be necessary, but I like to do it to help heat up the soil in a hurry. Keep this fire lit for about an hour or so and then allow it to die out.

Wait around 6 to 8 hours. When you're ready to serve, use a shovel and heavy leather grilling gloves to uncover the cloth package. Brush the top of the package as clean as possible before lifting it out. (It should still be hot, so be careful.) Move the package to your work surface and carefully unfold the cloth to avoid getting any dirt on the food. The squashes and potatoes should all be tender and soft. Ideally the meat should be fork tender and close to falling off the bone. If you were to check the internal temperature of the meat, you'd be looking for a temperature somewhere around 170°F or higher.

Feed a crowd and serve with condiments like Chimichurri, Salsa Verde, Red Pepper Aioli, or Harissa Aioli (pages 71, 350, 115, and 275) or the sauce of your choice.

SPECIAL EQUIPMENT

You'll want half the barrel; it doesn't matter if it has a bottom or not. It just needs to be a cylinder that's about 22 inches in diameter and 16 inches high. (You can use anything fireproof that you have with similar dimensions.) For ventilation, drill eight or nine 1-inch holes around the periphery that will become the bottom of your barrel roaster.

1 large piece of cloth, approximately 4 x 4 feet. Cotton tablecloths or untreated canvas are ideal (you can also use raw untreated burlap, or even thawed frozen banana leaves); keep in mind they will impart their flavor and aroma to the food.

A wheelbarrow load of hardwood firewood, split into small-diameter pieces. Ideally, you'd have a wheelbarrow full of firewood pieces that are 16 inches long and just 2 x 2 inches.

6 to 8 grapefruit-sized rocks. Get these from dry ground, not beneath water. Submerged rocks are dangerous because the water trapped inside will expand when heated and can send shards of rock blasting in all directions.

A few 5-gallon buckets of soil or sand. (You want it dry or semi-dry; you do not want mud.)

CLAY'S BEAR GREASE DUTCH OVEN BISCUITS

Clay Newcomb

In the South, biscuits accompany just about every meal. At my home here in the Ozarks, we make our biscuits with bear grease. Going back to Daniel Boone's frontier era, there's a long history of rural mountain folk using rendered bear fat in place of butter or pork lard since it remains shelf stable for over a year without refrigeration. I've learned that the fat from a fall black bear that has been gorging on acorns and berries is best; it renders down into a rich, golden oil that turns a pearly white when it cools. Bear grease is perfect not only for frying and especially for baking, but it's also rumored to cure baldness and forecast the weather! Folklore aside, bear grease is an important part of my heritage, and we cook with it almost every day. And there's no better way to end a long day of riding mules around in the Ozarks than with a plateful of warm, flaky bear-grease biscuits.

I usually double the recipe below. These can be baked in the coals in a Dutch oven with a lid or in a conventional oven in a baking dish or on a baking stone.

MAKES FIVE 3- TO 4-INCH BISCUITS

2 cups all-purpose flour, plus more for dusting

2½ tablespoons baking powder

1 teaspoon kosher salt

⅓ cup bear grease, chilled

5 tablespoons plus 1 teaspoon (⅓ stick) unsalted butter, chilled, plus more for greasing

½ cup milk

SPECIAL EQUIPMENT

10- or 12-inch-diameter (4- or 6-quart) shallow Dutch oven with lid for coal cooking

In a large mixing bowl, combine all the dry ingredients. Add the cold bear grease and grate the cold butter into the dry ingredients and lightly mix them in with a spoon. Then, using a pastry cutter, blend the fat into the dry ingredients until the mixture is clumpy but combined. Overall, you want to handle the dough as little as possible. Once you've reached the desired consistency, add the milk and mix together with your hands or a spoon until it becomes a dough.

Lightly flour a cold surface. Using your hands, place the dough on the surface and flatten it. Fold the dough over once (like a book), flatten it, fold it over again the opposite way, and flatten it. Repeat this three more times, making the final thickness about the height you want your biscuits to be. They won't rise much.

Cut the biscuits out with the open end of a small mason jar or circular cookie cutter. You should get 5 or 6 biscuits total. Chill the biscuits while you make your fire.

Prepare a campfire or a charcoal chimney for coal cooking in a fire pit or stone-lined fire circle. While the fire matures, prepare the Dutch oven for cooking. Using butter, thoroughly grease the Dutch oven and arrange the biscuits in the bottom. If you want soft-sided biscuits, keep the biscuits away from the sides of the Dutch oven. If you want hard, crispy sides, let them touch. Using the chart on page 152 as a guide for heat, place 10 coals in a circle on the ground and set the Dutch oven on top of the coals. Add 19 coals on top of the Dutch oven to create an oven that is approximately 425°F.

Check the biscuits after 12 minutes, but they may take as long as 20 minutes. They should be golden brown on top and browned but not scorched on the bottom. Eat them warm with butter, jam, or honey with your favorite camp meals.

HOW TO MAKE BEAR OIL

Clay Newcomb

At one time, making bear oil was a common practice among rural homesteads. But as a result of urbanization and industrialized food production over the last century, grain-based oils have all but eliminated the demand for this multipurpose fat in American kitchens. Today, the only place you're likely to see it is on the shelves of a few bear hunters who understand how valuable this resource is. Bear oil doesn't go rancid as quickly as pork lard and can be used for any type of cooking application. In my opinion, it's the best oil for frying, as well as making pastries, cookies, and piecrusts. Besides being a versatile cooking oil, it can also be used to lubricate guns and knives and to preserve leather.

HARVESTING THE BEAR FAT. In the fall, adult bears will have substantial amounts of whitish fat in between the hide and muscle. They usually have less fat in spring, but it's still worth harvesting. After skinning, use a sharp knife to carve off chunks of fat. You'll find most of the largest, thickest reserves of fat will be around the rump of the bear, but you'll find sizable external and internal deposits elsewhere on bears that are in exceptional condition. Remove as much fat as you can, but try not to get any meat mixed in with it.

Put all the fat in a game bag and get it cooled down immediately. Bear fat has a very low melting point, so if you can't get it to a refrigerator quickly, hang it in a cool, shady, breezy spot or put it in a cooler full of ice (keep the fat-filled game bag dry in a garbage bag). You can render the fat fresh or freeze multiple layers of big chunks together in a vac-sealed bag to reduce the potential for freezer burn. It's best to use it within 6 months of freezing.

PREPARING THE BEAR FAT. From frozen, I let the bear fat thaw about halfway before cubing it into 1-inch pieces. By cutting the fat when it's just above freezing, it slices more easily. You can render the cubes as is, but you'll get a lot more oil by grinding the fat after cubing. You'll also get better results if your grinder parts are thoroughly chilled in the freezer before grinding the fat.

RENDERING THE BEAR FAT. For rendering big batches of bear fat, I work outside with a propane outdoor cooker and a big heavy-duty aluminum cooking pot like you'd use to deep-fry a turkey. A low and slow approach with lots of stirring is the name of the game. If the fat gets too hot, it will develop a slightly burnt flavor. I prefer to cook bear fat at 225°F (use a candy thermometer to check the temperature). The slower you cook, the clearer the oil will be, and at 225°F, you can render down a pound of bear fat in about 25 minutes. It's best to work in batches, so be sure to plan your time accordingly. Stir constantly and use a wire strainer ladle to remove any large pieces of burnt cracklings that are floating on the surface. Leave the oil on the heat source until 90 percent of all solids are gone. A pound of ground bear fat should produce roughly one pint of bear oil, and slightly less if you're cubing it.

STORING THE BEAR GREASE. To store the grease, I mostly use half-pint common glass canning jars. I've found this is a convenient portion size, but pint-sized jars might be better if you have a lot of fat. Using a metal cooking funnel and triple-folded cheesecloth to strain it, carefully pour the hot oil into the jars. If you don't strain the oil, small, burnt particles of cracklings and meat will give the oil an off-flavor. I usually let the oil cool down for about 10 minutes with the lid off the jars, then put the lid on before storing it on a cool shelf in the cellar. You can also store it in the refrigerator or freezer.

Clay Newcomb is a seventh-generation Arkansan who lives on a farm in the Ouachita Mountains with his family and a whole bunch of critters. A hunter, mule skinner, curious naturalist, and student of rural culture, Clay is the host of MeatEater's Bear Grease podcast.

GOOSE AND DUMPLINGS

MAKES ABOUT 6 CUPS STEW AND 20 DUMPLINGS; SERVES 4 TO 6

This is a traditional-style bird-and-dumpling recipe, though we're using geese here instead of the chicken that's popular across the Midwest where many German immigrants landed. If you're intimidated by baking, don't worry. The dumplings are biscuit-like and are simply dropped onto the surface of the stew to be cooked. This is one that also works well in an oven at home if you're just trying to move through a stockpile of frozen goose breasts. The mushrooms add robust flavor to this dish.

PREPARE THE COALS. Prepare a campfire or a charcoal chimney with briquettes in a fire pit or stone-lined fire circle. The following instructions are for a 10-inch diameter (5-quart deep) Dutch oven. Use the chart on page 152 as a guide for the number of coals needed for your pot size to reach 375°F to 400°F. For a 10-inch pot, place 25 coals in a circle on the ground and set a Dutch oven over top of the coals. Start another chimney with 25 more coals.

FOR THE STEW. In the Dutch oven, melt 3 tablespoons of the butter with the oil. Season the goose with ¾ teaspoon salt and a few grinds of pepper. Add half the goose to the hot pot and cook until deeply browned on all sides, roughly 5 to 8 minutes. Remove to a plate. Add the remaining goose and cook until browned, another 5 to 8 minutes or so. Remove to the plate. Add the celery, onion, carrot, mushrooms, thyme and sage sprigs, 2 teaspoons salt, and a few grinds of pepper. Cook, stirring often, until softened and beginning to brown, 10 to 12 minutes. Add the remaining 1 tablespoon butter to melt, and then stir in the flour to coat the vegetables. Cook for 1 minute, stirring, to cook the flour. Return the goose and any juices to the pot. Add the game stock and 1 teaspoon salt. Stir to incorporate the ingredients and any flour stuck on the bottom of the pan. Using a leather grilling glove, remove the pot to the side to refresh the coals.

Arrange 8 new hot coals in the bottom of the fire pit. Place the pot over the coals, cover with the lid, and place the remaining coals on the lid. Let the stew come up to a boil (skim any scum that rises), and cover and simmer for about 1 hour, adding more stock or water if the liquid level gets low. Once the coals have died down, replenish them and cook until the goose meat is somewhat tender, for approximately another hour.

FOR THE DUMPLINGS. Mix together the flour, baking powder, salt, and sage in a medium bowl. Add the milk and stir to combine (see Make Ahead).

Remove the lid and make sure the goose is submerged in the stew. With two spoons, drop golf-ball-sized dollops of dough on the top of the stew. Return the lid, add new coals if needed, and cook until the dumplings are tender and cooked through, 15 to 20 minutes. Serve immediately, ladled in bowls and topped with fresh parsley or celery leaves, if desired.

STEW

4 tablespoons (½ stick) unsalted butter

1 tablespoon extra-virgin olive oil

2 prepared skinless goose breasts, lightly pounded with a mallet to tenderize, then cut into 1-inch cubes (about 1 pound 6 ounces total)

Kosher salt

Freshly ground black pepper

2 celery ribs, sliced ½ inch thick

1 large yellow onion, sliced ½ inch thick

3 medium carrots, sliced ½ inch thick

8 ounces cremini mushrooms (or foraged mushrooms), sliced ½ inch thick

2 bushy fresh thyme sprigs

1 fresh sage sprig

3 tablespoons all-purpose flour

4 to 6 cups blonde game stock or low-sodium chicken broth

2 tablespoons picked fresh flat-leaf parsley or celery leaves, for garnish (optional)

DUMPLINGS

2 cups (9.8 ounces) all-purpose flour, scooped and leveled

1 tablespoon baking powder

¾ teaspoon kosher salt

5 large fresh sage leaves, finely chopped (about 2 tablespoons)

1 cup milk

MAKE AHEAD. *You can make this stew at home and cook the dumplings on-site. Baking powder reacts when it comes in contact with wetness and heat, so mix the dry ingredients at home but wait to add the milk until you're on-site.*

DUTCH OVEN RABBIT BOUDIN WITH RED CABBAGE

Jean-Paul Bourgeois

Rabbit hunting with hounds is woven into the rural culture of the South. It's how I honed my shotgunning skills as a boy in Louisiana. It wasn't easy hitting a rabbit as it carved and cut through the shin-high grasses that surrounded the local sugarcane fields. I remember doing a lot of shooting, but most of the time I missed, so coming home with two or three cottontails was regarded as a big success. I was proud to contribute to the dinner table, and a couple rabbits could easily feed the whole family—if we used every edible part. This recipe honors those meals, by making boudin ("BOO-dan" as they say it in Louisiana) with the offal and leg meat, which then gets stuffed into the saddle portion of the rabbit. Boudin is a comforting staple of Cajun country; it is a cooked sausage traditionally made from pork, pork hearts and livers, and cooked rice, plus seasonings and aromatics. Boudin is often linked in hog casings, but it's also used as a stuffing for birds or, in this case, a cottontail rabbit saddle. One bite of this recipe and I'm right back in those cane fields of my youth, which is the ultimate compliment to the rich culinary traditions of my home state.

SERVES 4

RABBIT STOCK AND MEAT

2 whole skinned, cleaned rabbits, front and hind legs separated, saddles reserved

1 cup white wine

1 large yellow onion, quartered

1 carrot, cut into chunks

2 celery ribs, cut into large chunks

4 bay leaves

BOUDIN STUFFING

1 cup uncooked long-grain white rice

1 pound rabbit livers or chicken livers

Kosher salt and freshly ground black pepper

2 tablespoons bacon grease or vegetable oil

1 medium onion, diced small

2 garlic cloves, minced

1 bunch green onions (scallions), thinly sliced

½ bunch flat-leaf parsley, finely chopped

Hot sauce (I prefer Tabasco for this recipe, but Louisiana Brand and Crystal work great as well)

BRAISE

2 tablespoons bacon grease or vegetable oil

2 slices bacon, diced

¼ head shredded red cabbage (2 to 3 cups)

2 garlic cloves

½ medium onion, sliced

Hot sauce (optional)

1 tablespoon Dijon mustard (optional)

SPECIAL EQUIPMENT

Meat grinder

Butcher's twine

10- or 12-inch diameter (5- or 8-quart) deep cast-iron Dutch oven

FOR THE RABBIT STOCK. In a stockpot, place the cleaned rabbit legs, the wine, and water to cover. Add the onion, carrot, and celery (the mirepoix) and the bay leaves. Bring the liquids to a boil and then simmer for 1½ hours, or until the leg meat can be pulled from the bone. Once the rabbit is tender, allow it to cool in the broth until safe to handle with your hands.

Meanwhile, cook the rice. In a small pot, combine rice and 2 cups water over high heat. When the water boils, reduce the heat to low and cover. Cook for 20 minutes, or until fully done. Set the cooked rice aside; keep warm.

Recipe continues

FOR THE BOUDIN STUFFING. Season the rabbit livers with salt and pepper. (You can also add rabbit kidneys and hearts at this step.) In a hot skillet, add the grease and the rabbit livers and sear them on one side roughly 3 minutes. Rabbit livers should be cooked no more than medium and ideally still mid-rare when you remove them from the skillet. Set the livers aside. Add the onion, garlic, and green onions to the same skillet and sauté on medium-high heat until soft for 3 to 5 minutes.

Add 2 cups of the stock from the cooled rabbit-cooking liquid and continue to cook for 10 minutes, reducing the liquid by half. Once reduced, set aside.

Remove the rest of the rabbit pieces from the liquid and pick the meat from the bones. Reserve all of your rabbit-braising liquid (reheat and keep it hot). Roughly chop the pulled rabbit meat until it resembles coarse ground meat. Roughly chop the rabbit livers until they are a coarse mush.

ASSEMBLE THE BOUDIN SAUSAGE. In a large mixing bowl, combine the cooked hot rice, chopped rabbit livers, chopped rabbit meat, and onions with the liquid from the skillet. With a wooden spoon, begin to paddle your boudin together (mimicking the action of a standing mixer paddle). You will need to add reserved rabbit stock to the mixture as you work your boudin in the bowl. Be aggressive. The combination of starches being released from the rice, the silkiness of the livers, and hot rabbit stock is what gives boudin its iconic texture. The more stock you use, the more "wet" the mixture will be. For this recipe, you want the final product to resemble a thick rice pudding while it's still warm. Season the mixture with salt, pepper, and a couple dashes of hot sauce. Stir in the parsley and cool the mixture immediately (spread it out on a rimmed baking sheet, if needed, to expedite the process).

STUFF THE SADDLES. Once the boudin is cooled, stuff your rabbit saddles generously with the boudin, leaving enough space for the belly to overlap slightly (you'll use about 1½ cups boudin for the filling give or take). With butcher's twine, truss your saddles, tying knots every inch. (You will not use all of the boudin. See Cook's Note on uses for the remainder and how to store it.) Season the stuffed saddles with salt and pepper.

FOR THE BRAISE. Prepare a campfire with coals. Bring the Dutch oven out to the campfire and put about 10 coals underneath. Add the grease and sear the stuffed rabbit saddles until browned on all sides. Once well browned, remove the stuffed saddles to a plate and add the bacon pieces, stirring to render the fat. Add the cabbage, garlic, and onion, stirring to coat them with the fat. Add 1 cup of the rabbit stock. Place the saddles on top of your cabbage along with any juices that have collected and cover with the lid.

Add 14 coals on top of the lid (see the chart on page 152 for specifics) to approximate a 350°F oven temperature, and roast until the loin is cooked through and the filling is hot—the internal temp should register at least 135°F. Begin checking about 15 minutes in. It should be fully cooked between 25 and 35 minutes, but it could take longer.

Serve with hot sauce and Dijon mustard (if using).

COOK'S NOTE. *Should you have any extra boudin, vac-seal it as bulk sausage or patties, or throw it into a hog casing if you want to go through the effort. The sausage will keep in the fridge for up to 1 week and in the freezer for 6 months.*

Born and raised in southern Louisiana, Chef Jean-Paul Bourgeois spent his childhood surrounded by family, friends, and great Southern cooking. His mission is focused on honoring and celebrating humble beginning experiences with others.

04 **ON THE BURNER**

It's a bit of an oversimplification, but I've come to think of my own camping activities as being divided into two categories. The first category is camping for the sake of camping. I do this all the time with my family and we love it. Someone will say, "Let's go camping this weekend," and everyone knows what they're thinking about: hikes, looking at the stars, campfires, reading in a hammock, maybe some casual fishing. The second category of camping is when you go camping in order to accomplish something else that happens to occur in a location that requires you to camp. Let's say you want to hunt caribou on Alaska's North Slope or run a raft down the Salmon River Gorge. The only way to pull that stuff off is to camp out, though the camping portion of the trip is secondary to the primary mission.

Each version of camping has its own culinary traditions and necessities. When you're camping for the sake of camping, there's time to luxuriate in the process of cooking. You can pack along a carful of gear—griddles, grills, propane campstoves, kettles—and make fun stuff, including most of the delicious preparations found within this book. Things like Nutella and Banana Iron Pies (see page 321), Venison Chili (page 215), Ginger Catfish Stir-Fry (page 220), and The Late Eugene Groters's Beer and Apple Pancakes (page 245). When you're camping in order to accomplish something else, cooking processes can get stripped down to their bare essentials. Just how bare depends on how much time you have to cook and how much room you have for hauling cooking gear. On that rafting trip down the Salmon River Gorge, you could live large if you've got a big raft and you pack along coolers of produce, fresh herbs, and meat; a bin of sauces and seasonings; a grill

and utensils; and a spinning rod rigged for smallmouth bass. When hunting for caribou on the North Slope, you might be limited to a backpacking stove and quart-sized pot. Making dinner comes down to boiling creek water in order to rehydrate a sack of dried soup to be eaten inside a wet sleeping bag while mosquitoes and gnats maul the tops of your ears.

I picked up a lot of my outdoor skills and habits from my father, but this notion of mine about the two types of camp cooking is not one of those things. My dad had only a single mode as camp cook, and it didn't matter whether we were camping for the sake of camping or camping for the sake of hunting and fishing. As close as he could, he would replicate a home kitchen that was centered around a stovetop. He fought with the infantry in World War II and spent several summers canoeing the Boundary Waters between northern Minnesota and Canada with a troop of Eagle Scouts. Exposure to these rule-oriented, fastidious organizations led him to believe that there was one right way to do things and many wrong ways. The right way to set up a camp kitchen was to begin with the placement of a propane-powered two-burner Coleman campstove. Above this, you needed a spice rack along with a roll of paper towels suspended horizontally. Beneath the stove was a hanging rack of spoons and spatulas. Off to one side you wanted a double sink made of plastic basins mounted on a bench. To the other side were plastic milk crates stacked on their sides to form a bank of shelves for dried goods and cookware. Conveniently placed coolers functioned as a fridge, from which you'd draw butter and eggs. He'd even make a towel rack. In inclement weather, the kitchen got overhead protection from a woven poly tarp that he referred to as a "cook fly." Setting this whole thing up would take the better part of a day. Taking it down and packing it away took hours.

At home, my dad didn't do much of anything to assist my mom in the kitchen. He was in charge of fish fries, made using a deep fryer that was set up in our garage, but that was about the extent of his culinary responsibilities. In the woods, however, he was comfortable enough with pots, skillets, and griddles that you wondered why he never touched them at home. No disrespect to my mom, but he managed to cook better breakfasts in camp than my mom cared to make in the house—perhaps because cooking breakfast was a novelty to him, while my mom had long ago burned out. He made eggs-in-the-hole, beer-apple pancakes, and smoked trout hash. Standing on bare ground, with my head touching the low-slung cook fly and the morning sun shining through the trees, I loved to watch these meals take shape. I'd eat them seated in a folding chair, my plate propped on my knees.

Those early days of camping taught me to associate the use of standard cookware as much with the outdoors as indoors. Of course, there are certain things you're never gonna want to make outside. Things like soufflés or demi-glace come to mind. But other foods actually seem more fitting to the outdoors than they do the indoors, such as pan-fried trout. Looking back on my youth, I've come to see that the equipment my family used in those early days was hardly ideal. Our camp cookware consisted of thin, banged-up aluminum pots and pans that heated unevenly and were a major pain in the ass to clean. The cast-iron and nonstick camp cookware that is widely available today is so much better. You can get good results even with delicate foods, and you don't need to spend an hour trying to scrape away cooking debris with a Brillo pad. When it comes to gear, we're living in the good old days of outdoor cooking.

But don't go thinking that there's no adventure to be had while using cookware in the outdoors. A blackened cast-iron skillet laid on a bed of glowing coals is one of the most beautiful sights in the world of food. The flavors that can be achieved with this method will taste even better than they look—and it's a technique that is unique to outdoor cooking. This chapter will show how it's all done, from breakfast to dinner and from fires to the campstoves. We'll even show you how to throw the best fish fry of your life. Whether you're camping for the sake of camping or camping because you have to, you'll be slinging the finest grub ever. You won't even notice the skeeters.

SKILLETS, GRIDDLES, AND POTS: WHAT YOU NEED TO KNOW

There's a lot more to cooking outside than just grilling and smoking. Sometimes, you want to bring the type of cooking you'd normally do on your indoor range into the outdoors, but you want it to be easy and efficient. It could be something big like a batch of chili that will feed a bunch of tailgaters or something more elaborate like making paella on the beach. No matter the specifics, you're going to need at least a basic selection of cookware, including pots, pans, and griddles. From a practical standpoint, you simply can't get by without this stuff if you want to boil, simmer, sauté, fry, or even bake foods outside. Even if all you want to do is reheat a precooked, vac-sealed meal (see page 217), you'll need to warm it up in a pot of hot water. I know plenty of people who at least partially outfit their outdoor cooking kits with pots and pans that have been retired from normal kitchen duty, and this works okay in some cases. I've also seen my fair share of meals burnt to a crisp because they were cooked in the cheap aluminum cookware you'll find in the camping aisle at discount stores.

Don't take that to mean you need to spend a fortune, but you will be way better off with a dedicated set of quality pots and pans that are built well enough to withstand the rigors of outdoor cooking. And remember that whatever specific items you ultimately end up including in your arsenal will depend a lot on what recipes you'll be preparing and for how many people. Aluminum and stainless-steel cookware with or without a nonstick coating is suitable as long as you're working with a burner that mimics an indoor stovetop. If you'll be doing some of your cooking over a campfire, carbon-steel cookware is a better choice. And, of course, the same kind of cast-iron skillets, griddles, and Dutch ovens that American settlers were using on the frontier two hundred years ago are still the most versatile choice for all types of outdoor cooking.

In some cases, however, you can't get by without a special piece of equipment that's designed for certain outdoor cooking applications. For instance, a big crayfish or seafood boil requires a pot that goes way beyond the normal stockpots you might have in your cupboard. Likewise, standard kitchen cookware won't cut it on a backcountry camping trip; at a minimum you'll want a small, ultralight, nonstick titanium or anodized aluminum pot. The following illustrations cover a range of common outdoor cooking techniques that utilize some type of pot, pan, or griddle.

Propane Stoves

Various types of two-burner propane stoves are far and away the most popular workhorse cooking appliance for most car campers. As noted earlier, fire bans make them a must-have for camp cooking in the West. You may need to account for the smaller surface area and lower Btu output of some models when choosing which size pots and pans will work best.

Outdoor Cookers

You can do a lot with these simple single propane burners and a giant pot. They have a very high Btu output, so they're great for quickly steaming crustaceans and shellfish or getting a big kettle of grease hot enough for deep-frying. The adjustable burner can also be turned down low enough to simmer stews and chilis.

Griddles

The two-burner stove shown here has a convenient built-in griddle system that makes it unnecessary to pack a separate griddle on car-camping trips. However, it's still worth owning a cast-iron skillet for other cooking setups. If nothing else, they make flipping pancakes, eggs, and burgers a lot easier.

Backcountry Stoves

Prepackaged freeze-dried or dehydrated meals make up the majority of meals that are "cooked" with backpacking stoves. But don't take that to mean that fresh ingredients are off the menu. I've used my campstove to cook everything from deer tenderloins to foraged mushrooms to cubes of bear meat. Just remember, backpacking pots and pans like the one pictured here are designed specifically for use with an appropriate stove. Avoid the temptation to cook over fires or hot coals with them.

CAST-IRON PRIMER

Cast-iron cookware has been around so long that it's developed an aura of mystique and romance in the culinary space. Stories about Grandma's favorite skillet abound, and there are entire cookbooks devoted to cast iron. You'll find plenty of those kinds of recipes in this book, but we're more focused on the practical than the romantic. For starters, cast iron holds and distributes heat better than many other types of metal cookware, which makes it the ideal vessel for everything from searing steaks to simmering stews. It's also indestructible; cast iron easily withstands the abuse that would otherwise destroy more typical household cookware if it was used to cook over open fires and coals. And the great thing about cast iron is you don't have to spend a bunch of money to reap its benefits. If you're looking for something affordable, you won't be disappointed with cast iron from Lodge or Camp Chef. Garage sales and flea markets are a great place to find inexpensive cast-iron cookware, too.

For your camp kitchen, start with the basics: a skillet, a Dutch oven, and a griddle. A 10-inch skillet is big enough for just a couple people; otherwise a 12-incher is the way to go. A Dutch oven in the 5- to 7-quart range is ideal unless you regularly cook for large groups. Cast-iron griddles are available in round, rectangular, and square shapes. A rectangular model that's roughly 10 × 20 inches will rest nicely on most two-burner stoves. Go with a square 10 × 10-inch version for use on a single burner. Regardless of size, make sure to get a griddle with a raised edge that prevents grease from dripping over the side.

Most cast-iron cookware comes "seasoned" right out of the box. If your cookware didn't come pre-seasoned, you'll need to do it following the manufacturer's instructions. A seasoned cast-iron pan has been oiled and heated to achieve a semi-permanent, glossy nonstick coating. You may also need to re-season a well-used piece of cast iron cookware now and again. To do this, just wipe the pan with a thin layer of vegetable oil and place it upside down on a baking sheet in a 350-degree oven for an hour.

I mentioned earlier that cast iron is indestructible, but that's only the case if you take proper care with it. Cast-iron cookware's only weaknesses are moisture and neglect. If exposed to moisture for as little as a few hours, cast iron will rust, and the pan will need to be thoroughly cleaned with steel wool or a wire brush and re-seasoned.

To avoid this scenario, cast-iron cookware should be washed and dried after each use. You may have been told the harsh chemicals in dish soap will destroy cast iron's seasoned nonstick coating and impart off-putting flavors into the metal itself. While you can often get away with just wiping cast iron cookware down with paper towels or a rag, you can in fact wash it with soap if warranted. Just use the minimum amount of soap necessary, rinse thoroughly, dry, and wipe down with a lightly oiled cloth.

SPICY FISH CAKES

MAKES 12 CAKES; SERVES 6

I'm a big fan of crab cakes and fish cakes. One thing I like about them is that you can stretch a small amount of seafood into a much more substantial offering, thanks to the added ingredients that go into the cake. I shared one of the versions that I like, Sucker Balls with Magic Sauce, in *The MeatEater Fish and Game Cookbook*. This recipe for spicy fish cakes uses fresh fish fillets. There are also a couple of ways you can make these in advance for a camping trip (see the Make Ahead note below). While the standard practice is to top fish cakes with a squeeze of lemon and dab of tartar sauce, here I've paired them with a tomato mayo inspired by Escoffier's variation of béarnaise called "sauce choron." It's rich and tangy and works great on grilled or foil-packed fish, too.

FOR THE SAUCE. Stir together the mayo and tomato puree in a small bowl. Grate the garlic into the sauce and add the tarragon. Stir to combine. Cover and refrigerate until ready to use.

FOR THE FISH CAKES. Cut the fish fillets into 2-inch pieces (don't worry about pin bones in small fish) and place them in a food processor fitted with a metal blade. Add the eggs to the processor, lock on the lid, and pulse the machine 25 to 30 times, until the mixture resembles a slightly coarse sausage filling. Add the mustard, scallions, serranos, lemon zest, Creole Seasoning, salt, and ¾ cup of the panko, then pulse the machine another 10 to 15 times, until all the seasonings are fully distributed. If you're cooking the fish cakes right away, transfer the mixture to an airtight container and refrigerate the mixture for at least 30 minutes before making cakes and cooking them; to cook them later, see Make Ahead.

Place the remaining 2½ cups panko on a large plate. Divide the chilled fish cake mixture evenly into 12 portions. Form each into a 2½-inch-wide, 1-inch-thick cake, gently squeezing and rotating the mixture while shaping so it holds together. Pat the edges to smooth them and place the cakes on the plate of panko. Completely coat each fish cake with panko, gently pressing the panko into the cake.

Heat a large cast-iron skillet over medium-low heat on a propane campstove for about 3 minutes to warm it up. Add 3 tablespoons of the oil and tilt the skillet to coat.

Place 6 cakes in the skillet. Cook for about 6 minutes, or until browned on the bottom. Carefully flip and cook for another 5 minutes, or until browned. Remove the fish cakes from the pan and cool on a wire rack. Season with a pinch of salt. Add remaining oil and cook the rest of the cakes.

Serve with the tomato mayo sauce and lemon wedges.

TOMATO MAYO SAUCE

Makes ½ cup

½ cup mayonnaise

2 tablespoons tomato puree, or 1 tablespoon tomato paste (not tomato sauce)

1 small garlic clove

½ teaspoon dried tarragon

FISH CAKES

2 pounds skinless fish fillets

3 tablespoons spicy brown mustard

2 large eggs

4 scallions, minced

4 small serrano chiles, minced

2 lemons, zested and cut into wedges

4 teaspoons Creole Seasoning, homemade (page 347) or store-bought

1½ teaspoons kosher salt

3¼ cups panko

6 tablespoons vegetable oil, plus more as needed for cooking

MAKE AHEAD. *You can make the fish cake mixture a day in advance, but it's best not to form the cakes. Instead, store the mixture in a resealable container in the refrigerator. Transport the container to camp, well-chilled in a cooler. Form into cakes and coat with panko crumbs at the campsite and then cook. The tomato mayo sauce can be made in advance and stored for up to 4 days refrigerated or in a cold cooler. The cakes can also be formed and kept in a freezer for 3 months.*

MOROCCAN-ISH VENISON MEATBALLS
IN SPICY TOMATO SAUCE

MAKES 30 TO 32 MEATBALLS; SERVES 4 TO 6

SPICY MORROCAN-STYLE TOMATO SAUCE

Makes 3 cups

3 tablespoons extra-virgin olive oil

½ medium yellow onion, diced

1 tablespoon kosher salt

⅛ teaspoon ground black pepper

2 garlic cloves, thinly sliced

2 tablespoons harissa paste (see Cook's Note)

1 teaspoon ground cinnamon

1 teaspoon ground coriander

1 teaspoon ground cumin

1 (28-ounce) can crushed tomatoes

¼ cup cilantro leaves, coarsely chopped

MEATBALLS

½ cup panko crumbs, or 1 bread slice

½ cup whole milk

1½ pounds ground game meat

1 large egg, lightly beaten

½ medium yellow onion, grated

2 garlic cloves, grated

½ bunch cilantro, leaves finely chopped

½ bunch mint, leaves finely chopped

2 teaspoons kosher salt

1½ teaspoons ground coriander

1 teaspoon ground cinnamon

1 teaspoon ground cumin

1 teaspoon paprika, preferably smoked or hot

¼ teaspoon ground ginger

¼ teaspoon ground turmeric (optional)

⅛ teaspoon ground black pepper

¼ cup extra-virgin olive oil, for cooking

Mini-meatballs are a fun way to utilize that stash of ground game meat that you may have piled up in the freezer. Many cultures around the world share America's love of meatballs, so there are plenty of places from which to draw inspiration. This is a Moroccan-inspired meatball that is bathed in a spicy tomato sauce. It's great as an appetizer and would also make a whip-ass meatball sub. These meatballs work well with all ground big game. An 80/20 blend of meat to fat is the perfect burger ratio, but you can go richer or leaner without messing anything up.

FOR THE SAUCE. Heat the oil in a large nonstick skillet over medium heat on a propane stove. Add the onions, salt, and pepper and stir to coat with oil. Cook, stirring occasionally, until the onions are soft, about 8 minutes. Add the garlic, harissa, cinnamon, coriander, and cumin and stir to coat the onions. Let cook about 1 minute, or until fragrant. Add the tomatoes to the pan. Add ½ cup water to the empty tomato can, swirl it around, then pour it into the pan. Reduce the heat to maintain a simmer and cook, stirring occasionally, until the sauce thickens slightly, 20 to 30 minutes. Add more water if the sauce starts to get too thick. Stir in the cilantro right before adding the meatballs. (See Make Ahead tips.)

FOR THE MEATBALLS. Combine the panko and milk in a small bowl and set aside to soak about 5 minutes. Place the meat in a large bowl. Add the egg and sprinkle the onions, garlic, cilantro, mint, salt, coriander, cinnamon, cumin, paprika, ginger, turmeric (if using), and pepper over the burger. Crumble the panko paste over the meat mixture. *Gently* mix the ingredients with your hands until combined. Forming the mixture into 1½-inch balls yields about 32 balls. (See Make Ahead tips for storing and transporting.)

TO COOK. For cooking at camp, preheat a skillet with the extra-virgin olive oil, and over medium-high heat on a propane campstove cook the meatballs in batches. At home, you can cook these outside or in a propane or pellet grill with the lid down or in a 400°F oven on a greased rimmed baking sheet.

TO SERVE. Transfer the meatballs and all the juices and oil to a plate and reheat the tomato sauce. When warm, add the meatballs and juice to the sauce and stir gently to coat. Serve with sliced crusty breads that are lightly grilled or toasted over a campfire.

ALSO WORKS WITH. *Pretty much any ground meat, such as beef, sheep, wild hog, venison, goose, duck, and so on.*

Crusty bread or pita or other flatbread, lightly grilled, for serving

---

COOK'S NOTE. *Harissa paste comes in both spicy and mild versions. Choose a spicy one for this sauce. In a pinch, substitute ½ teaspoon cayenne pepper for the harissa.*

MAKE AHEAD. *You can precook the meatballs and freeze them in a vac bag; the sauce can also be made ahead and frozen in a sealable container. Transport both chilled in a cooler.*

PORTUGUESE-STYLE PANFISH AND POTATO SOUP

SERVES 4 TO 6

Believe me, I understand the temptation to fry every last perch, bluegill, crappie, or porgy that you can get your hands on. They taste great that way! But in order to develop as a cook and a husband (my wife gets burned out on fish fries), I've learned to dedicate a meaningful percentage of my panfish haul to things besides baths in hot grease. If you're in a similar position, please consider this excellent panfish and potato soup. It's perfect for a pile of small fillets. The addition of the linguiça sausage adds a lot of character and heartiness, but you can substitute any other spicy sausage. And if you're not a panfish enthusiast, don't worry. You can chunk up pretty much any firm-fleshed fish (or shellfish) and use it for this delicious preparation.

Add 1 tablespoon of the olive oil to a heavy 4-quart pot. Place over medium heat on a propane campstove. Add the sausage and cook until lightly browned and the fat has rendered out. Remove the sausage to a separate plate. Discard most of the fat from the pan.

Add the remaining 2 tablespoons olive oil, the onions, garlic, and a pinch of salt to the pot. Cook over medium heat until the onions are translucent, tender, and browned slightly at least 8 minutes. Add the celery, bell peppers, bay leaves, allspice, and cayenne. Stir to toast the seasonings and sauté the vegetables for 3 to 4 minutes.

Add the potatoes and enough of the stock to cover them (about 3 cups). Bring to a low boil and cook for about 8 minutes, or until just tender. Add the crushed tomatoes and cooked sausage and bring to a boil again. Season with salt and black pepper to taste. (You could prep the entire soup up to this point and bring it refrigerated or frozen to camp.)

Add the fillets (if the fillets are large, cut each into a few pieces) and additional broth, if needed, to cover the fillets. Cook at a low simmer for 5 minutes, stirring very gently once or twice. Remove the soup from the heat for 5 minutes (the fish will continue to cook).

Serve warm in bowls with crusty bread, lemon wedges, hot sauce, and chopped cilantro or parsley.

3 tablespoons olive oil

12 ounces linguiça or andouille sausage (about 4 small links), sliced into ¼-inch half-moons

1 medium onion, diced small

3 garlic cloves, minced

Kosher salt

2 celery ribs, diced small

½ red bell pepper, seeded and diced

2 bay leaves

¼ teaspoon ground allspice

Pinch of cayenne pepper

1½ pounds Yukon Gold potatoes, diced small (about a ⅓-inch dice)

5 cups homemade fish stock or a combination of chicken and clam broth

2 cups whole peeled tomatoes, crushed by hand (14.5-ounce can)

Freshly ground black pepper

1 to 1½ pounds boneless panfish fillets or other similar fish

TO SERVE

Crusty bread

Lemon wedges

Hot sauce

Fresh cilantro or flat-leaf parsley leaves, chopped

ALSO WORKS WITH. *Any panfish, tautog, striped bass, and other fish with light, firm flesh. Also shrimp, clams, and mussels.*

MISO UDON NOODLE SOUP WITH SALMON

SERVES 2 GENEROUSLY

8 ounces skinless salmon fillet, cut into 1½- to 2-inch chunks

1 teaspoon kosher salt

1 scallion, thinly sliced, whites and greens kept separate

2 (9-ounce) packages frozen udon noodles (see Cook's Notes)

1 baby bok choy, quartered (1⅝ ounces)

4 tablespoons dashi-miso paste (see Cook's Notes)

Sesame oil, for drizzling (optional)

COOK'S NOTES. *Udon noodles can be purchased in a variety of forms. The frozen, precooked variety is the best for camping or backpacking because preparation time is super quick. If you can't find the frozen ones, cook dry noodles according to the package instructions, drain, rinse with cold water, then drain again. Store in a zip-top bag with a splash of toasted sesame oil or neutral oil and bring to camp in a cooler.*

Dashi-miso paste is available online and in Asian grocers. Dashi (a Japanese soup base) is sold in large bags, and it's also available in tea-bag form online, which is very convenient. You can add the dashi tea bags to the miso paste that's sold in plastic tubs to achieve similar results. Otherwise, plain miso paste will work, too.

ALSO WORKS WITH. *All species of salmon, trout, char, and whitefish. Also cooked and shredded chicken, wild turkey, upland bird, rabbit, and squirrel.*

This is a versatile framework for a satisfying camp soup. It's a good option for families. It gives kids what they want, which is noodles, combined with something they should learn to love, which is fish. We're using salmon here for a few reasons. One is that my family catches a lot of salmon, so I'm always looking for good things to do with them. Another is that salmon is widely available in grocery stores, so it's impossible for landlocked cooks not to find the stuff. But you can swap out the salmon for any number of fish species, and it'll be equally good. In fact, this could be ideal to make with fresh-caught fish on a backcountry backpacking trip.

Combine the salmon, salt, and scallion whites in a bowl and set aside.

In a large pot, bring 3 quarts water to a boil over high heat on a campstove. Add the noodles and cook for 1 minute, stirring occasionally, until the noodles can be separated. Divide the noodles between two large soup bowls. Discard the water.

Add 4 cups water to the same pot and bring it to a boil. Blanch the bok choy for 60 seconds. Remove from the pot and divide it between the bowls. Reduce the heat to maintain a simmer and whisk in the dashi-miso paste.

Add the chunks of salmon to the pot. Simmer until barely cooked, about 1 minute, then remove and divide it between the bowls. It will finish cooking in the bowls. Add the soup to the bowls and top with scallion greens and a drizzle of sesame oil, if using.

Serve immediately.

VENISON CHILI

MAKES 4 QUARTS

Growing up in Michigan, it was common for people to think of whitetail deer and chili as being inextricably linked. (I'm talking about the kind of Midwest chili that has a lot of beans and not a lot of heat.) In fact, people back home would hunt for whitetails with the stated purpose of securing their chili meat for the year. My personal love of the dish has not waned over the decades that I've been away from Michigan, though I have come to appreciate versions of the dish that would be acceptable to folks living outside of the Great Lakes region. This one uses ground meat, but it could also be made with precooked, cubed, or shredded elk or deer shoulder. It works doubled or tripled, so you can make it to handle a crowd. And with some prep work (see the Make Ahead instructions), it's a great choice for campsite cooking.

FOR THE PASTE. Heat the oil in a large skillet over medium heat. Cook the onions for about 5 minutes, stirring occasionally, until they soften slightly. Add the poblanos, jalapeños, garlic, and salt and pepper and cook 10 to 15 minutes, stirring often, until the chiles soften. Add the ancho powder, brown sugar, cumin, oregano, chipotle, and adobo sauce. Mix well. Cook for about 3 minutes, stirring often, until the paste darkens in color. Transfer to a container to cool. If saving for later, refrigerate or freeze until ready to use.

FOR THE CHILI. Heat the oil in a large Dutch oven or other heavy pot over medium-high heat on a campstove. Crumble the meat into the pot in batches and sprinkle lightly with the salt and pepper. Cook, stirring often, until the meat browns. Add the chili paste to the pot and stir to combine. Add the tomatoes, beans, and beer to the pot and bring to a simmer. Reduce the heat as low as possible while still maintaining a simmer. Cook, partially covered and stirring occasionally, until the meat is tender and the flavors have melded, about 1 hour. If using meat other than burger, such as cubed shoulder meat or turkey legs, pre-braise them in game stock to save on cook time here. Add water as needed to loosen the chili if it gets too thick.

FOR SERVING. Serve the chili with shredded cheese, sour cream, cilantro, onions, and corn chips.

MAKE AHEAD. *We've designed this recipe to be an efficient 1-hour cook on-site. For that approach, make and freeze the chili paste mixture in your home kitchen, then reheat it and add the meat and canned ingredients at camp. Or, you can prepare the whole dish as directed, then vac-seal and freeze it at home and reheat it on-site. For reheating instructions, see page 217.*

ALSO WORKS WITH: *Pretty much any ground meat, such as beef, sheep, wild hog, venison, goose, duck, and so on.*

CHILI PASTE

Makes 2¾ cups

3 tablespoons canola oil

1 large white onion, chopped

4 poblano peppers, seeded and diced

4 jalapeño peppers, seeded and diced

10 garlic cloves, thinly sliced

1 teaspoon kosher salt

¼ teaspoon ground black pepper

2 tablespoons ancho chile powder

2 tablespoons dark brown sugar

2 tablespoons ground cumin

1 tablespoon dried oregano, preferably Mexican, crumbled

2 chipotle peppers in adobo sauce, plus 1 tablespoon sauce

CHILI

2 tablespoons canola oil

3 pounds ground venison (substitute some ground pork if your meat is very lean)

2 teaspoons kosher salt

½ teaspoon ground black pepper

2 (28-ounce) cans canned crushed tomatoes

2 (15-ounce) cans small red beans or kidney beans, rinsed and drained

1 (12-ounce) bottle beer

FOR SERVING

Shredded pepper Jack, or sharp cheddar

Sour cream

Chopped fresh cilantro leaves

Diced red or white onion or sliced scallions

Corn chips, tortilla chips, or cornbread

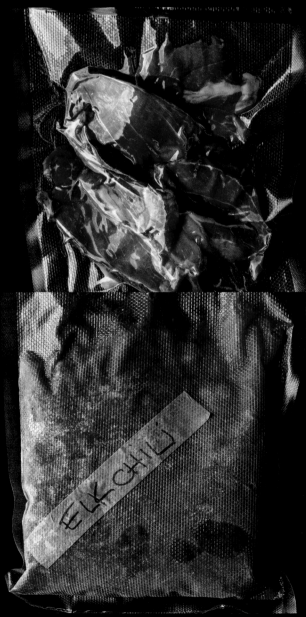

VAC-SEALING:
REHEATING PRECOOKED MEALS AT CAMP

These days vacuum sealers are standard kitchen equipment for just about everyone, and like most folks, you probably use yours primarily for storing food in the freezer. But vacuum-sealed bags of premade dinners can also save you a ton of time and eliminate cleanup when you're in camp. This method of food prep does require a little advance planning, as you need to make and freeze meals (or freeze leftovers) ahead of time. While we spotlight a few meals that lend themselves to vac-sealing in the list below, this system works great for anything that is suitable for freezing ahead of time, from sloppy Joe and taco meat to all of the soup, stew, and stir-fry sauce recipes in this book.

You'll basically be doing a camping version of the sous vide process to reheat the food, which can be completely frozen or just chilled. Get a pot large enough to hold your vac-sealed meal and fill with water about halfway to two-thirds full; if it's a small bag of food for one or two people, you can reheat it in a shallow pan filled halfway with water. Bring the water to a low boil, add your bag, and cook until the interior contents are at least at 160°F to 165°F. When the food is hot, ladle it directly out of the bag and add any fresh garnishes or toppings, if needed.

The following recipes are ideal for vac-sealing. Any cooked or smoked wild game or birds will vac-seal well and keep in the freezer for 3 to 6 months, especially when in a liquid or gravy. Vac-sealing smoked fish works well, but we don't recommend vac-sealing cooked fish; in general the quality of the protein degrades and is less palatable. Below are recipes for meats, soups, stews, and complex marinades that make easy work of outdoor meals if prepared ahead and frozen.

Beaver Confit (page 20)
Boston Baked Beans (page 305)
Brined and Smoked Turkey Breast (page 128)
Brown Sugar Wild Hog Ham (page 103)
Bulgogi Marinade (Bulgogi Lettuce Wraps, page 38)
Camp Sausage (page 36)
Cooked beans (page 306)
Deer Shoulder in a Barrel (page 176)
Dutch Oven Rabbit Boudin (page 184)
Fish Sausages (page 115)
Goose and Dumplings (page 183)
Ground Venison Sauce (page 223)
Layered Fish Chowder (page 290)

Lentil Stew (page 311)
Moroccan-ish Venison Meatballs in Spicy Tomato Sauce (page 208)
Penne with Sausage and Peas (page 225)
Peruvian-Style Marinade for Duck with Ají Verde (page 78)
Portuguese-Style Panfish and Potato Soup (page 211)
Smoked Duck (page 130)
Smoked Moose Nose Hash (page 133)
Smoked Venison (page 118)
Spatchcocked birds (page 75)
Summer Sausage (page 100)
Turkey Chili Verde (page 285)
Venison Chili (page 215)
Weeknight Butterflied Steak (page 45)

CUBAN-STYLE RICE WITH RABBIT

SERVES 6 TO 8

RABBIT

5 large garlic cloves, minced (3 tablespoons)

1 tablespoon kosher salt

1½ teaspoons dried oregano

2 tablespoons apple cider vinegar

1 tablespoon olive oil, plus more as needed

2 or 3 wild rabbits (4 to 5 pounds total), each cut into 4 leg pieces and a saddle

RICE

Makes 8 cups

Olive oil

1 large red bell pepper, seeded and cut into medium dice

1 large cubanelle pepper, seeded and cut into medium dice

1 large onion, chopped

3 garlic cloves, thinly sliced

1 packed cup fresh cilantro leaves and tender stems, chopped, plus more for garnish

1½ teaspoons Sazón Coriander & Annatto Seasoning (from 1½ packets)

2 teaspoons ground cumin

2 teaspoons dried oregano

1 teaspoon paprika

3 bay leaves

Kosher salt and freshly ground black pepper

3 cups homemade game stock

1 (8-ounce) can tomato sauce

1 tablespoon drained capers

2 cups medium-grain rice, rinsed

½ cup frozen peas, thawed

½ cup pimiento-stuffed whole olives

Lime wedges, for serving

Here's a nod to the excellent chicken-and-rice dishes that abound in the Caribbean. Many of those preparations belong to that wonderful category of foods that taste better as leftovers than they do the first time around. We're making this version with cottontail rabbit, which I like to refer to as "thinking man's chicken." If you're not a rabbit hunter and you don't know any rabbit hunters, let's just hope that you're a squirrel hunter. Those work just as well here. Homemade stock makes the difference in this dish, however. Rabbit stock is even better, but you can get by with store-bought broth.

SPECIAL EQUIPMENT. Wide, heavy-bottomed 8- to 10-quart pot with a lid.

FOR THE RABBIT. Mix the minced garlic, salt, oregano, vinegar, and oil in a small bowl. Add the rabbit pieces to a zip-top bag, pour in the marinade, and seal the bag. Massage the rabbit through the bag to distribute the marinade over all the surfaces. Refrigerate for at least 1 hour but preferably overnight.

Heat a wide pot with a lid over medium heat on a camp propane burner. Add 1 tablespoon oil and swirl to coat. Pat the rabbit dry, removing the minced garlic if you can. Cook the rabbit in batches; try not to overcrowd the pot so each piece gets a good sear. Turn the meat as it browns. Each batch should take 4 to 5 minutes. Add more oil as needed between batches and lower the heat if the brown bits on the bottom of the pan start to burn. Remove the pieces to a plate as they brown.

FOR THE RICE. Once all the rabbit is browned, heat 1 tablespoon oil, or more as needed, in the pot and add the peppers, onions, sliced garlic, and cilantro. Stir to scrape up any browned bits, then add the Sazón, cumin, oregano, paprika, bay leaves, 2 teaspoons salt, and several grinds of black pepper. Cook, stirring, until softened, 5 to 8 minutes. Add the stock and bring to a simmer. Return the rabbit to the pot, nestling the pieces into the liquid. Cover and cook for about 1 hour, stirring occasionally, until the meat begins to get tender. (Older animals may need more time.)

Stir in the tomato sauce, capers, and rice. Over just enough heat to maintain a simmer, cover and cook 25 to 30 minutes, until the liquid is absorbed and the rice is tender. Remove from the heat, top with the peas and olives, cover the pan, and let sit for 10 minutes. Serve with lime wedges and garnish with cilantro.

ALSO WORKS WITH. *Wild turkey, upland birds, snowshoe hare, squirrels, nutria, or domestic rabbit and chicken. You could also try this with alligator or snapping turtle meat.*

GARLIC MISO SHRIMP

SERVES 2

I trap shrimp every summer with my family up at our fish shack in southeast Alaska. We eat them pretty much every night while we're there, usually just boiled for a quick minute and dipped in cocktail sauce. By the time we get back home to Montana, I'm usually burned out on that simple preparation, and I'm ready to make something a little more unique and exciting with the shrimp that I bring home. This marinated shrimp recipe is the perfect fix for that. It works especially well with shrimp, but the marinade can be made ahead of time for all kinds of seafood and shellfish. It's an elegant appetizer for dinner parties, and so damn good that I'm prepared to violate tradition and make a big batch the next time I'm at my shack. Those Alaskan shrimp have never had it so good.

The marinade would also work with thinly sliced big game and upland birds that will be grilled or roasted to finish. This dish can be made on a propane stove or a hot grill set up with direct and indirect heat zones.

FOR THE MARINADE. Place all the marinade ingredients except the serrano pepper in a container large enough to hold the shrimp and mix thoroughly. Add the shrimp and serrano pepper and marinate for 1 hour in the refrigerator.

FOR THE SHRIMP. Preheat a large cast-iron skillet over medium-high heat on a propane camp burner for 5 minutes. When the pan is hot, add the peanut oil and spread it evenly in the skillet. Remove the shrimp from the marinade, reserving the marinade. Carefully add the shrimp to the pan in a single layer, being very careful as the oil may pop and spit a little due to the moisture in the marinade. Cook the shrimp for 2 to 3 minutes on each side, until just barely cooked through. Lower the heat and transfer the shrimp to a plate.

To make the glaze, combine the butter, garlic, shallots, and cayenne in the pan and cook, stirring often, for 1 minute. Pour the marinade into the pan along with the rice vinegar and lime juice. Give everything a stir and let the sauce simmer for 2 minutes, or until it has thickened slightly.

FOR SERVING. Remove the pan from heat, place the shrimp back in the pan, and toss them thoroughly in the glaze. Sprinkle the shrimp with sesame seeds, cilantro, and scallions and serve with rice, if using, and lime wedges.

ALSO WORKS WITH. *Prawns, spiny lobster, crayfish, scallops, clams, mussels, and any firm, white, flaky fish.*

MISO MARINADE

Makes about 2 cups

4 tablespoons white miso

3 tablespoons soy sauce

6 tablespoons mirin

2 tablespoons honey

1 tablespoon Worcestershire sauce

1 tablespoon fresh lime juice

1 tablespoon toasted sesame oil

¼ cup warm water

½ teaspoon freshly ground black pepper

1 serrano pepper, halved lengthwise

SHRIMP

1 pound large shrimp, shells on and deveined

4 tablespoons peanut oil

4 tablespoons (½ stick) unsalted butter

15 large garlic cloves, minced (about 4 tablespoons)

1 large shallot, minced (3 tablespoons)

½ teaspoon cayenne pepper

1 teaspoon rice vinegar

2 tablespoons fresh lime juice

FOR SERVING

2 tablespoons toasted sesame seeds

½ bunch cilantro, leaves picked (1 cup loosely packed)

1 bunch thinly sliced scallions, white and green parts (1 cup)

Cooked white rice (optional)

Lime wedges

SPECIAL EQUIPMENT

12-inch cast-iron skillet

GINGER CATFISH STIR-FRY

SERVES 4 TO 6

MARINADE

1 tablespoon Shaoxing wine or dry sherry

¼ teaspoon kosher salt

⅛ teaspoon ground white pepper

1 tablespoon cornstarch

1 to 1½ pounds skinned catfish fillets, cut into 1½-inch pieces

SAUCE

½ cup fish, chicken, or vegetable stock

1 tablespoon soy sauce

¼ teaspoon sugar

1 tablespoon cornstarch

⅛ teaspoon ground white pepper

1 tablespoon Shaoxing wine or dry sherry

3 tablespoons vegetable or neutral oil

½ cup julienned peeled ginger

1 garlic clove, finely chopped

2 scallions, trimmed and thinly sliced

2 ounces snow peas, ends trimmed, sliced into ½-inch strips on the bias

½ red bell pepper, seeded and thinly sliced

Cooked white rice, for serving

ALSO WORKS WITH. *When it comes to fish, you name it: walleye, northern pike, bluegill, crappie, pompano, snapper, grouper, redfish, speckled trout, and peeled shrimp. Also, upland bird breast meat cut into bite-sized pieces.*

Here's a solid option for a shore lunch or camp dinner on your next fishing trip. The recipe's combination of ginger and fish is popular in Hong Kong and the southwestern region of China. The bold ginger flavor works particularly well with a host of fish species, including catfish. You can make the marinade, broth, and vegetables in advance. Then all you need to do is procure the fish and you're ready to cook. Or drag some fish out of the freezer and use that. The marinade will help cover any off-flavors that might have come about from extended freezer times.

FOR THE MARINADE. Combine the wine, salt, white pepper, and cornstarch in a bowl. Add the catfish and marinate for 5 minutes.

FOR THE SAUCE. Mix the stock, soy sauce, sugar, cornstarch, white pepper, and wine.

In a large nonstick pan or wok, heat 1 tablespoon of the oil on medium-high heat on a propane campstove. When hot, add the pieces of catfish. Cook for 2 minutes, until lightly browned on the bottom, and flip. Cook for 1 to 2 more minutes until lightly browned on the other side. Remove the fish to a plate, and don't worry if it isn't cooked all the way through.

Add the remaining 2 tablespoons oil to the pan and cook the ginger, garlic, and half of the scallions for 1 minute. Then add the snow peas and bell peppers and cook for another minute. Add the sauce to the vegetables in the pan. Cook, stirring, for 30 seconds. Add the fish and continue to cook, gently stirring, for 1 minute, or until the cornstarch has thickened, the fish is cooked through, and the sauce is translucent.

Garnish with the remaining scallions and serve with white rice.

COOK'S NOTE. *Don't be put off by the amount of ginger in this dish, as it goes well with fish. Feel free to substitute broccoli, string beans, zucchini, or whatever else you like for the snow peas.*

MAKE AHEAD. *The two mixtures, the marinade and the sauce, can be made in advance, stored in separate airtight containers, and brought to camp ready to use. Use a small whisk or fork to emulsify them if they have separated.*

TOSSED NOODLES WITH GROUND VENISON SAUCE

(ZHA ZHIANG MIEN)

SERVES 6 TO 8

This recipe was adapted from a Chinese dish called zha zhiang mien, which translates rather clunkily to "fried sauce noodle." It's traditionally made with finely ground or chopped pork, though it works beautifully with ground game. More authentic preparations rely on a sweet bean sauce typically found in Asian specialty markets. For the sake of convenience, we built this recipe to achieve similar flavors using ingredients that are much easier to find. Big thanks to Jeannie Chen, who is friends with my collaborator, Krista Ruane. Jeannie helped us with the necessary adaptations to make this recipe achievable for folks who can't get to the big city for their ingredients.

In a large pot of boiling water, cook the dried noodles according to the manufacturer's instructions. Drain and toss them in a bowl with the sesame oil. (I like to blanch the edamame in this water after the noodles have cooked.)

FOR THE SAUCE. In a medium bowl, mix together the broth, hoisin, oyster sauce, soy sauce, wine, cornstarch, salt, and sugar. Set aside.

In a large cast-iron or nonstick skillet, heat the oil over medium-high heat and cook the garlic and scallions until fragrant, about 30 seconds. Add the ground meat and chopped mushrooms and cook, stirring often and breaking up the meat, until the meat is cooked through, 3 to 4 minutes. Add the sauce and stir until it thickens, 2 to 3 minutes.

To serve family-style, place the noodles in a large, wide platter, then compose the toppings over the noodles, top with all the sauce, and toss well. For individual portions, toss the noodles with the meat sauce, portion into bowls, and top with the vegetables. Eat while hot.

COOK'S NOTES. *Shaoxing wine is found in Asian markets but can be replaced with dry sherry. Dried udon noodles (look for the brand Kame) can be found in big supermarkets. The topping quantities and ingredients here are guides; use as much or as little as you like. The sauce can be tossed without the noodles with a selection of fresh vegetables for a quick, easy camp meal.*

MAKE AHEAD. *This meat sauce can be frozen to use later, which means it's an ideal sauce to keep dishes innovative on camping trips. After making the sauce, you can allow it to cool down and vac-seal to freeze the full quantity, or portion out serving-sized quantities. Either can be frozen up to 3 months. If freezing: To thaw the sauce, thaw quickly in warm water before heating thoroughly in a pan.*

12 ounces dried udon noodles (see Cook's Notes)

1 tablespoon toasted sesame oil

SAUCE

½ cup chicken or vegetable broth

2 tablespoons hoisin sauce

2 tablespoons oyster sauce

2 tablespoons soy sauce

1 tablespoon Shaoxing wine or dry sherry

1 teaspoon cornstarch

½ teaspoon kosher salt

¼ teaspoon sugar

3 tablespoons vegetable oil or neutral oil

6 garlic cloves, minced

2 scallions, ends trimmed, white and green parts, thinly sliced

1 pound ground venison

4 ounces white mushrooms, finely chopped (1⅓ cups)

VEGETABLE TOPPINGS

(see Cook's Notes)

1 cup unpeeled cucumber, julienned

½ cup julienned carrots

2 radishes, halved and thinly sliced

½ cup shelled and cooked edamame

ALSO WORKS WITH. *Pretty much any ground meat, such as beef, sheep, wild hog, venison, goose, duck, and so on.*

VENISON STIR-FRY WITH CABBAGE

SERVES 4

MARINADE

1 pound venison backstrap, cut into slices against the grain about ⅛ inch thick and 1½ to 2 inches long

2 tablespoons soy sauce

1 tablespoon Shaoxing wine or dry sherry

1 teaspoon toasted sesame oil

2 teaspoons cornstarch

SAUCE

1 teaspoon fennel seed

1 teaspoon cumin seed

¾ cup homemade game stock or chicken broth

1 teaspoon cornstarch

1 tablespoon soy sauce

2 teaspoons rice vinegar (optional)

2 tablespoons vegetable oil

2 or 3 Thai bird chiles or any chiles with heat, thinly sliced (see Cook's Note)

2 garlic cloves, finely chopped

1 teaspoon minced fresh ginger

½ head cabbage, outer leaves removed, cored, halved again, and leaves separated (about 4 cups)

⅛ teaspoon kosher salt

Cooked white rice, for serving

SPECIAL EQUIPMENT

Spice grinder or a flat stone and a rounded stone

MAKE AHEAD. *The marinade and sauce components can be made in advance and even frozen.*

This venison stir-fry is packed with a lot of big flavors from fennel, cumin, ginger, and garlic. It's reminiscent of the cumin lamb stir-fries that you might see on Chinese menus in the United States. In general, lamb recipes work well with venison. This one is no exception. It's especially good when combined with a sweet, hearty vegetable like cabbage. You'll see that we call for some pulverized spices in this preparation. You could be a lame-o and use a spice grinder. Or you could take the backwoods approach and grind your spices between a couple of rocks. Without getting too deep into geology, you'll want to use rocks with a lot of structural integrity for this. Crumbly rocks could give you a lot of unwanted grit in your spice. That ain't yummy.

FOR THE MARINADE. In a medium bowl, marinate the sliced meat with 2 tablespoons of the soy sauce, wine, sesame oil, and 2 teaspoons of the cornstarch.

FOR THE SAUCE. Toast the fennel and cumin seeds in the pan over medium-low heat until fragrant and slightly toasted, 2 to 3 minutes. Transfer the seeds to a spice grinder and grind into a powder. (At camp, you can put the spice seeds on a flat rock and use a rounded, rough stone to pulverize the spices as finely as you can. If some whole spices remain, it's fine). Put the ground spices into a dish and set aside.

Mix ½ cup of the stock, the remaining 1 teaspoon cornstarch, the remaining 1 tablespoon soy sauce, and vinegar (if using) in a bowl.

TO COOK. In a 12-inch pan, heat 1 tablespoon of the vegetable oil over medium-high heat on a camp burner. Add the ground fennel and cumin seeds and cook for 30 seconds, or until fragrant. Add the marinated meat in one layer. Do not move it for 1 minute to allow it to brown, then stir it around for another 30 to 45 seconds, until it's cooked to rare. Remove the meat to a bowl.

To the same pan, add the remaining 1 tablespoon vegetable oil, the chiles, garlic, and ginger and stir-fry for 30 seconds, until fragrant. Add the cabbage and stir to coat it with aromatics. Add the remaining ¼ cup stock and the salt. Stir-fry for 3 to 4 minutes, until the edges of the cabbage are a bit browned. Add the partially cooked meat back to the pan with the vegetables and stir to combine. Add the flavored broth and stir until the sauce is slightly thickened. Remove from heat and serve with rice.

COOK'S NOTE. *You can add more chiles if you'd like a little additional heat.*

PENNE WITH SAUSAGE AND PEAS

SERVES 4 OR 5

In my home freezer, I always keep a stash of homemade sausages packaged in vacuum-sealed bags. You can thaw these sausages with lightning speed by dropping them into a tub of cold water. They're perfect for last-minute meals when I fail to pull something out of the freezer ahead of time. In these situations, it's tempting to just slap a grilled sausage on a bun with a squirt of mustard. But that doesn't need to be your only trick. The recipe satisfies the same urgency for speed, but it hits entirely different notes. It's ideal for quick weeknight family dinners. It freezes really well, too, so it makes a good addition to your car-camping repertoire. You could even make this on a backcountry trip—just swap the frozen peas for canned.

FOR THE SAUCE. In a bowl, crush the canned tomatoes by hand. Set aside.

Cut the sausage links into ¾- to 1-inch pieces. Add 1 tablespoon of the olive oil and half of the sausage to a hot pan. Cook the sausages until they begin to brown and release from the pan. Stir or flip the sausages with tongs and continue cooking for about 8 minutes to brown the other side. Season with a pinch of salt. Remove the browned sausages from the pan and repeat with the remaining sausages, adding more oil if needed. When all the sausage is cooked, drain the fat from the bottom of the pan and move the sausage to a heatproof bowl.

Add the remaining ¼ cup oil to the pan with the red pepper flakes, onions, and garlic. Cook on high heat for 30 seconds to 1 minute, until fragrant; do not allow the garlic to brown. Add the hand-crushed tomatoes and 1½ teaspoons salt and stir. With the heat still on high, return the sausages back to the pan and bring to a simmer. Cook, simmering and stirring occasionally, for 20 minutes, until the flavors meld. Taste the sauce and add more salt if needed. Turn the heat to low to keep warm while the pasta cooks.

FOR SERVING. Meanwhile, bring a 6-quart pot of water to a boil and add the salt and the penne. Cook according to the package instructions for al dente. Add the peas and stir to thaw. Drain off the water and transfer the pasta and peas back into the pot. Add the hot tomato sauce and stir to incorporate.

Serve warm with grated cheese and additional red pepper flakes (if using).

SAUSAGE SAUCE

1 (28-ounce) can whole peeled tomatoes

4 Camp Sausages (page 36), or 1½ to 2 pounds Italian-style game sausages or bulk sausage

¼ cup plus 2 tablespoons extra-virgin olive oil

Kosher salt

1 teaspoon crushed red pepper flakes, plus more (optional) for serving

1 medium onion, chopped (about 1¼ cups)

4 large garlic cloves, thinly sliced

FOR SERVING

3 tablespoons kosher salt

1 pound penne pasta (or any other shape you like)

1½ cups frozen peas

Grated pecorino or Parmigiano-Reggiano cheese

MAKE AHEAD. *If freezing, transfer the cooled sauce to a vac-seal bag, seal, and freeze for up to 6 months. (See details on reheating on page 217.)*

ALSO WORKS WITH. *Any nonsmoked game sausage made from big game, small game, or upland birds.*

LOUISIANA-STYLE CRAYFISH, BLUE CRAB, AND SHRIMP BOIL

SERVES 8 TO 10

CRAYFISH BOIL

8 pounds live crayfish

10 live blue crabs, preferably large male crabs

2 or 3 (10-pound) bags ice

3 pounds large Gulf shrimp, shell on, split, and deveined

3½ cups Low Country Seafood Seasoning (page 348)

3¾ cups store-bought liquid seafood boil

½ cup kosher salt

6 bay leaves

2 leeks, trimmed, cut lengthwise into 4 pieces

6 medium sweet onions, quartered

6 garlic heads, halved crosswise

4 celery ribs, halved crosswise

Juice of 4 lemons

2 pounds andouille sausage, cut into 2-inch pieces

6 ears of sweet corn, halved

4 pounds new potatoes, halved

2 baguettes

SPECIAL EQUIPMENT

Propane outdoor cooker

Stainless-steel 40-quart pot with perforated steamer basket

One of the things that I love about the Atlantic Seaboard and Gulf Coast regions of the United States is how territorial everyone gets around the subject of seafood boils. On the Eastern Shore of Maryland, some cooks get so nitpicky about how to boil and eat blue crabs that they actually insist on the type of table covering to be used—brown butcher paper is standard. Some Gulf Coast Texans will tell you that the table covering has to be layers of newsprint, as though this selection will impact the flavor of the crabs. I have never seen or heard of anyone stipulating what specific publication's newsprint should be used, but I wouldn't be surprised by it. In Louisiana, I've seen otherwise laid-back people get feisty in debates regarding nuanced details of how to properly conduct the "soak" phase of a crayfish boil, even though the soak phase is literally just letting the cooked crayfish passively soak in their cooking liquid. I mention all of this because certain folks are guaranteed to receive this recipe with open hostility, as it contradicts their firmly held convictions about how seafood boils should be conducted. Our version borrows from the flavor profile of the classic Louisiana-style boil, but our combination of blue crabs and crayfish might strike some Louisianans as pure sacrilege. The only rule we insist on is that you invite a bunch of people over when you make this preparation. It's as much about camaraderie and friendly arguments as it is about the flavors.

FOR THE SEAFOOD. Place the bag of crayfish in a cooler and rinse them thoroughly with a hose or running water to remove any excess mud, grit, and debris. Repeat the rinsing process until the water runs clear; this may take four or five cycles of rinsing. Place them in a paper bag or another cooler. Rinse the blue crabs under fresh water and place them in a large paper bag. Drain any excess water from the cooler and lay down two or three bags of ice. Cover the ice with a piece of burlap or a couple large kitchen towels and place the crayfish and blue crabs on top of the burlap. Rinse the shrimp lightly in fresh water and place in a strainer to drain. Transfer the shrimp to a plastic bag and place in the cooler. Refresh the ice as needed and drain any excess water as the ice melts so the crayfish and crabs are not submerged in water.

FOR THE SEAFOOD BOIL BASE. Combine 2½ cups of the Low Country Seafood Seasoning, 3 cups of the liquid seafood boil, the kosher salt, and bay leaves in an airtight container and refrigerate. Combine the leeks, onions, garlic, celery, and lemon. Squeeze the lemons and add their juice and store in a separate airtight container.

TO COOK. Set up your propane outdoor cooker and add 5 gallons water to a 40-quart stainless-steel stockpot with a perforated steamer basket. Place the pot on the burner and add the seafood boil base ingredients. Stir the contents and cover. Light the burner and set the heat to high. Once the liquid reaches a boiling point, add the andouille sausage, corn, and potatoes to the pot. Cover the pot and cook for 5 minutes. After 5 minutes, remove the lid and put the crayfish and crabs in the pot. Bring everything back to a boil. As soon as you notice steam coming out of the sides of the lid, shut off the burner. Let the seafood steep for 10 minutes. Remove the lid, toss in the shrimp, and cover the pot for another 3 minutes. With leather grilling gloves, carefully pull the steamer basket out of the pot and rest it on the top of the pot to drain for a couple minutes.

Dump the contents of the steamer basket into a clean cooler or onto a table covered with several layers of newspaper. Cover the food with the remaining ¾ cup liquid boil, ½ to 1 cup of seafood seasoning, and 1 cup of the hot boil liquid from the pot. (If you're not a fan of spicy food, omit the last step of tossing in additional seafood spice.)

Toss everything very well until the spices are evenly distributed. Serve with large pieces of baguette.

COOK'S NOTE. *If you don't want to make your own Cajun-inspired seafood seasoning, you can substitute Zatarain's or a similar Louisiana seafood-boil spice. The Low Country Seafood Seasoning recipe makes more than needed for the recipe. It can be used as an all-purpose seasoning for any fish dish, including a fried fish fry, a fish stew, or enriched brine.*

HOW TO FRY FISH

Parker Hall

There is a weird "itchiness" that my hands get after spending half a day cleaning a cooler full of catfish. I don't know if it's a thousand micro cuts or irritation from the fish slime or a combination of the two, but I really like it. It means the freezer is getting filled up, and we are about to fire up the grease with friends and family.

Some of my earliest memories involve running trotlines. My father would operate the leaky, tiller-handled johnboat while he baited hooks, tossed fish into the cooler, and shouted at my brother and me. We were young and basically useless on the water. My dad would get so frustrated that he'd simultaneously tell us to "sit down!" and "grab the net" without realizing how confusing that was. But at the end of the day, we usually had a boatload of fish.

Back home, we helped Dad clean and process the fish. My brother and I weren't very good at it. Dad cleaned ten fish to our one, and there's no telling how many fillets we mangled. When the cleaning was done, he would then take control of cooking the fish on a double-burner propane fryer that he made himself. We weren't allowed to help, because, of course, we didn't know what we were doing. My dad still maintains that sentiment today. Whenever I cook fish, my dad always has some sort of negative comment about the amount of seasoning, temperature of the grease, or the utensil I'm using. It's all in good fun . . . I think.

Despite my dad's opinion of me, I have learned a few things over the years. Without a doubt, cleaning catfish properly is one of the most important components of having a good fry. Some folks like to claim that catfish have a muddy taste, but I've found this usually boils down to lazy preparation on the part of whoever is cleaning them. Like all fish, catfish have a bloodline that we call "red meat." I trim most of that out, particularly on larger fish. However, catfish fat is really what gives them that off-flavor. It's important to remove all of it. Catfish fat is generally light yellow in color and has a somewhat gooey consistency. Of the three species of catfish we eat—channel cats, flatheads, and blue cats—the largest and fattiest is the blue cat. No matter the species, I trim off every last bit of fat I can see, and then I give the meat a rinse with a hose using a good bit of water pressure. Soaking the fillets in ice-cold salt water for an hour or so can help, too.

For frying, I like to cut the fillets into pieces that take about two and a half bites to eat. I don't know the exact measurements, but you get the idea. If the meat is cut too small, all you will taste is fried cornmeal. If the bites are too big, they take too long to cook. The two- to three-bite size seems just about right.

If you have ever fried fish inside of your house, you are already well aware that the oily fried-fish smell will stick around for a few days. For that reason, I almost always do my frying outside. Any kind of heat source will work as long as you can get the grease up to temperature and keep it that way. I prefer a propane-powered outdoor cooker. Wind is your enemy when frying outside, as it takes the heat away rapidly. This cools the grease, and cool grease results in soggy fish. Nowadays, there are cookers with wind shields, but a pickup truck, a big tree, or a piece of plywood will also get the job done. If you are cooking anywhere other than on the grass or dirt, keep in mind that frying fish can be a messy ordeal. Consider putting down some cardboard or plywood under your fryer if you're cooking on a deck or carport.

Through the years, I have seen hundreds of combinations of pots, cookers, and stirring and dipping implements utilized while frying fish. My favorite frying container is a large cast-iron pot. Cast iron does the best job at holding heat with the least fluctuation in temperature. Granted, it takes a little longer for the grease to get up to temperature than it does with a thin steel or aluminum pot, but cast iron is more forgiving. Those other types of pots can work well, too, but attention must be paid when either adding fish (temp goes down) or when you remove a batch of fish (temp goes up). As for utensils, everyone that I know has a favorite tool for flipping, stirring, and removing fish. My dad uses a relatively short-handled wire-slotted skimmer spatula with a deer antler stuck on the end. My brother will use whatever he can find, including tongs. I like a long-handled wire-type dipping utensil called a spider strainer. I think it is also important to have a finer strainer to remove excess meal from the grease. That's especially key when cooking for a large group and running many batches of fish through the grease. If it's not removed, the meal will sink to the bottom of the pot and get scorched. This will shorten the life of the grease and give the fish a burnt taste.

Any number of kinds of grease can be utilized to fry fish, but I usually use either vegetable oil or peanut oil. Peanut is my favorite, since it has a higher smoke point than vegetable or canola oil, but it is pricier. I generally like my temperature to be somewhere right around 350°F. If I am frying large, thick pieces, like flathead belly or wild turkey strips, I like my grease just a bit cooler so the meat cooks all the way through without burning the breading. If I am doing something smaller, like a bunch of bluegill fillets, I may bring up the temperature a little as the meat is more delicate and cooks really fast. Just remember that if your temperature gets too hot, you'll end up with scorched grease and burned fish fillets. You also need to correctly match the amount of fish to the size of your pot. If you overload the grease, it will cool off and your fish will get soggy. All of your friends and family will call you horrible names if this happens. You will be pushed out of the way, and a more "experienced" fish cooker will take over. (If it's my family, they all think they are the best.)

Another important step is seasoning and breading the fish. Everyone likes it a little different, but for seasoning, I use three ingredients: black pepper, garlic powder, and Cajun seasoning, which has added salt. For breading, some folks like to add commercially produced fish-fry breading or a little flour to their meal. I do not. I use just plain yellow cornmeal. It is important to season the fish itself, not the cornmeal. Some people give in to the devil's temptation of adding spices to the cornmeal. This can be referred to as a faux pas, a vocabulary word I learned in school thirty years ago. The definition of the term is "grave social error." In this case, it means that you will find out your first batch of fish doesn't have enough seasoning, and your last batch has way too much.

Start by firing up the grease. Then lay out all the fish that you plan to cook on a cutting board, a piece of cardboard, or even newspaper. If the fish is wet, take a paper towel and soak up the excess water off the fillets. If you don't, the cornmeal will get "clumpy," and the moisture will cool your grease, popping and splattering all the while. After the fillets are mostly dry, season both sides with the three spices. Don't overdo it with the Cajun seasoning. Remember, you can always hit it again after it comes out of the grease if you need to. Once you have put on the black pepper, add a little more. It is hard to overdo it with the black pepper. The same can be said for the garlic powder.

I season the fillets while the grease is coming up to temperature. Next, I empty a bag of yellow cornmeal into a large foil pan. These work great for seasoning fish as well as for serving them. When the thermometer says the oil is about 340°F, I put six to eight pieces into the meal and coat them well, then I gently ease the fillets into the grease by hand. Don't drop them in or you will splash hot oil onto yourself, and a grease burn is the gift that keeps on giving. While this first batch is in, pay attention to your temperature and adjust accordingly. You want it to maintain that 340°F to 350°F range. While the fish are cooking, throw your next batch into the cornmeal for coating. Then take a look at the fish in the fryer. When they are close to being done, which should take only a few minutes, they will begin to float. I like to

turn them over a time or two and leave them in for another minute or so.

The first batch of fish is usually the worst for me. The oil is still new, and your pieces won't be really golden brown. It's a good time to hand a piece to your friend and have them test your seasoning to see if you need to add anything. Do that as soon as it comes out of the fryer, so you can watch your friend instantly spit the fish out because they burned their lips. The frying usually gets better after a couple of batches, but you will want to start to collect the excess meal that is in the oil to prevent it from becoming scorched, all the while watching your temperature. Another good tip is to keep a rag or towel in your back pocket in case you need to remove the pot from the burner for a minute if the oil is getting too hot. Repeat the process until you are done. As the cook, you'll probably end up eating the last batch because the rest will have already been devoured by everyone else. If you like, squeeze some lemon on and dip it in tartar sauce, cocktail sauce, or whatever other kind of sauce you like.

Remember, you can reuse your grease. I can usually get several cookings out of one potful. Just let it cool and pour it back into the original container.

I live in Florida now and don't eat as much catfish as I used to. However, my intake of what my friends and relatives call "saltfish" has increased exponentially. "Saltfish" is anything that comes out of the ocean that is foreign to my family or friends. They have no idea what it is, except that it is fish that came out of the ocean, not off a trotline or jug. That said, the process for saltfish is the same. Black pepper, garlic salt, Cajun seasoning, cornmeal, 350°F. Heck, I do the same for wild turkey, shrimp, ducks, and squirrels. You can't go wrong with anything cooked this way.

Parker Hall is the state director for the USDA/APHIS Wildlife Services Program in Florida.

MILANESA TORTA WITH WILD TURKEY

MAKES 6 SANDWICHES

Tortas are commonly known as "Mexican sandwiches" in the United States. What really sets tortas apart is the bread. Traditionally, they are served on a soft, oval roll called a telera. In Mexico City, you can find torta vendors who are regionally famous for their craft. While the rolls they use are fairly standard, the sandwiches themselves can be stuffed with all manner of different fried or grilled fillings. For this sandwich here, a Milanese-style torta, you'd normally use a pounded chicken cutlet. We're going with wild turkey instead.

FOR THE CUTLETS. Cut the turkey breast crosswise against the grain into 6 pieces. (Cut out any large pieces of silverskin or connective tissue.) Place between two sheets of plastic wrap and pound them flat into ¼- to ⅓-inch-thick cutlets. The flattened cutlets should be well-tenderized and slightly larger than your torta roll.

TO SET UP THE FRY STATION. Gather three large, deep plates. Place breadcrumbs in the first large plate and stir in the taco spice. Crack the eggs into the second plate and whisk in the hot sauce. Distribute the cornstarch on the third plate.

Dip the cutlets, one by one, first in the cornstarch, shaking to remove any excess, then in the egg, and then finally into the breadcrumbs. Try to cover the entire surface of the cutlet with breadcrumbs by pressing them into any exposed areas.

TO FRY. Place a 12-inch cast-iron skillet over medium-high heat on a propane campstove and add ½ inch canola oil to the pan. Heat the oil until it hits 350°F. Test the temperature with a pinch of breadcrumbs: If they sizzle, pop, and begin to brown, the oil is hot enough.

Working in batches of 2 pieces, fry the turkey cutlets for 3 to 4 minutes on each side, until golden brown and crispy. Remove the cooked turkey, set it on a draining rack or paper towels, and season each piece with a pinch of salt. Repeat with remaining 4 pieces.

FOR THE TORTAS. Slice open the chipotle peppers and scrape out the seeds. On each roll, spread the crema on the top half and a ¼ cup refried beans on the bottom half of each roll. Place turkey on top of the beans and then shredded cheese, 2 or 3 chipotle pepper pieces, salsa verde, tomato slices, pickled jalapeños, shredded lettuce, and lastly a couple avocado slices.

Eat immediately or save the tortas for later, wrapping them tightly in parchment paper and then in foil.

TURKEY CUTLETS

1 skinless, boneless wild turkey breast (about 1½ pounds), cut into six 4-ounce pieces

1½ cups plain breadcrumbs

3½ tablespoons store-bought taco spice or Taco-Style Seasoning (page 348)

3 large eggs

1 tablespoon hot sauce, like Cholula

½ cup cornstarch

Canola oil (about 1½ cups for a ½-inch depth in a 12-inch cast-iron pan)

TORTAS

1 (16-ounce) can refried black beans, or 2 cups homemade Refried Black Beans (page 307)

2 (8-ounce) cans chipotles in adobo sauce

6 telera rolls or oval-shaped soft rolls

6 tablespoons Mexican crema

12 ounces Oaxaca cheese, shredded

1½ cups salsa verde, store-bought or homemade (see page 350)

2 tomatoes, sliced

¾ cup pickled jalapeños

1 head iceberg lettuce, shredded

1 large avocado, sliced

SPECIAL EQUIPMENT

12-inch cast-iron skillet

THERMOS RAMEN

MAKES ENOUGH FOR ONE 18-OUNCE THERMOS; SERVES 1

½ (3.5-ounce) package dried ramen noodles (1.75 ounces), broken in half lengthwise

½ of the flavor packet from dried ramen noodles (see Cook's Note)

¼ cup frozen shelled edamame or any leftover vegetables from camp (see list below)

¼ cup sliced, shredded, or dehydrated leftover cooked protein

1¾ cups boiling water

SPECIAL EQUIPMENT

18-ounce wide-mouthed food thermos

COOK'S NOTE. *You can substitute 1 bouillon cube for the half ramen flavor packet.*

ALSO WORKS WITH. *Dehydrated mushrooms and scallions, fresh herbs, thinly sliced vegetables, any cooked and shredded big game or small game meat, or dehydrated meat like hard sausage, jerky, or dried smoked fish.*

Here's a quick and easy (and highly transportable) backcountry meal that'll have you thanking yourself on cold days in the field. You can use this recipe as inspiration and then substitute the ingredients with whatever you happen to have on hand. One package of dried ramen is good for two of these meals. Assemble the soup at home or camp in the morning and then throw it in your backpack. At lunchtime, the noodles are soft, all the ingredients are rehydrated, and the soup is still hot.

Use your backcountry stove to boil 2 cups water. Pour the boiling water into the thermos and add the half package of ramen noodles. Put the lid on for 1 to 2 minutes to soften the noodles, then add half the flavor pack, vegetables, and leftover protein and tightly close the thermos.

Allow to sit for at least 10 to 13 minutes (or the duration of your hike) before eating and then open and stir everything together.

CAMP BREAKFASTS, LUNCHES, AND SNACKS

SOUPED-UP TOAD IN A HOLE

SERVES 4

There are dozens of names for this dish. Egg in a hole, bird in a nest, and the far less appetizing name that I grew up with—toad in a hole—are just a few. Apparently, in some parts of the country it's referred to by the equally unappetizing moniker "spit in a hole." Some say it was made famous by the 1987 romantic comedy *Moonstruck* (where it's called *ouvo in cestino,* or "egg in a basket"), but my dad was cooking it on his camp-stove griddle way the hell before that.

    This version does play with the Italian American flavors of the *Moonstruck* version. You can strip this one down as much as you'd like, but if you want something really special, you should follow through on this preparation in its entirety.

Preheat a two-burner griddle over medium-low heat on a campfire stove. Add the pancetta to one side and crisp it while the griddle heats up, flipping halfway through, about 2 minutes. Set aside when done.

Meanwhile, using a 2½-inch round cookie cutter or biscuit cutter, cut a hole in the center of each slice of bread. Set aside.

Melt 2 tablespoons of the butter on the unused side of the griddle. Put both the bread and rounds on the buttered area. Place ½ tablespoon of the butter in each hole, then set an artichoke heart, cut-side down, in the hole and press down so it splays. Crack an egg into each hole, top each with some of the giardiniera, and season with salt and pepper. Let the bread toast until golden, about 1 minute.

Move the bread slices to the side of the griddle and melt the remaining 2 tablespoons butter where the bread was. Carefully flip the bread slices and rounds over. Cook until the bread is golden on the bottom and egg is cooked to the desired doneness, about 1 minute for a runny yolk.

Transfer the egg in a nest and bread rounds to four plates and serve with a side of the pancetta.

4 thin slices pancetta or bacon (4 ounces)

4 slices sandwich bread

6 tablespoons (¾ stick) unsalted butter

4 canned artichoke hearts, drained, dried, and quartered lengthwise

4 large eggs

Kosher salt and freshly ground black pepper

3 tablespoons giardiniera, any large pieces coarsely chopped

COOK'S NOTES. *All giardinieras are not made equal. If you can get your hands on the giardiniera in oil that hails from Chicago delis, get it. It's superior to all others.*

You can invert foil pie tins over two pieces of toast to help the eggs cook faster.

ALSO WORKS WITH. *Smoked ham, game bacon, domestic duck eggs.*

HOW TO MAKE GOOD COFFEE IN THE OUTDOORS

Just like food, coffee tastes better outside. I've been drinking it daily since I was a teenager, and I'm a hopeless addict. We keep things simple at home by using a standard electric coffee maker that requires very little thought or planning. I could get that thing up and running with a blindfold on. In the outdoors, getting a coffee fix requires a little more effort. It's not that big of a deal if I'm using the kitchen stove in my camper or a two-burner stove on a car-camping trip, where I have the space to pack my French press (I love the shatterproof GSI JavaPress). But things can get a tad more specialized on back-packing trips. Back in the old days, I'd carry a zip-top baggie of Folgers instant coffee that I'd premix with powdered creamer. While I wouldn't go so far as to say I'm a coffee snob, these days I'd say I'm something close to it. Which means that I get burned out pretty quickly on Folgers instant coffee. Day one of that stuff is not so bad. But day seven is pretty awful.

Thankfully, outdoor coffee has come a long way over the years. Now you can find instant coffee that's at least 70 percent as good as the real stuff. Alpine Start and Starbucks both produce pretty tasty instant coffee that comes in single-serving packets. For coffee snobs who might balk at the weaker flavor of freeze-dried stuff like Alpine Start, the Starbucks Via packets are a mixture of freeze-dried and micro-ground coffee that are available in a range of popular blends. Either way, you just dump the packet into hot water and stir to dissolve the powder. Another simple, and arguably better, option for car camping and backpacking trips is the single servings of real ground coffee packaged in tea bags that are made by Black Rifle Coffee Company and others. To make a cup of coffee, just steep the bag in a mug of hot water for several minutes. I've yet to find a brand that will do the trick with a single packet. Instead I always start with two. Speaking of mugs, there are plenty of ultra-light backpacking models to choose from. I use a GSI mug while backpacking, but I stick to a double-walled, vacuum-insulated mug with a spill-proof lid for everything else. They keep hot coffee hot for a long time without scalding your hands, and you don't have to worry about your buddy's boot kicking your mug over and spilling the goods.

If you really can't get by without brewed coffee, then you'll want to head to REI or another bougie camping retailer and you'll be blown away by the options for packable coffee presses and pour-over devices. The MSR MugMate weighs less than an ounce and filters a single serving of brewed coffee. If you've got a really big backpack, the GSI JavaPress that I mentioned can handle 30 ounces of coffee.

Finally, if you're patient and don't mind a little grit in your morning cup of joe, there's always cowboy coffee. For those of us who tend to rely on quick-and-easy outdoor coffee, making the cowboy version is something of a lost art. But all you need to do is bring a metal coffee kettle or pot of water to a boil. (Some people throw in a pinch of salt.) Historically, this was done over a campfire, but feel free to use a stove. After it reaches a boil, take the kettle off the heat to cool for a minute before adding the appropriate amount of coffee grounds. (Don't add the grounds while the pot is boiling over the flames or you risk burning the grounds and making a horrible-tasting pot of coffee.) Stir the grounds in, put the lid back on, and wait for a couple minutes. Stir again and wait a couple more minutes. Sprinkle a little cold water into the pot and tilt the pot slightly so it's resting at a bit of an angle. This will allow the grounds to settle in one corner of the pot. To serve, pour the coffee slowly without disturbing the grounds on the bottom of the kettle. Chances are there will be a few grounds floating around in your mug anyway, but I guarantee you, it'll taste a helluva lot better than instant Folgers crystals. When it's time to clean up, dump out the used grounds and rinse the pot in a creek. If you're anything like me, that'll get you wondering if trout are easier to catch when they're jacked up on coffee.

THE LATE EUGENE GROTERS'S BEER AND APPLE PANCAKES

MAKES 6 TO 8 MEDIUM PANCAKES

When I was growing up, one of my dad's fishing buddies was an eccentric junk collector and hobbyist inventor named Eugene Groters. Into his seventies, Groters kept a large mirror fastened over the bed in his log cabin that he shared with his wife, Beatrice. He kept a wild collection of oddities in the living room, including a pair of whitetail fawns stored inside a glass jar filled with what must have been formaldehyde. Overhead racks stored his gun collection, which included a gun for every year he'd been alive. He once told me that he'd made a mistake and had accumulated one more gun than he had birthdays. He then pulled a Winchester Model 94 down from the rack and gave it to me. I used to love waking up in the mornings at Groters's cabin, because he made the best pancakes in the world. He was an avid beer drinker and that's what he used to make his pancakes. He added apple slices, too. When you try these, you'll understand why he made them that way. This recipe can be doubled or tripled, depending on how many people you're feeding.

1 recipe (about 1¼ cups) Modular Pancake Dry Mix (see Cook's Note)

¾ cup American-style pale lager beer

2 tablespoons vegetable oil or melted unsalted butter

1 large egg

1 apple, peeled, cored, and sliced

Unsalted butter, as needed for cooking and (optional) serving

Maple syrup, for serving

In a medium bowl, combine the pancake mix, beer, oil, and egg, stirring until no flour is visible—don't overmix the batter. Allow it to sit for 5 minutes while you preheat a camp-stove griddle or nonstick pan over medium-low heat. (Alternatively you can use a greased cast-iron pan over a keyhole fire; see page lv.)

Melt a pat of butter on the griddle and distribute it evenly. Pour ¼ cup of the batter for each pancake on the griddle and arrange a few apple slices on top. Cook the first side until bubbles appear on top, 3 to 4 minutes, then flip with a spatula and cook the second side for 2 to 3 more minutes until golden brown on the bottom. Remove to a plate and keep warm. Repeat with remaining batter.

Serve warm topped with more butter (if using) and maple syrup.

COOK'S NOTE. *This recipe utilizes a make-ahead dry pancake mix that is featured on page 326. The mix can be used to make all sorts of batters, pancakes, and desserts, so it's a handy item to bring on camping trips.*

MONTE CRISTO SANDWICH

SERVES 4

3 large eggs

½ cup milk

¼ cup Dijon mustard

¼ teaspoon kosher salt

¼ pound Gruyère cheese

2 tablespoons unsalted butter

½ pound sliced smoked ham or Brown Sugar Wild Hog Ham (page 103)

8 slices sturdy white sandwich bread

Confectioners' sugar, for dusting (optional)

Apricot jam, for serving (optional)

Maple syrup, for serving (optional)

ALSO WORKS WITH. *Any smoked game or domestic ham or slices of Summer Sausage (page 100).*

This sandwich has a hell of a lot going for it, as it's made with good ingredients and then battered and fried. What more could you ask for? It's great for breakfast, lunch, or dinner. You can get fancy and French up the top with confectioners' sugar or apricot jam. For breakfast, go with a splash of maple syrup. This one is easy to prep in advance, so you can have it ready in a hurry when it's time to cook.

TO PREP. Up to 24 hours ahead, whisk the eggs, milk, mustard, and salt in a large bowl. Pour into a pint storage container. Refrigerate until ready to use. Grate the cheese and store in a resealable bag.

TO ASSEMBLE AND COOK. Melt 1 tablespoon of the butter in a large cast-iron skillet over medium heat on a propane campstove or keyhole fire (see page lv). Pour the batter into a shallow dish. Place half of the ham on 4 of the bread slices. Evenly top with the shredded cheese. Then place the remaining ham on the cheese. Top with the remaining 4 bread slices. Holding the sandwich closed, carefully submerge it in the batter and let it soak for at least a minute to evenly soak the bread. Place 2 sandwiches at a time in the skillet and cook until golden brown, 3 to 4 minutes per side. Wipe out the skillet and repeat with the remaining ingredients.

Dust with confectioners' sugar (if using) and top with a dollop of jam or douse with maple syrup (if using) before serving.

05 ON THE SPIT

As soon as I finished college, my brother Danny and I went down to Mexico's Yucatán Peninsula to spend a month fly-fishing for bonefish in the shallow lagoons south of Tulum. We'd camp on the beaches for three or four nights and then hitchhike our way back north to get resupplied with food and water. Sometimes we'd just hitch to Tulum, which was a hell of a lot emptier and grimier in the mid-1990s than it is today. Other times we'd get on a bus in Tulum and ride even farther north to Playa del Carmen.

We had pretty good fishing on that trip—actually much better than I thought we would—but the thing that really surprised me was the eating. There were a few places near the bus stop in Tulum that served these beautiful and muscular little chickens that they'd marinate in a garbage can. The chicken was grilled over an open flame, slowly and carefully, and then they'd dice the spatchcocked bird into small pieces using a tree stump for a chopping block and a machete. This was the best grilled chicken in the world, and I'm not just saying that because I was half starved every time I ate it. I'm saying that because it was the best grilled chicken in the world.

When we continued north to the town of Playa del Carmen, we were motivated in part by the nightlife there, which was great. But the tacos al pastor in Playa del Carmen were even better. These were small tacos made with corn tortillas and thinly sliced pork shoulder that had been marinated in citrus juices and herbs. The tacos were topped with onions and cilantro. What blew me away about the tacos was more than just the taste; I was mesmerized by the visual display of the cooking contraption, known as a trompo. A mountain of thinly sliced pork was layered on the trompo's vertically mounted rotisserie spit. The meat formed a roughly cylindrical shape about the size of a big raccoon. The cylinder was capped with a skinned-out pineapple. The rotisserie turned in front of a vertical burner. They added achiote paste to the marinade, so that the roasted meat turned a reddish pink. The rough edges of the cylinder became lightly charred in the burner's heat, and the pineapple juice running down the meat made it glisten. For maximum visual display, taco vendors positioned their trompo at chest height. They'd use long knives to whack off slices of the meat and pineapple that they'd catch in a tortilla held in their hand like a baseball mitt. Then they'd top it with cilantro and diced onion. Like I said, mesmerizing.

After eating several dozen tacos al pastor over the course of that month in Mexico, I was committed to the idea of someday owning my own trompo. I finally got around to it as I was planning the day of my wedding. I wanted to host an all-day volleyball tournament in my home state of Michigan to entertain my friends before the evening ceremony. It seemed like tacos al pastor would be the perfect thing to serve at lunch. If you hated volleyball and didn't know what to do with yourself, you could at least watch that glorious cylinder of meat spin round and round.

My buddy Ronny, who's a fabricator, welded me a beautiful trompo from stainless-steel scraps that he pilfered from a plant in Virginia that makes and packages the ultra-pasteurized single-serving half-and-half containers you see in gas stations. Instead of a propane burner, he fitted it with a rectangular charcoal box. The meat-facing side of the box was expanded

metal grating. The day before my wedding, we sliced a pile of venison roasts and added them to a marinade. The next morning, we layered the slices on the spit, topped it with a pineapple, and set that thing to turning in front of the charcoal box. Of my whole wedding day, that's pretty much the only thing I remember with any level of detail: spiking volleyballs and hammering tacos al pastor.

You can't argue against the pageantry of anything that's cooked on a spit. It's fun and it looks cool. Most of us get our first experience with this form of cooking when we're kids. Thread a hot dog or a marshmallow on a stick and then let it burn to a black mess over a campfire. My kids love cooking like this. I made them each custom marshmallow sticks with a steel rod set into a deer antler handle as Easter presents. These got zero traction. The kids much prefer taking a machete over to a stand of aspens in our backyard and whacking down their own.

If roasting marshmallows is the elementary school of cooking on a spit, the shish kebab is junior high. Linguists believe that the word *kebab* comes from an Arabic word for roasted meat. If you do things right, you can get perfectly cooked bites of meat, seafood, and veggies on a kebab without a whole lot of hassle. The presentation of a classic kebab can be beautiful, with those contrasting colors of intermixed green and yellow peppers, purple onions, and white mushrooms. But eventually you figure out that keeping the meat separate from the veggies allows you to tailor cooking times to the particular needs of each ingredient. That gives you the magic of having buttery, cooked-through mushrooms alongside rare cubes of steak on your picnic table at the same time.

This chapter will take you on a journey that goes way beyond the classic kebab, into a huge and wild world full of spit-cooking possibilities. You'll go from skewered hearts to the showstopping trompo to caveman-style ducks spatchcocked on sharpened saplings. You'll even take a detour into tripod cooking, where you'll use various contraptions to suspend cookware in the heat of a fire. Some of this might seem like a lot of work, but it's well worth it. It's certainly a lot easier than backpacking up and down the Yucatán coast for a month in search of your next fix of tacos al pastor. Besides, I've heard that part of Mexico has gotten really built up. They say it's not what it used to be.

SPITS AND SKEWERS: WHAT YOU NEED TO KNOW

Spits and skewers come in many forms, from hot dog sticks carved out of twigs to the asado crosses used in Argentina to roast whole lambs. No matter the design or material, their function is basically the same: Spits and skewers allow food of varying sizes to be easily rotated or flipped during cooking. Entire hogs, whole game birds, piles of thinly sliced or chunked meat, and all manner of vegetables can be impaled and roasted this way. In this next section, you'll find examples of the different types of spits and skewers used for the recipes in this chapter.

When you think of a skewer, you're probably envisioning a typical combination of meat and vegetables threaded in an alternating pattern onto a thin piece of metal or wood. Building skewers that way is a great idea in theory, but a better plan is to follow the rule of keeping like with like. In other words, your veggies all go together on one set of skewers and the meat goes on another. Taking this approach means no more mediocre skewers with one ingredient that's undercooked, the next that's overcooked, and some that are burnt to a crisp. Instead, each singular ingredient will be cooked to perfection before being combined on your serving platter. Although they're usually cooked on a grill (or coals) over direct heat, skewers need to be rotated, much like a miniature spit, to achieve the desired results of meat with a tender interior and a crispy, caramelized exterior.

Skewers

You can make your own skewers with the same simple tools and materials used to make a DIY spit like the one above, or you can buy them. For a few dollars, you can get a hundred throwaway spits made out of bamboo, but you have to soak them for 30 minutes in water prior to use or they tend to catch fire on the grill. Skip the hassle and get a set of reusable metal skewers; they aren't much more expensive and they'll last forever. For backyard grilling, 8- to 12-inch skewers work well, but you may want some longer skewers in the 16- to 24-inch range for campfire cooking. Flat skewers, which are most commonly used across the Mediterranean and Middle East, are intended for ground meat; you'll find a recipe using those on page 276.

Backcountry Campfire Spits

As long as there's some green, live wood nearby (willow and alder are ideal), you can fashion a sturdy campfire spit system with just a pocketknife and maybe a hatchet or small handsaw. Look for limbs at least an inch in diameter for the support poles—anything smaller may burn up and collapse, dumping your meal into the ashes. And size up your spit sticks as needed to support whatever you're cooking. This setup is ideal for cooking whole squirrels, rabbits, and small game birds in the backcountry.

Rotisserie Devices

From small electric attachments that integrate with propane grills to whole-hog charcoal spit roasters or homemade devices like the trompo pictured above, there's no shortage of innovative rotisserie options out there. Some rotisseries must be turned manually, while others are motorized. What they all have in common is allowing the user to constantly rotate roasting meat, often for a long period of time, so it cooks evenly throughout or can be shaved off as it cooks, in the style of a trompo or shawarma.

HOW TO MAKE A DIY SPIT FOR MALLARDS AND OTHER GAME BIRDS

All you need to cook game birds or small game animals over a campfire is a pocket knife and access to some green wood. First, build the support frame for the Backcountry Grate on page 12 over a bed of hot coals. Then cut your sharpened spits long enough so they can rest in the frame and hold the bird or critter while it roasts.

1. Spatchcock your bird (see instructions on page 75).

2. Use a sharp knife to make two slits through the back of each side of the bird. (Use the same technique for rabbits or squirrels.)

3. Insert the spits through the slits.

4. Using two spits keeps larger birds in position while they are suspended over the fire.

5. If the cavity is tight, use a third spit to open the bottom of the bird wider for more even cooking.

6. Suspend your birds on spits over an outdoor spit frame skin-side down to start.

7. Baste the birds as you cook, rotating them skin-side down and skin-side up as needed to ensure even cooking.

8. When the meat is cooked through and skin is golden, it's ready.

SICHUAN SKEWERS

MAKES 8 TO 10 SKEWERS; SERVES 2 TO 4 AS A MAIN OR 6 AS AN APPETIZER

This method is inspired by Sichuan street vendors who start by dipping skewers into hot fat before throwing them on the grill for a few minutes. After that, they repeat the dipping and grilling process, and then finally they hit the skewers with an array of aromatic spices. Often prepared with beef or lamb, this dish can be made with all kinds of big game meat. The skewers are addictive, and they're a great way to use up all of your odds and ends. You do need to plan ahead to have the right vessel for the hot fat. And it should go without saying that you need to be attentive when you have hot grease near a flaming grill. A splatter of grease can catch fire fast and easy, so be careful.

FOR THE INFUSED FAT. Put the fat, star anise, bay leaves, cinnamon sticks, cloves, Sichuan peppercorns, and fennel seeds into a small, heavy-bottomed saucepan that is tall and narrow. You want the fat to reach at least halfway up the pot. Heat the fat and spices over medium-low heat. Let the spices steep in the fat for 1 hour. Reduce the heat to low if the fat is bubbling. Carefully strain through a fine-mesh sieve into a heatproof bowl. If you're not using it immediately, let it cool, then cover and refrigerate. Otherwise, wipe out the pot with a dry paper towel and return the fat to the pot.

FOR THE SPICE MIX. In a small, dry cast-iron or other heavy-bottomed skillet, toast the cumin seeds over medium heat, shaking occasionally, until they are fragrant and turn a darker shade of brown. This should take only a minute. Transfer the cumin to a plate. Add the Sichuan peppercorns to the same skillet and toast for 30 seconds, again shaking occasionally, or until fragrant. Transfer to a plate and let both spices cool. Add the toasted cumin seeds and peppercorns to a spice or coffee grinder or a mortar and pestle and pulverize them. Add 2 teaspoons of the red pepper flakes and the fennel. Pulse or grind the spices until coarsely ground. Stir in the remaining 1 teaspoon red pepper flakes, the granulated garlic, and salt and transfer to a small bowl.

Prepare a grill at medium-high heat for two-thirds direct and one-third indirect grilling.

Thread the meat onto metal skewers, pushing the meat to the tip of the skewer. Set aside on a plate.

SAFETY TIPS BEFORE GETTING STARTED. Pour the fat into the tall and narrow pot. Be sure you have a towel or leather grilling gloves handy. It is

Recipe continues

SPICE-INFUSED FAT

Depending on the size of your pot, you may want to double this infused fat so that it's deeper in the pot (see the Cook's Note).

Makes about 2 cups

14 to 16 ounces rendered fat (preferably bear, goose, or duck)

5 whole star anise

3 bay leaves

3 cinnamon sticks

5 whole cloves

½ teaspoon Sichuan peppercorns

½ teaspoon fennel seeds

SICHUAN SPICE MIX

2 teaspoons cumin seeds

2 teaspoons Sichuan peppercorns

1 tablespoon crushed red pepper flakes

2 teaspoons fennel seeds

2 teaspoons granulated garlic

2 teaspoons kosher salt

1 pound big game round, cut into ½- to 1-inch cubes

SPECIAL EQUIPMENT

1½-quart metal bain-marie or tall, narrow pot (see Cook's Note)

10 (8- to 10-inch) metal skewers

COOK'S NOTE. *A narrow (4 to 6 inches in diameter), tall (6 to 8 inches high) pot or bain-marie is ideal for preparing the fat and dipping the skewers in this recipe. (If you have an asparagus pot, this might be your chance to use it.) If you're lacking a pot with the right dimensions, the best option is to use a small 1- to 1½-quart pot and baste the skewers with a brush or a spoon; you'll get approximately the same results. Make sure to use a pot with metal handles that are safe for the grill.*

ALSO WORKS WITH. *All hooved big game animals, wild turkey, geese, and ducks.*

best if you can warm the pot of fat on a grill side burner. If this isn't possible, use the grill itself, making sure the grill is level and stable. Heat the fat until hot but not smoking, then move it to the indirect side of the grill.

TO GRILL. Use a brush to coat the meat lightly with the seasoned fat. Grill very lightly on all sides, less than 30 seconds per side. Working with about four skewers at a time, carefully plunge them into the pot of fat, at an angle if necessary, to cover as much of the meat with the fat. If the fat does not completely cover the meat, spoon or brush the hot fat over the meat several times to baste it. Carefully pull the skewers from the fat and let the fat drip back into the pot.

Return the skewers to the grill and sprinkle generously with the spice mix. Cook until lightly charred in spots and to the desired doneness. Remove the skewers from the grill and sprinkle with more spice mix. Transfer to a platter and serve.

SHEEP SKEWERS (ARROSTICINI)

SERVES 6

Arrosticini are a traditional skewered dish from the Italian province of Abruzzo. Sheepherding goes back untold centuries in the Abruzzese mountains, so naturally skewers from the region are made with lamb. They're cooked on a narrow, channel-shaped grill called a canala or furnacella by street vendors who pack cubes of meat and fat closely together. The high heat sears and caramelizes the meaty bits as the fat melts and bastes the meat. The skewers are simply seasoned with sea salt and sometimes rosemary after grilling.

Wild sheep and feral sheep are an excellent wild game substitution for lamb, but be sure to choose tender cuts. Here we're substituting pancetta in place of lamb fat.

In a medium bowl, combine the meat, rosemary, salt, garlic, and oil until well coated. Cover and refrigerate for at least 5 hours or up to 24 hours. Bring to room temperature 1 hour before cooking. Toss with the lemon juice right before skewering. Prepare a medium-hot grill for direct grilling. Discard the garlic. Thread the cubes of meat onto skewers, with small pieces of pancetta between every 2 pieces of meat. Be sure to pack the skewer tightly without any space between the chunks of meat.

Grill the skewers, turning often, until they are slightly charred on the outside and medium-rare on the inside. This may take only 3 to 4 minutes total. Try to avoid flare-ups.

Sprinkle the skewers with additional salt as they come off of the grill. Serve immediately with crusty bread.

1½ pounds sheep top round, trimmed and cut into ¾-inch cubes

1 tablespoon fresh rosemary leaves, coarsely chopped (from 1 sprig)

1 tablespoon kosher salt, plus more for sprinkling

4 garlic cloves, smashed

2 tablespoon extra-virgin olive oil

1 tablespoon fresh lemon juice

6 (¼-inch-thick) slices pancetta, cut into ¾-inch chunks

Crusty bread, lightly grilled, for serving

SPECIAL EQUIPMENT

Metal or wooden skewers (see Cook's Note)

ALSO WORKS WITH. *Wild hog, antelope, deer, domestic lamb, feral sheep, and goats.*

COOK'S NOTE. *If you're using wooden skewers, soak them in water for at least 30 minutes to prevent them from burning on the grill.*

BIG GAME HEART SKEWERS

SERVES 6 TO 8

1 (2-pound) big game heart

1 tablespoon extra-virgin olive oil

2 teaspoons flaky sea salt, such as Maldon

6 fresh bay leaves, snipped crosswise into ¾-inch-wide strips

5 garlic cloves, smashed

Crusty bread, lightly grilled, for serving

ALSO WORKS WITH. *Deer, elk, moose, or pronghorn heart, cleaned and sliced, or whole rabbit, turkey, and upland bird hearts.*

Hearts are one of the finest-tasting parts of game animals—my oldest boy will say the very best part—and they're the perfect medium for grilled skewers. This simple Portuguese preparation with bay leaves and garlic lets the mild flavor and tender texture of hearts shine through. Be careful not to overcook them—they are at their very best medium-rare. This recipe uses thin slices of big game hearts. Slicing them thin makes them easier to fold on the skewer and helps the meat stay tender. Smaller hearts from ducks or rabbits can be cooked whole. If you're not familiar with how to clean a big game heart, see the sidebar below.

PREP THE HEART. Clean and prep the heart according to the instructions below, and cut it into ¼-inch-thick slices. Put the slices into a large bowl and toss with the oil, sea salt, bay leaves, and garlic. Cook immediately or marinate for up to 2 hours.

TO ASSEMBLE. Thread the slices of heart onto the skewers in a tight folding S or accordion pattern. Occasionally insert the bay leaves and garlic in between the slices of meat. Push the meat together tightly.

TO GRILL. Prepare a medium-hot grill for direct grilling. Place the skewers on a well-oiled grill grate. Grill, turning occasionally, for 6 to 8 minutes, until the meat is slightly charred on all sides but not overcooked.

Transfer to a plate and serve with crusty bread. Discard the bay leaves before eating.

HOW TO PREPARE A HEART FOR SKEWERS

Rinse the heart, pat dry, and place it on a cutting board. First trim the hard, white fat off the outside of the heart. Next, slice off the gristly top "cap" of the heart to expose the interior chambers. Butterfly the heart by making a lengthwise incision from top to bottom, but don't cut all the way through. Lay the heart out flat on the cutting board—this may require a couple more additional cuts. Now trim all interior fat, arteries, and fibrous connective tissue until you're left with clean muscle. Lastly, cut the heart into lengthwise slices about ⅛ to ¼ inch thick.

CRYING TIGER SKEWERS
WITH HEARTS OF DUCK OR UPLAND BIRD

SERVES 4

These skewers are influenced by "crying tiger," a grilled beef dish from Thailand. They're served with a spicy dipping sauce called *jaew* (see Cook's Note) that's made with dried Thai chile flakes. While it is customary to finish the sauce with ground toasted rice, it's also delicious without it. The sauce pairs well with most grilled foods and would be a welcome accompaniment to a simple seared steak.

My strategy for bird hearts is to keep storing the hearts in my freezer until I've got enough to make a dish with them.

FOR THE MARINADE. In a wide, shallow container, stir together the soy sauce, oyster sauce, fish sauce, oil, granulated sugar, and black pepper until the sugar dissolves.

Add the duck hearts to the marinade, stirring to coat them well. Cover and marinate in the refrigerator for at least 3 hours, or keep them refrigerated in a storage bag with the marinade for up to a day.

FOR THE DIPPING SAUCE. Toast the rice (if using) in a small, dry cast-iron skillet over medium heat, swirling often, until golden brown, 5 to 7 minutes. Transfer the rice to a plate to cool. Using a spice or coffee grinder or a mortar and pestle, grind the rice into a powder. Set aside until ready to use.

Mix the fish sauce and lime juice with the brown sugar until the brown sugar dissolves. Add the red pepper flakes, cilantro, scallions, and shallots. Add more red pepper flakes for spicy skewers, if desired. Cover and refrigerate until ready to use. This sauce can also be made in advance and stored in the fridge. Stir in the rice powder (if using) just before serving.

GRILL. Prepare a medium-high hot grill or campfire for direct grilling. Thread the hearts onto the skewers. Lightly brush the hearts with oil. Grill on a well-oiled grate, turning often, until seared on all sides, 3 to 4 minutes for rare.

Transfer to a platter and serve with the dipping sauce.

MAKE AHEAD. *The marinade can be made in advance and stored in a leakproof container at room temperature for up to a month.*

ALSO WORKS WITH. *Hearts from hooved big game animals, upland birds, waterfowl, and small game. If using big game, see How to Prepare a Heart for Skewers on page 268.*

MARINADE

2 tablespoons soy sauce

2 tablespoons oyster sauce

1 tablespoon fish sauce

1 tablespoon neutral oil, plus more for grilling

2 tablespoons granulated sugar

¼ teaspoon freshly ground black pepper

---

1 pound duck hearts

DIPPING SAUCE (JAEW)

Makes ⅔ cup

1 tablespoon uncooked jasmine or glutinous rice (optional but highly recommended)

¼ cup fish sauce

3 tablespoons fresh lime juice (about 2 limes)

3 tablespoons packed dark brown sugar

1 to 2 tablespoons crushed red pepper flakes or gochugaru, plus more as needed

1 tablespoon finely chopped fresh cilantro

1 scallion, white and green parts, finely chopped

1 medium shallot, thinly sliced crosswise (about 2 generous tablespoons)

COOK'S NOTE. *Jaew is a spicy dipping sauce. Start with 1 teaspoon of red pepper flakes and then add more to taste. Stir the ground rice into the sauce to thicken right before serving.*

VEGETABLE SKEWERS

SERVES 4 TO 6 AS A SIDE

1 pint cherry tomatoes

10 ounces medium mushrooms, cleaned and trimmed

2 small onions, peeled and cut lengthwise into 6 wedges each

2 zucchini, cut in half lengthwise, then cut into ½-inch half moons

Extra-virgin olive oil, for drizzling

Kosher salt and freshly ground black pepper

SPECIAL EQUIPMENT

10 (8- to 12-inch) metal skewers

Mushrooms don't cook at the same rate as cherry tomatoes, and cherry tomatoes don't cook at the same rate as onions. Which is to say, you'll get the best results if you don't mix different types of vegetables on the same skewer. Go ahead and mix aromatics for flavor if you want to combine a vegetable with citrus slices or a hearty flavor enhancer (such as sage, thyme, rosemary, or even scallions) that can stand up to the heat of the grill. You can make simple vegetable skewers by brushing them with a touch of olive oil and then sprinkling them with a bit of salt and pepper. For a little variety, try hitting them with a seasoned mushroom or garlic salt or one of the many spice rubs on page 355. You can also brush on one of the glazes from page 355 just before removing the vegetables from the grill. And, of course, grilled vegetables will pair well with many of the condiments in this book (see pages 349 to 355). Here's an easy recipe to get you started.

Skewer the vegetables, using 4 skewers for the tomatoes and 2 each for the mushrooms, onion wedges, and zucchini. Dress with a drizzle of olive oil and season with salt and pepper. Prepare a grill for direct heat. When hot, lay down the skewers with space in between them. Cook each to your desired doneness. Char and caramelization add flavor; it should take 3 to 5 minutes per side for the tomatoes and zucchini, and 6 to 8 minutes per side for the onions to get some color and cook through. Rotate the mushrooms as they cook. They will steam a little and then begin to crisp in parts after 10 to 12 minutes.

Remove the skewers to a plate and serve warm or at room temperature, with or without a condiment of your choice.

TUNA AND/OR YELLOWTAIL SKEWERS

AND SALAD WITH CARROT-MISO DRESSING

SERVES 2 TO 4

This dish will be familiar to anyone who's explored the menus at Japanese American restaurants across the United States. The glaze is magical and doesn't need to be used exclusively on skewered foods. It'd be just as good brushed across a grilled or baked fillet of fish. Here, I'm using a couple of my favorite ocean residents—yellowfin tuna and yellowtail (known on sushi menus as ahi and hamachi, respectively)—but you could replace these with any number of fish species. And you can put just about any vegetable under that carrot-miso dressing and it'll disappear just as quickly. Be aware of issues consuming raw fish. Always keep fish chilled until it's ready to eat, and eat fresh raw fish that has never been frozen at your own risk. Flash freezing kills off any parasites that might be lurking within.

FOR THE GLAZE. In a small saucepan, combine the soy sauce, brown sugar, honey, vinegar, ginger, and garlic. Simmer over medium-low heat, stirring occasionally, for 15 minutes, or until the sauce reduces slightly. While the sauce is simmering, in a small bowl whisk together the cornstarch and 1 tablespoon water until smooth. Whisk the cornstarch mixture into the sauce and continue to cook, stirring, until the sauce thickens. Set aside. The sauce will continue to thicken as it cools.

FOR THE SKEWERS. Prepare a medium-hot grill. Thread two skewers, alternating with the tuna and scallions; set aside. Repeat with the yellowtail. Lightly brush the skewers with neutral oil and place them on a well-oiled grill grate. Grill on each side until grill marks appear, 5 to 10 seconds per side. Generously brush with the glaze, then return to the grill for another 5 to 10 seconds per side. Remove the skewers from the grill, brush again with the glaze, and transfer to a platter or tray. Scatter serrano slices over the skewers.

FOR THE SALAD. In a large bowl, mix the lettuce, cucumbers, carrots, and tomatoes. Drizzle with ¼ cup dressing and toss to evenly coat. Add more dressing to taste. Divide the salad between two bowls and serve each salad with one skewer of tuna and one skewer of yellowtail.

GINGER-SOY GLAZE

Makes about 1 cup

½ cup soy sauce

¼ cup packed dark brown sugar

¼ cup honey

2 tablespoons unseasoned rice vinegar

1 (3-inch) piece fresh ginger, peeled and grated (about 5 teaspoons)

2 garlic cloves, grated

2 teaspoons cornstarch

SKEWERS

9 ounces sushi-quality skinless tuna fillet, cut into 1-inch cubes

2 or 3 scallions, white and green parts, cut into 1-inch pieces

5 ounces sushi-quality skinless yellowtail fillet, cut into ¾- to 1-inch cubes

Canola oil or other neutral oil, for brushing

1 serrano chile, thinly sliced, for garnish

SALAD

3 cups iceberg lettuce cut into bite-sized pieces

3 Persian cucumbers, cut into thick half-moons

2 (3½-ounce) medium carrots, julienned or shredded on the large holes of a box grater

½ pint grape tomatoes (about 6 ounces), quartered

1 recipe Carrot-Miso Dressing (page 302)

WOVEN CALAMARI SKEWERS
WITH HARISSA AIOLI

SERVES 4 TO 6

One of my earliest magazine stories was about the nocturnal culture of squid jiggers in Seattle who come to the downtown piers on winter nights to fish for *Loligo opalescens,* otherwise known as the market squid. Many years after writing the article, I ended up living in Seattle, where my kids and I joined the ranks of the nighttime squid jiggers on a regular basis. The squidding season runs pretty much from Thanksgiving to Valentine's Day, during that period of long, dark nights and short days. On a bad night we wouldn't get any, but on a good night we might get fifty or sixty squid measuring anywhere from four to eight inches, not counting the tentacles. During the few years that I lived in Seattle, we made many mounds of fried calamari, as well as various versions of stuffed squid and braised squid. I wish I had figured out this preparation back then, because it would have been a welcome way to switch things up even more. Crowding the squid rings together means they get seared quickly on the outside and steamed to cook through to the center. Done properly, you'll get squid that is tender but not overcooked. It looks really cool, too. You can use any size of squid for this, as long as you adjust the recipe for the weight. You'll see our recipe calls for larger pieces, while the photograph shows smaller squid. Both options are more than fine.

FOR THE AIOLI. In a mini food chopper, pulse the garlic until minced. Add the lemon juice, salt, and egg and pulse to combine. With the motor running, slowly drizzle in the oil until the mixture is emulsified and thickened. Add the harissa and pulse to mix thoroughly. Adjust salt if needed. Cover and refrigerate until ready to serve or chill in a cooler for car camping. The aioli will keep for up to 4 days; it's best when enjoyed within a day or two.

FOR THE SQUID. Cut the calamari tubes crosswise into 1-inch-wide rings. Cut the tentacles in half. In a large bowl, toss the calamari rings and tentacles, oil, lemon juice, salt, and pepper until well coated. Fold a calamari ring in half to make a small bundle, roughly 1 inch in size, and thread it onto a skewer. Repeat and thread all the rings of calamari onto a skewer, stacking them tightly so no bare skewer appears between the pieces. Next, fold and skewer the tentacles.

Prepare a medium-hot grill for direct grilling. Place the calamari skewers onto well-oiled grates of the grill. Grill, turning occasionally, until the calamari are charred on all sides, 4 to 5 minutes. Transfer to a plate, sprinkle with a little more salt, and serve with harissa aioli.

HARISSA AIOLI

Makes 1 cup

3 garlic cloves

2 tablespoons fresh lemon juice

½ teaspoon kosher salt, plus more as needed

1 large egg

¾ cup extra-virgin olive oil

2 tablespoons prepared harissa paste (see Cook's Note)

SQUID

1 pound cleaned squid tubes and tentacles, patted dry

1 tablespoon extra-virgin olive oil

1 tablespoon fresh lemon juice

¾ teaspoon kosher salt, plus more as needed

⅛ teaspoon freshly ground black pepper

Neutral oil, for greasing

COOK'S NOTE. *Harissa paste is a flavorful, rich hot chile–based paste that comes from the Maghreb region of North Africa. It has roasted red peppers and an array of aromatics and spices including garlic, caraway, cumin, and coriander. It is now widely available at most grocery stores, but if you have difficulty finding it, check a high-end grocery store or order it online.*

ALSO WORKS WITH. *Octopus, scallops.*

VENISON KOFTA KEBABS

WITH SALAD, YOGURT SAUCE, AND PITA BREAD

SERVES 4 (2 KEBABS AND 1 PITA PER PERSON)

KEBABS

1 small yellow onion, cut into chunks

1½ pounds finely ground big game meat (see Cook's Note)

1 teaspoon ground cinnamon

1 teaspoon ground coriander

1 teaspoon ground cumin

1 teaspoon paprika

½ teaspoon ground nutmeg

½ teaspoon ground black pepper

½ teaspoon ground white pepper

1½ teaspoons kosher salt

YOGURT SAUCE

½ cup plain whole-milk yogurt (not Greek)

1 small garlic clove, minced or grated

1 teaspoon fresh lemon juice

2 teaspoons olive oil

¼ teaspoon kosher salt

10 fresh mint leaves, finely chopped

SALAD

1 small yellow onion, halved crosswise and thinly sliced with the grain

½ bunch fresh flat-leaf parsley, leaves torn (about 1 cup)

1 tablespoon fresh lemon juice

1 tablespoon olive oil

¼ teaspoon kosher salt

1 recipe homemade Pita (page 314)

Neutral oil, for grilling

SPECIAL EQUIPMENT

8 flat metal 12-inch skewers

This kebab is made from ground meat that gets formed into a tight tube around a skewer. It's based on kofta, a preparation that is credited to the ancient Arabs and today is a staple of the Middle East, Turkey, and North Africa. Traditional kofta is made of finely chopped meat (it's called kofta whether it's placed on a skewer or formed into meatballs), but we're using ground meat, or burger, instead. These skewers are best enjoyed with all of the components, so make an event of it. Store-bought pita will do if there's no time to make it yourself. If you have access to a Middle Eastern market and can find the seasoning mix called Lebanese seven spices, go for it. Pick up some sumac while you're at it—it'll add extra zing to the salad. Both sumac and the spice mix are available online, but we've worked a homemade version of it into our kebab mixture below.

FOR THE KEBABS. Blitz the onion in a food processor. Put the ground meat in a large bowl. Add the onion, spices, and salt. Mix thoroughly. Using about 3 ounces of the meat per skewer, form tight tubes 7 to 9 inches long around each skewer. You need to squeeze the meat to make sure it sticks to itself and to the skewer. Be sure to seal it well so it doesn't fall off. Keep it well chilled until grilling, which will also help it stay on the skewer during cooking.

FOR THE YOGURT SAUCE. Stir together the yogurt, garlic, lemon juice, oil, salt, and mint in a small bowl.

FOR THE SALAD. If desired, soak the onions in water to cover for 5 minutes to make it less pungent. Drain, then toss the onions with the parsley, lemon juice, oil, and salt.

TO GRILL. Prepare a campfire or grill for direct heat with a grate fitted over the top. If making the pitas, follow the instructions on page 314 to make and cook the pitas before grilling the kebabs.

Clean and oil the grates. Place the kebabs over the coals and grill, turning occasionally with the help of a metal spatula to keep them from sticking, until nicely browned, juicy, and cooked to 160°F, 15 to 20 minutes.

For each serving, hold a pita in your hand and grab the kebab to slide it off the skewer. Repeat with a second kebab. Drizzle the kebabs with some yogurt sauce and top with salad.

COOK'S NOTE. *The meat should be finely ground for this kebab.*

SPIKED FOWL

This preparation is more of a technique than a recipe. It'll gather curious onlookers, for sure, who'll want to stand around debating whether or not it'll actually work out. The answer is yes, it will, if you have the patience to let the meat cook in the ambient and reflected heat from the fire rather than crowding it too close to the flames and scorching it. Variations on the technique are more commonly used for roasting lambs in Argentina or cooking batches of whole salmon that are opened like books and fixed to vertically mounted stakes set in the ground. But we're doing it here with whole game birds, which is a lot of fun and tastes really special. Make sure that your birds are plucked and not skinned, as the intact skin will help prevent the meat from drying out and a steady spritz of a salty brine will keep it moist and flavorful.

FOR THE BIRDS. We found that whole plucked game birds like quail, ducks, pheasant, and grouse are the perfect size for this technique. The skin shields the meat from drying out, and birds of this size don't need to cook too long, relatively speaking. You can absolutely try larger portions of big game meat that demand a longer roast; just keep in mind that the lack of fat can lead to a dry, chewy eating experience.

You can add other flavors like apple cider vinegar or citrus zest and juice, even herbs, to this solution. Just let the solution sit for at least 2 hours to absorb some of the flavors.

STAKE THE BIRDS. Whittle the bottom tip of the stake so you can pound it into the ground. Hammer a nail about 2 feet above the bottom. This will be the "stop" for your bird, should it slide. Wipe the stake down with a clean, wet rag to remove any dirt or bugs. Insert the stake into the cavity of the bird and nestle it just above the nail. Using the twine, truss each bird tightly around a stake. The back ribs will likely overlap on the stake as it's wrapped.

PLAN THE FIRE. It's a good idea to plan this out before you truss the birds or start the fire. Make sure you've got enough stakes, metal, and room to make it work. The key to this cooking setup, which essentially functions like a large oven, is the heat reflector, which is a metal perimeter that wraps around the fire. Use a flexible metal 3 to 4 feet wide that comes in sheets or rolls, like corrugated steel. Avoid galvanized steel, as it can

Recipe continues

FOR EACH BIRD

1 green stake from a willow or other pliable tree, 3 to 4 feet long and 1 to 2 inches in diameter

1 nail

Length of string

Mallet or a rock

1 bird, backbone removed with game shears

SALINE SOLUTION

In a spray bottle, combine:

1¾ cups water

¼ cup kosher salt

FOR THE FIRE

10 to 16 logs of firewood

Pieces of flexible metal such as corrugated steel or sheet metal (non-galvanized), 4 feet tall and approximately 15 to 21 feet in length

Shovel to dig a trench

release toxins at high temperatures. You'll need several yards, depending on the circumference of your fire pit. Arrange your firewood in an oval shape. Dig a short trench that will lead under the metal from the outside of the reflector to the edge of the fire to draw in oxygen.

Use a mallet to pound the stakes into the ground with the birds breast-side toward the fire in a semicircle about 2 feet from the fire's edge and about 1 foot from where you'll place the metal reflector. Wrap the reflector around the fire, about 1 foot behind the semicircle of birds on stakes and 3 feet from the fire. Leave a small gap in the metal perimeter where you can enter and exit. You can wedge the metal into soft ground or use makeshift exterior supports to hold it up.

ROAST THE BIRDS. Cook until the birds become golden brown, periodically spraying them with the saline solution throughout the process, about every 5 to 10 minutes. Total cooking time will vary depending on the size of the birds, the heat from your fire, and the ambient temperature. Lean the stake closer to the fire if needed. For a grouse or pheasant, the internal temperature should register 155°F deep in the breast and at the thigh joint. Expect an hour or more for birds of this size and much less for a quail. Duck breast is excellent medium-rare to medium, so don't overcook and pull the duck at 140°F. Keep in mind the legs and wings won't cook at the same rate as the breasts, so they might end up a little tough—but they're still tasty and fun to gnaw on.

Serve with any of the condiments and sauces on pages 349 to 355.

HOG ON THE TROMPO

SERVES 12 TO 16

If you want the full story behind this recipe's inspiration, you can read about my experiences on the Yucatán Peninsula back in the mid-1990s on page 253. If you're short on time, here's a truncated version: I came to love tacos al pastor while traveling in Mexico in search of bonefish. About ten years later, I pestered my buddy Ronny into welding me a trompo so that I could produce my own version for friends on my wedding day. An even shorter version of the story would simply be this: Trompos are badass. This recipe is scaled up for throwing big ol' taco parties where you might want to put 5 pounds of marinated meat on the spit. You'll find a scaled-down version with a smaller yield for 1½ pounds of meat on page 346. As for how to make friends with a welder, you're on your own.

FOR THE MARINADE. Heat a heavy, dry skillet over medium heat until hot but not smoking. Toast the guajillo chiles until they blister slightly, about 15 seconds per side. Transfer the chiles to a large bowl. Pour hot water over the chiles to cover. If necessary, place a small plate into the bowl to keep the chiles submerged. Soak the chiles 30 minutes to 1 hour, until soft. The longer they soak, the easier they will be to blend smoothly. Pour ¼ cup of the soaking liquid into a blender. Drain the chiles and add them to the blender. Wipe the bowl dry and set aside.

Chop half of the onions, transfer them to a bowl, cover, and refrigerate until ready to serve. Coarsely chop the remaining onions and add them to the blender. Add the garlic, chipotles, vinegar, achiote paste (if using), sugar, 2 tablespoons of the salt, oregano, cumin, and black pepper. Blend until a smooth thick paste forms.

Transfer the marinade to a large bowl and add the hog slices. Massage to coat them well. Cover and let marinate, refrigerated, for at least 8 hours or up to 48 hours.

FOR THE MEAT. You don't need a custom-made trompo for this recipe. Any electric rotisserie setup will work. Stack the slices of meat in layers on the skewers. Depending on the size of each slice, you may need to pierce a corner so that the bulk of the piece extends away from the skewer. Continue this process, creating a wide circular base. The meat should be packed tightly. Repeat until all the meat is stacked tightly on the rotisserie, leaving enough room to add the pineapple on top.

Recipe continues

MARINADE

Makes 5¼ cups

12 dried guajillo chiles, stems and seeds removed (21 ounces total)

3 large white onions

12 garlic cloves

3 chipotle chiles in adobo sauce

½ cup plus 1 tablespoon apple cider vinegar

⅓ cup achiote paste (3 ounces; optional but recommended)

⅓ cup plus 1 tablespoon sugar

2 to 3 tablespoons kosher salt

1 tablespoon dried oregano, preferably Mexican

1½ teaspoons ground cumin

½ teaspoon freshly ground black pepper

MEAT

5 pounds wild hog backstrap and roasts, thinly cut into ¼-inch slices

1 whole fresh pineapple, peeled with top still on

FOR SERVING

32 corn tortillas, warmed

Fresh cilantro leaves

Lime wedges

ALSO WORKS WITH. *Domestic pork and tender venison cuts from the backstrap and hindquarter. I'd be curious to try turkey breast, but haven't done it yet.*

If you're using an electric rotisserie, add the skewered meat and turn on the device. For a propane grill rotisserie, add the skewered meat, fire up the grill, and turn on the rotisserie. If your trompo uses charcoal like mine, heat up a chimney and add the hot coals to the coal chamber. Start the motor and cook. Keep the meat spinning until the outside is charred a bit and the internal temperature about 2 inches in reaches 160°F for wild hog meat (this is important as it is a precaution against trichinosis). This could take 1 to 2 hours, depending on the heat output of your contraption. With mine, I often add a reflector with foil wrapped around the front to create some additional ambient heat and keep the heat closer to the meat. This helps to speed things up.

Once your thermometer reads 160°F in multiple places at a 2-inch depth, you can shave off the outer edges of the meat directly into corn tortillas. Carve a slice of the pineapple and serve with the cilantro, lime wedges, and the reserved chopped onions.

Repeat this process of checking the internal temp and carving meat from the outside. Keep in mind that it is not necessary or even desirable to bring venison like deer or elk to 160°F; feel free to start eating as soon as it hits rare or medium-rare (about 135°F).

TURKEY CHILI VERDE

MAKES ABOUT 8 CUPS; SERVES 4 TO 6

The time-honored Mexican combination of stewed birds (usually chickens) and tomatillos makes for a hearty and exciting meal that is perfect for Dutch oven campfire cooking. In my previous book, *The MeatEater Fish and Game Cookbook,* I shared a slow cooker turkey posole with hominy grits that is similar to this dish. But this version is more of a thicker, stewier, stick-to-your-ribs recipe that you'll truly appreciate on a cold night. Be sure to consider the age of your turkey; an old tom will likely need a bit more time on the fire than a young jake (adolescent male). We give the legs a head start by par-braising them before adding them to the dish. If you're a frugal butcher, throw the wings in as well.

TO BRAISE THE TURKEY. Pat the turkey legs dry. Add 1 tablespoon of the oil in the bottom of a large stock pot. Season the turkey legs with salt and pepper and cook until browned, turning every 3 to 4 minutes. Remove to a plate. In the stockpot, combine the beer, stock, green chiles, oregano, cumin, and 1 tablespoon salt over high heat and bring to a simmer. Carefully lower the turkey legs into the liquid (the liquid should almost cover the legs; if not, add more stock or water). Cover the pot and maintain a gentle simmer over low to medium-low heat for 2 to 4 hours. Check for the tenderness and add more broth and water as needed to keep the liquid level barely covering the meat. Once the legs are close to tender, add the breast pieces and remove the lid. Keep the pot over the lowest heat possible to maintain a low simmer and continue to cook until the leg meat pulls apart easily with a fork.

Remove the breast meat and turkey legs from the liquid and let cool until you can comfortably shred the meat with your hands. Discard the bones. Strain the cooking liquid (about 4 cups) through a fine-mesh strainer. Transfer the cooking liquid and the shredded turkey to two separate airtight containers and refrigerate for up to 1 week or freeze until ready to use.

PREPARE A CAMPFIRE. In a campfire stone circle, build a fire and set up a grate for high direct heat. When hot, heat a cast-iron griddle on the grate for at least 10 minutes. Lightly brush with oil. Place the tomatillos, onions, jalapeños, garlic, and poblanos on the griddle and cook, turning frequently, until charred all over. Remove to a bowl and let cool until you can easily handle them. Remove the seeds from the poblanos and jalapeños and the skins from the garlic.

If you have access to electricity, add the charred vegetables to a large blender in two batches and puree. If not, use a manual food mill to puree

Recipe continues

---

2 skinned turkey legs

1 tablespoon vegetable oil, plus more for grilling

Kosher salt and freshly ground black pepper

2 (12-ounce) bottles lager beer

4 cups homemade game stock or store-bought chicken stock

2 (4.5-ounce) cans chopped green chiles

1 tablespoon dried Mexican oregano

1 tablespoon ground cumin

1½ pounds skinless, boneless wild turkey breast, cut into 4 or 5 pieces

1½ pounds tomatillos, husked and rinsed

1 large white onion, quartered

1 or 2 jalapeño peppers or serrano chiles, halved

6 garlic cloves, unpeeled

3 poblano chiles

1 small bunch fresh cilantro

OPTIONAL GARNISHES

Thinly sliced radishes

Sliced jalapeños or serranos

Sour cream or crema

Cotija cheese

Fresh cilantro leaves

SPECIAL EQUIPMENT

Tripod with chain and hook

10-inch-diameter deep Dutch oven with bailing handle (about 5 quarts). (A bailing handle is a handle designed to keep the pot from slipping on the hook. Without it, be careful to keep the pot balanced when stirring.)

Manual food mill (if camping without electricity) or blender

MAKE AHEAD. *Braise the turkey legs and shred the meat in advance for camping trips. The step of charring and pureeing the tomatillo-poblano mixture can also be done in advance, then vac-seal the puree or store it refrigerated in an airtight container for 2 weeks or in the freezer until ready to use. You can also make the entire meal ahead of time, vac-seal, and reheat it in a pot of water at camp.*

ALSO WORKS WITH. *Thighs and drumsticks from goose, duck, and various upland birds. Also shoulders or shanks from deer, elk, and wild hog.*

or chop them finely with a knife. (Make sure someone is watching your fire if you step away.)

FOR TRIPOD COOKING. Set a tripod over the campfire circle. Lower the chain so that the pot hovers 6 to 12 inches above the flames or hot coals. Suspend the Dutch oven and let sit for a few minutes to make sure the heat is penetrating the pot (add a splash of water into the pot; if it sizzles and evaporates, it's hot). Lower the pot closer to the fire or build the fire up, if necessary.

Add the puree to the pot and stir in 2 teaspoons salt. Cover and bring to a simmer, stirring occasionally, and cook until the puree thickens a bit and turns a duller green color, about 5 minutes. Add the shredded turkey and 2 cups of the reserved cooking liquid and simmer for about 20 minutes until it comes to a boil and is bubbly and hot. Stir to avoid scorching on the bottom. Add more cooking liquid as needed to reach the desired consistency.

Ladle the chili into bowls. Garnish with toppings as desired.

LATVIAN SOĻANKA SOUP

Janis Putelis

I was awestruck by the gigantic black, straight-out-of-Harry-Potter witches' cauldron that was emanating lovely smells to our hungry group of hunters. The cauldron was being heated by a wood fire, and inside was a very simple dish called soļanka (pronounced sol-YAN-kah), which is not thick enough to be called stew, but too thick and hearty to be considered soup. It was a cool, rainy October afternoon on my first day of a driven hunt in Latvia, one of the three Baltic countries in eastern Europe. Latvia borders Russia to the east and sits across the Baltic Sea from the southern tip of Sweden. My family all came from Latvia, and I grew up speaking the language, but this was my first time visiting. Our group of forty had already finished two drives, harvesting two moose and one red deer. The hunters, and especially the drivers who walk all day to push the game to the hunters, were famished.

All of us were gathered around the warm pot of soļanka, and while bowls were being passed around, I asked the cook for a recipe. In less than two minutes, she explained how to make it, though she didn't offer any strict guidelines on how much of any one ingredient to use. It's one of those preparations that's made based on intuition, experience, and how many people you'll be feeding.

Here's what she told me: Brown bite-sized venison chunks in a pan and add them to a big pot of boiling water. When the meat is tender after an hour or two, add chopped and browned smoked sausages, chopped carrots, chopped onions (one onion for every pound of meat), and one cup of ketchup for every gallon of water. Next, add chopped potatoes. When the potatoes are soft, toss in a couple handfuls of chopped pickles and season with salt, pepper, a bay leaf, and any general-purpose seasoning you like. Garnish the soup with olives, lemons, and sour cream and serve with a slice of buttered bread.

This soup has the familiar tastes of a traditional hearty "American" game stew, but the sour cream and pickled garnishes are a regional touch that make it a uniquely Latvian dish.

After a decade of guiding fly fishermen and elk hunters in Colorado and Arizona, Janis Putelis started with MeatEater as a wilderness production assistant. He went on to become the director and producer of the MeatEater television show and The MeatEater Podcast. *Today Janis hosts his own show,* MeatEater Hunts, *along with the Gear Talk podcast.*

LAYERED FISH CHOWDER

MAKES 4 TO 5 CUPS; SERVES 4 TO 6

¼ pound thick-cut bacon, cut crosswise into ¼-inch strips

1 large yellow onion, chopped

3 small, bushy fresh thyme sprigs

2 bay leaves

2 russet potatoes (about 1¼ pounds), peeled and sliced ⅛ to ¼ inch thick

Kosher salt

Freshly ground black pepper

1½ pounds thin, flaky white fish, such as flounder

1¾ cups oyster crackers

2 tablespoons unsalted butter

4 cups fish stock or bottled clam juice, plus more as needed

¼ cup heavy cream

½ bunch fresh flat-leaf parsley, chopped, for garnish (optional)

SPECIAL EQUIPMENT

10-inch-diameter (5-quart) deep Dutch oven

Leather grilling gloves

This is my take on one of the oldest chowder recipes ever printed in the United States—going back to 1751 in the *Boston Evening Post*. The technique of layering ingredients (almost like a gratin) was popular back then, and we're using it here. It's a unique way to pull the comforting flavors of a New England–style chowder into a casserole-like dish.

It's best to cook this over a bed of coals rather than flames; since there is so little liquid, you don't want to risk scorching it with intense heat. But it still works hanging from a tripod.

FOR THE FIRE. Set up a tripod over a fire pit or campfire. When there is a bed of glowing coals, suspend a cast-iron Dutch oven 3 to 6 inches over the coals. Maintain the coals and fire for the duration of the cooking process.

FOR THE CHOWDER. Cook the bacon in the pot until it begins to crisp and brown, 10 to 12 minutes. Add the onions, thyme, and bay leaves and cook about 10 minutes, or until the onions soften and the bacon gets crispier. Remove the pot from the fire. Scoop half of the onion-bacon mixture into a bowl.

TO LAYER. Arrange the onion-bacon mixture in an even layer (see illustration) in the bottom of the pot. Lay half of the potato slices over the onions and sprinkle with ½ teaspoon salt and a few grinds of pepper. Lay half of the fish over the potatoes and sprinkle with ¼ teaspoon salt and a few grinds of pepper. Scatter half of the oyster crackers over the fish. Scatter half of the onions over top. Lay the remaining potatoes and ½ teaspoon salt on top and a few grinds of pepper. Lay the remaining fish and ¼ teaspoon salt and a few grinds of pepper on top. Scatter the remaining oyster crackers and then the remaining onions on top. Dot with the butter. Pour in enough stock to just cover everything, roughly 2 to 3 cups. (If you need more than 4 cups of stock to cover, add water.) Do not stir.

Cover the pot, return it to the fire, and suspend it 3 to 6 inches over the glowing coals—adding more as needed—and simmer until the potatoes are tender and the fish is cooked through, about 30 minutes. (Check periodically and raise the pot as needed to avoid burning.) Remove the pot from the fire. Pour in the cream and gently push it into the chowder with a spoon or ladle. Cover the pot and let it stand for 5 to 10 minutes to warm and distribute the cream. Discard the thyme sprigs and bay leaves and garnish with parsley (if using).

06 ON THE SIDE

SALADS, SIDES, DESSERTS, AND DRINKS

Our current home has a covered deck with a fireplace at the east end. We like to sit out there on summer evenings, especially when friends are over. A few summers ago, we decided to buy a couple of outdoor couches that could sit next to the fireplace. My wife and I argued about what color to get. I thought that brown made sense. It would hide a lot of the grime that is inevitable to outdoor furniture, I figured. My wife felt that white "would be easier to clean," whatever that means. She happened to win that particular debate, and so we went with white. Since then, the kids and the dog have managed to get ridiculous amounts of soot and mud and goo on those couches. While I still don't know about "easier to clean," I'd definitely agree with the statement that they need to be cleaned way more frequently.

It's so bad that it's funny, literally. For a while I had on my phone a video that was taken while various kids from around the neighborhood were all roasting marshmallows in the fireplace. I can't even remember what was actually being filmed in the video, because one's attention focused strictly on what was happening in the background. You could see our youngest boy, Matthew, trying to figure out what to do with the gobs of melted marshmallow that were hanging off his fingertips. You see him consider the couch's fabric as a familiar napkin. He even extends his hands in that direction. But then he catches himself and pauses, perhaps contemplating the dire warnings that he's received from his mother and father about not trashing the furniture so badly. He then pauses in a moment of indecision before committing himself wholeheartedly to wiping his hands down the front of his T-shirt. Satisfied with the results, he runs off.

I watched that video a dozen times and laughed. My kids even laughed at it. It captured, beautifully, the fun and mess of outdoor cooking as well as the beauty and sticky sweetness of summer. For reasons that are hard to explain, this chapter makes me think of that video. The recipes here aren't all summertime preparations, and they're admittedly light on marshmallows, but you will find here the lighter and funner (and yes, sweeter) side of outdoor cooking. It's a trove of drinks (boozy and otherwise), desserts, salads, sides, and breads. It's the stuff that rounds out and completes any great outdoor meal, though much of it would be just as at home indoors as outdoors. I'm sure you'll enjoy it all. Just try to keep it off the furniture, okay?

HOW TO MAKE A KILLER SALAD

Every summer, I grow some combination of lettuce, kale, herbs, radishes, onions, peas, and tomatoes in my garden. Just as fish taste better when you catch them yourself, veggies taste better when you grow them. I like to build salads with the stuff from my garden; it's all the better when you can eat them outside with friends and family.

Making a killer salad isn't complex. In fact, the beauty of a salad lies in its simplicity. There's no need to overwork it. If you go by this tried-and-true method, you'll make a killer salad every time without a lot of fuss.

There are three elements every salad needs: greens, some zip, and a dressing. Here's what I mean.

1. Base of Greens

I'm a fan of combining varieties of lettuces. It makes for a visually appealing salad, and you'll add texture and interest without too much effort.

Try combining soft lettuces like Bibb with a few leaves of crunchy romaine, or green or red leaf lettuces with oak leaf or iceberg. Any combination will work.

- Crunchy: romaine, iceberg, red and green leaf

- Soft: Little Gem, Bibb, oak leaf

- Baby/mixed: mesclun, baby mizuna, spinach

2. Add Some Zip

Add punch to your salad with color, texture, and/or flavor. Fresh herbs, bitter greens, and onions (added sparingly) give zip and spice to any salad. This element doesn't always have to be a plant—a handful of nuts or pickled things, even crushed corn chips, can be a game-changer. Keep it simple, though. One or two items from the below list is all you need.

- Herbs and leaves: mint, dill, parsley, basil, or celery leaves

- Chicories: radicchio, endive, or frisée

- Bitter greens and vegetables: arugula, watercress, purslane, radishes, or young mustard greens

- Alliums: chives, scallions, red onions, or yellow onions

- Crunchy: nuts, pickles, or even corn chips

- Leftover anything: cooked beans, grilled vegetables, roasted peppers, or potatoes

3. The Dressing

Choose something that lets the naturally bright flavors of the lettuces and herbs shine through. My go-to dressing is simple—olive oil and red wine vinegar (usually sherry wine vinegar) or olive oil and lemon juice—but I've also included in the pages that follow some of my favorite ways to dress things up. It goes without saying that a store-bought salad dressing is equally acceptable.

4. Add a Star Ingredient

If you've done steps 1 through 3 above, you've already got a fantastic salad. But if you have a star tomato, cucumber, avocado, some foraged mushrooms, or a wedge of noteworthy cheese, slice it up and add it in.

THE DRESSINGS

OLIVE OIL AND VINEGAR

MAKES ABOUT ¼ CUP

Quality counts here, so don't skimp on the oil. You can do a 3:1 or 2:1 ratio of oil to acid, depending on your preference for acidity. If you're doing this like Krista's Italian mother, you'd mix the components of the dressing directly into the salad with your hands. You'd start with the olive oil, mixing it gently together with your greens to coat, then add salt, mix gently again, and finally add your vinegar and toss with serving spoons. She prefers a salad on the zippier side, so use a 2:1 ratio for full authenticity.

3 tablespoons extra-virgin olive oil

½ teaspoon kosher salt

1½ tablespoons sherry wine vinegar, lemon juice, or a combination of red wine vinegar and balsamic vinegar

BASIC VINAIGRETTE

MAKES ABOUT ¼ CUP

This basic vinaigrette is a standard for any salad. Bump it up with herbs or swap out the vinegar for a different kind. It's one to commit to memory.

Whisk the red wine vinegar (use 1 tablespoon vinegar for a standard vinaigrette, 2 tablespoons if you like yours a little more acidic), salt, pepper, and Dijon in a small bowl. Slowly drizzle in the extra-virgin olive oil to emulsify. Taste and adjust seasonings.

1 to 2 tablespoons red wine vinegar

½ teaspoon kosher salt

½ teaspoon freshly ground black pepper

½ teaspoon Dijon mustard

3 tablespoons extra-virgin olive oil

SOY VINAIGRETTE

MAKES ¾ CUP

Whisk together the vinegar, lime juice, wasabi, shallots, sugar, salt, and soy sauce. Add the sesame oil and 1 tablespoon water, then slowly whisk in the canola oil.

1 tablespoon rice vinegar

1 tablespoon freshly squeezed lime juice

2 teaspoons prepared wasabi

1 small shallot, finely chopped (about 1 tablespoon)

½ teaspoon sugar

¼ teaspoon kosher salt

2 tablespoons soy sauce

1 tablespoon toasted sesame oil

½ cup canola oil or other neutral oil

CARROT-MISO DRESSING

MAKES 1¼ CUPS

2 carrots, coarsely chopped

1 (2½-inch) piece fresh ginger, peeled and coarsely chopped (1½ tablespoons)

5 tablespoons rice vinegar

2 tablespoons canola oil or other neutral oil

2 tablespoons white miso paste

1 teaspoon toasted sesame oil

1 teaspoon granulated sugar

This dressing pairs with the salad in the Tuna and/or Yellowtail Skewers recipe on page 273, but you can put it on just about any vegetable and it will be consumed with lightning speed.

In a food processor or blender (for a smoother texture, choose the blender), combine the carrots and ginger and pulse until finely ground. Add the vinegar, miso, sesame oil, and granulated sugar, and process until smooth. Cover and refrigerate until ready to use; the dressing will keep for up to 1 week in the refrigerator.

FRESH RANCH DRESSING

MAKES ABOUT 2¼ CUPS

¾ cup mayonnaise

½ cup sour cream

1 tablespoon distilled white vinegar

1 teaspoon Worcestershire sauce

4 dashes hot sauce

1 tablespoon garlic powder

2 teaspoons onion powder

1 teaspoon kosher salt

½ teaspoon freshly ground black pepper

2 tablespoons finely chopped fresh parsley

1 tablespoon finely chopped fresh dill

1 tablespoon finely chopped fresh chives

½ cup buttermilk, plus more as needed

Stir together all of the ingredients except the buttermilk. Add enough buttermilk to thin the dressing so that it's pourable. Cover and refrigerate.

TWO MORE DRESSINGS

Kelp Goddess Dressing (page 60)

Marjoram-Mint Dressing (page 308)

COLESLAW

SERVES 8

There are endless variations on coleslaw. It's good to have at least a couple favorites in your repertoire, because slaw is a quick and easy side dish for outdoor gatherings. Feel free to personalize this recipe. You can give it extra zip with the addition of jalapeños or serranos or by dousing it with sriracha at the end. If you like more color, julienne one or two bell peppers or use a mix of purple and green cabbages.

Combine the cabbage, scallions, carrots, and jalapeños (if using) in a bowl. In another bowl, mix the dressing ingredients until smooth. Dress the cabbage mixture and toss completely to combine; season to taste. Refrigerate for at least an hour before serving to cut down on the cabbage's crunch (see Cook's Note). Store, covered, in the refrigerator or cooler until ready to serve.

1 medium head green cabbage, shredded

8 scallions, white and green parts, sliced on a bias

2 carrots, grated

2 julienned jalapeño peppers or serrano chiles (optional)

DRESSING

1 cup mayo

½ cup apple cider vinegar

2 tablespoons Dijon mustard

2 tablespoons granulated garlic

1 tablespoon kosher salt, plus more as needed

2 teaspoons onion powder

2 teaspoons freshly ground black pepper

COOK'S NOTE. *To speed up the wilting process, don't add the salt to the dressing—instead, add the salt to the vegetables and massage it into the leaves. Let sit for 10 minutes, then add the dressing (and more salt to taste, if needed).*

MAKE AHEAD. *If prepping for a long camping trip, the dressing and vegetables can be prepped and stored separately until ready to use to avoid getting watery.*

BOSTON BAKED BEANS

MAKES 6 TO 7 CUPS COOKED BEANS (MORE INCLUDING LIQUID); SERVES 6 TO 8

This is a New England–style baked bean preparation, rich with animal fat and sweetened with molasses. (If you're looking for cowboy-style beans that taste more like a chili, this ain't that.) It's possible that the technique of sweetening baked beans was shown to colonists in the Northeast by Native Americans, who used maple syrup instead of molasses as their sweetener. The molasses came later, as it was a surplus by-product of sugar production from southern sugarcane plantations.

Precooking your beans saves time when you're trying to feed a group of hungry campers, so this recipe calls for cooking your beans ahead of time in an Instant Pot. But you can cook them however you please (see our stovetop method on page 306) or even use canned beans in a pinch. Keep in mind, though, that home-cooked beans really raise the level of flavor and texture, so for this dish I'd urge you to take the extra step.

PRECOOK THE BEANS. Put the beans into a large saucepot and cover with water by 2 inches. Turn the heat to high and bring to a boil. Once at a boil, remove from the heat, cover the pot, and let stand for 1 hour. Drain and rinse the beans.

Put the beans in a 6-quart Instant Pot and add fresh water to cover by 2 inches (about 8 cups water). Add the quartered onion, carrot, celery, bay leaves, thyme, and salt. Secure the lid and set at manual high pressure for 4 minutes. When the cooking time is up, let the pressure naturally release for 10 minutes, then manually release the remaining pressure. You should have 6 cups cooked beans and 5 cups cooking liquid.

Discard the aromatics and let the beans cool. Then store the beans in their cooking liquid in the refrigerator until ready to use.

FOR FINISHING. Prepare a charcoal chimney with briquettes (or a hardwood campfire) in a fire pit or stone-lined fire circle. Use the chart on page 152 as a guide for the number of coals needed for your size pot to reach 350°F. (For a 10-inch Lodge pot, place roughly 21 coals in the chimney.)

Strain the beans from their cooking liquid (reserve the liquid) and put them into the Dutch oven. Add the salt pork and chopped onions to the pot. In a small bowl, whisk together the molasses, mustard, and ½ cup of the cooking liquid, and then stir this into the beans. Pour enough of the remaining cooking liquid to just barely cover the beans (roughly 1 cup) and stir together to combine. Put on the lid.

Recipe continues

1 pound dried navy beans, rinsed

1 medium onion, quartered, plus 1 large onion, chopped (about 1¾ cups)

1 medium carrot, cut into large pieces

1 celery rib, cut into large pieces

3 bay leaves

3 fresh thyme and/or rosemary sprigs

1 tablespoon kosher salt, plus more as needed

⅓ pound salt pork or fatback, rind removed, cut into ¼-inch dice (see Cook's Notes)

½ cup molasses (not blackstrap; see Cook's Notes)

2 tablespoons spicy brown mustard

Freshly ground black pepper

SPECIAL EQUIPMENT

10- or 12-inch-diameter (5- or 8-quart) deep Dutch oven with a lid for coal cooking

COOK'S NOTES. *If your salt pork is super fatty without much meat, use ⅓ pound, as above. If it's meatier, feel free to up it to ½ pound. You can also use a slab bacon from any animal, which will add a smokier flavor.*

We recommend regular molasses here, not blackstrap, because we're using it for sweetening. Blackstrap molasses is excellent for many applications; it's high in iron and calcium but contains very little sucrose and thus has a bitter flavor and won't sweeten the beans without added brown sugar or another sweetener.

Once the coals are ready and hot, arrange 7 coals in the campfire pit, put the Dutch oven on top, and arrange the remaining coals on the lid. (Or break up coals from a spent log and gather the equivalent coals. Keep the wood fire going as you'll need more coals later). After 30 minutes, light a new chimney with 21 briquettes. Let the beans cook at a low simmer, adding new coals as needed, for 45 minutes to 1 hour. Move the pot, remove the lid, and lay down a fresh hot set of coals from the chimney or fire coals. Place the Dutch oven on top and cook the beans uncovered for 1 to 1½ hours, until a thick, stewy liquid has developed. Remove from the heat, taste the beans, and season with salt and pepper as needed. Serve warm.

COOKING DRIED BEANS ON THE STOVE

If you don't have an Instant Pot on hand, here's our preferred method for cooking dried beans on the stovetop. We're using Italian ingredients for flavoring, but you can add alternate aromatics—jalapeños and tomatoes for Mexican-style beans or smoked bacon for a rustic kick. Double or triple as desired.

Step 1: Choose your soaking method

Overnight soak: Add 1 pound of beans to a large bowl, cover with water by 2 inches, and lightly cover with plastic wrap. Let soak overnight on the countertop in a cool place. (Note: If it's very hot where you are, soak for only 4 to 6 hours, or use the quick soak method below so the beans don't sprout overnight.) Drain and rinse the beans, picking out any stones or odd-shaped beans.

Quick soak method: Put 1 pound of beans into a large saucepot and cover with water by 2 inches. Turn the heat to high and bring to a boil. Once at a boil, remove from the heat, cover the pot, and let stand for 1 hour. Drain and rinse the soaked beans, picking out any stones or odd-shaped beans.

Step 2: Cook

Put the beans in a 12-inch-diameter (8-quart) deep Dutch oven and cover the beans with fresh water by 2 inches (about 8 cups water). Add a halved head of unpeeled garlic and 1 halved, peeled white onion. Bring the beans to a boil, stirring occasionally and skimming off any scum that arises. Add 2 teaspoons kosher salt and more water, if needed, to keep the liquid level 2 inches above the beans. Cook the beans at a bare simmer for 45 minutes to 1½ hours more, checking for tenderness at 30 to 40 minutes. Check the beans more frequently at the end—every 10 minutes or so—they should be tender but not mushy. Once tender and just cooked, remove from the heat and add 1 cup olive oil to the pot and 2 fresh rosemary sprigs. Season the beans and cooking liquid to taste with additional salt and stir to combine. Let stand for 1 hour in the pot while they cool to finish cooking.

Step 3: Store

Ladle the cooled beans into vac-seal bags or resealable freezable containers, covering the beans with the liquid. If you're freezing the cooked beans, leave 1 inch of headroom to allow for expansion. Freeze the beans for up to 8 months. If you're refrigerating the beans, use within 1 week.

REFRIED BLACK BEANS

MAKES 1¾ CUPS

You can reheat a store-bought can of refried beans or make this extra-delicious version.

Put a small saucepan over low heat. Allow the pan to heat up for 3 minutes and then add the lard, onions, garlic, spices, and salt. Cook, stirring often, for 3 minutes, or until the onions and garlic soften. Stir in the beans, cover the pan, and lower the heat to maintain a simmer. Cook for another 5 minutes, then remove the lid and stir in the lime juice. Remove the pan from the heat and let the beans cool before using.

1 tablespoon lard

3 tablespoons finely chopped white onion

3 garlic cloves, finely chopped

½ teaspoon Mexican oregano

½ teaspoon ground cumin

¼ teaspoon kosher salt

1 (16-ounce) can refried black beans

Juice of ½ lime

CAMPSTOVE RICE

MAKES 6 CUPS; SERVES 4 TO 6

Wash the rice in a sieve until the water is slightly more clear and place it in a 3-quart pot with a lid. Add the cold water and cover. Bring to a boil and then reduce the heat to a low simmer. Cook for 15 minutes, or until the water is absorbed. Leave it covered for another 5 minutes, then fluff with a fork and serve hot with your choice of dish.

2 cups basmati or long-grain rice

3 cups cold water

COOK'S NOTE. *Cooking fluffy, dry rice comes down to a ratio. If you don't have an actual measuring cup, simply use the same vessel (like a thermos cup or a ladle) to measure your rice and water. Use the ratio above—2 cups rice to 3 cups water, or about 1:1.5 rice to water. For a wetter rice, the ratio can go up to 1:2 rice to water. Another method that works well is to eyeball it: Fill your pot with enough water to come up to your first knuckle when the tip of your finger is touching the rice.*

GRILLED EGGPLANT, CHICKPEAS, AND MARJORAM-MINT DRESSING

SERVES 2

MARJORAM-MINT DRESSING

Makes ⅓ cup

1 tablespoon sherry vinegar

2 teaspoons Dijon mustard

½ teaspoon kosher salt

⅛ teaspoon freshly ground black pepper

1 garlic clove, grated

¼ cup extra-virgin olive oil

1½ teaspoons chopped fresh mint

1 teaspoon chopped fresh marjoram leaves

CHICKPEAS AND VEG

1 (15-ounce) can chickpeas, drained

1 tablespoon extra-virgin olive oil

1 teaspoon kosher salt

⅛ teaspoon ground black pepper

2 ripe but still firm Campari tomatoes, cored and quartered

2 large fresh marjoram sprigs

1 small red onion, cut into 6 wedges, core attached

EGGPLANT

1 (1¼-pound) medium eggplant with stem attached, halved lengthwise

2 tablespoons extra-virgin olive oil

1 teaspoon kosher salt

⅛ teaspoon freshly ground black pepper

Neutral oil, for the grill

Here's a good one for when the vegetarians come to dinner. It's hearty enough to serve as a main dish, or it can be a substantial side dish. It's especially good for folks who raise eggplants in their gardens and then struggle to find interesting ways to use them.

Prepare a medium-hot grill, allowing three-quarters of the grill for direct grilling and the remaining quarter for indirect grilling.

FOR THE DRESSING. In a large bowl, combine the vinegar, mustard, salt, pepper, and garlic. Whisk in the oil until combined. Stir in the mint and marjoram and adjust the seasonings. Set aside.

FOR THE CHICKPEAS. In a 10-inch cast-iron skillet, combine the chickpeas, oil, salt, pepper, tomatoes, marjoram, and onions. Place the pan on the grill and cook, stirring occasionally, until the chickpeas are browned, about 5 minutes. Remove from the heat. Discard the marjoram. Add the chickpea mixture to the bowl of dressing and toss to coat well. Set aside.

FOR THE EGGPLANT. While the chickpeas are cooking, deeply score the flesh of the eggplant halves in a crosshatch pattern without cutting through the skin. Brush the eggplant flesh with the olive oil, allowing the oil to be fully absorbed. Sprinkle with salt and pepper.

Place the eggplant halves, flesh-side down, on well-oiled grill grates and grill until lightly browned, 2½ to 3 minutes. Flip the eggplant flesh-side up and continue to grill, moving it to the cooler side of the grill if the skin starts to scorch, about 8 minutes. You'll need to move the eggplant around as the stem ends and blossom ends take longer to cook. Squeeze gently with tongs to see if it's soft enough. Transfer the eggplants to two plates, top with the chickpea mixture, and serve.

COOK'S NOTE. *Marjoram is widely available. If you can't find fresh marjoram, young oregano or thyme can be substituted for a different yet still aromatic flavor.*

ALSO WORKS WITH. *Zucchini or summer squash, portobello mushrooms. This is meant to be a vegetarian dish, but the eggplant can be swapped with big game steak or hearts, meaty fish like tuna or halibut, or small spatchcocked game birds like doves or quail.*

LENTIL STEW

MAKES 10 CUPS (2½ QUARTS)

Dried lentil soups are quick and easy to pull together on a campstove, over a campfire, or to make ahead and then vacuum-seal for later use. If making a soup, add some smoked ham or smoked upland bird wings to bump the flavor and meatiness. Or lower the liquid ratio and use the lentils as a side. They can form a bed for fried or poached eggs. They can be stirred in with white rice. Or they can be chilled and added to salads for a protein boost.

In a bowl, rinse and drain the lentils two or three times, picking through them to remove any stones or discolored pieces.

In a 4- to 6-quart pot, heat the oil over medium heat until it shimmers. Add the diced onion and cook until translucent, about 6 minutes. Add the carrots, celery, and salt and cook until the vegetables are tender, 8 to 10 minutes. Stir in the drained lentils and garlic and cook for 60 seconds. Add the water or stock so that the liquid sits at least ½ inch above the surface of the lentils. Bring to a boil over high heat. Skim off any scum that rises to the surface. Add the thyme, bay leaves, and pepper to taste. Lower the heat and simmer, uncovered and stirring occasionally, for about 40 minutes, until the lentils are tender; if the liquid level lowers below the lentils before they are tender, add more water. (See Cook's Note on adjusting liquid levels.) Once tender, taste and adjust the seasonings with salt and lemon juice.

Ladle the lentils into bowls and serve hot with crusty bread.

1 (1-pound) bag brown lentils or green French lentils

3 tablespoons extra-virgin olive oil

1 medium onion, diced small

2 medium carrots, sliced into thin quarter rounds

3 celery ribs, diced small

2 teaspoons kosher salt

3 garlic cloves, smashed and peeled

2 quarts water or light game stock, or a combination, plus more as needed

3 fresh thyme sprigs

3 bay leaves

Freshly ground black pepper

Juice of ½ lemon

Crusty bread, for serving

COOK'S NOTE. *If you're making a soup, add stock or water (or a mix) to keep the liquid level at your preferred consistency. If you're making lentils as a side, they can be on the drier side: Cook with just enough liquid to keep them submerged and cook the lentils through. Try not to add too much toward the end after they have rehydrated. Use a slotted spoon to remove cooked lentils to a serving dish.*

KAINTUCKIE BUTTERMILK CORNBREAD

SERVES 8 TO 10

8 handfuls yellow self-rising cornmeal mix (3 cups)

2 big pinches kosher salt (¾ teaspoon)

½ handful sugar, plus sugar to taste after the batter is made! (2 tablespoons measurement)

3 large eggs

2 big gobs of butter, melted (2 tablespoons)

4 to 6 big splashes of warm buttermilk (1¼ cups)

Lard, for cooking

SPECIAL EQUIPMENT

12-inch cast-iron skillet

This recipe comes to us via Kevin Murphy, the World's Greatest Small Game Hunter, straight from Kentucky—or Kaintuckie as he reverently calls it. This is a quick-style cornbread that uses a cornbread mix with the baking powder and baking soda included in the base. If it's good enough for Kevin Murphy, it's good enough for you. It makes an ideal accompaniment to his BBQ-Style Squirrel recipe on page 127.

Kevin likes to use a natural "yellow" variety of corn-bread mix best, so look for that kind.

Preheat the oven to 425°F. When at temperature, place a 12-inch (man-track-sized) skillet in the oven to heat up.

In a large bowl, combine all the dry ingredients. Then, while stirring with a wooden spoon, add all the wet ingredients. The mix should be like a thick-flowing batter! Add more wet (buttermilk) or dry (cornbread mix or all-purpose flour) if it's not!

Remove the skillet from the oven and add a gob of lard to melt. It should sizzle when you drop a bit of batter in it! Pour the batter into the skillet.

Bake for about 20 minutes, until the crust is crispy. A note from Kevin: "Stick a 'coon baculum in the center to check for doneness—it's just right to eat when it pulls out shiny. You can use a wooden skewer or a toothpick if you don't have a raccoon's pecker bone layin' around."

SAVORY CHEESE BISCUITS

MAKES 8 BISCUITS

These are basic biscuits that can be made in a Dutch oven or even a skillet with a tight-fitting lid that's been placed over coals or inside an oven. They freeze well when raw, so they're also a good make-ahead staple to keep on hand for when you need them. These are flavored with black pepper and Parmigiano-Reggiano cheese, but you can tailor them to your own liking by adding herbs and/or cheddar cheese.

Preheat your grill or oven to 425°F. If cooking over live coals, prepare a campfire or a charcoal chimney for coal cooking in a fire pit or stone-lined fire circle. Lightly grease a cast-iron skillet with a lid or shallow 10-inch-diameter (4-quart) Dutch oven with a lid and set aside.

In a large bowl, whisk together the flour, baking powder, salt, and pepper. Add the cheese and toss gently with your fingers. Cut in the chilled butter with two butter knives. When the butter is pea-sized and somewhat incorporated, form a well in the shaggy dough and pour the milk into the center. Pull the sides of the well in and knead together lightly until the mixture forms a solid mass.

Sprinkle some flour onto a cutting board. Pat the dough into a ½-inch-thick rectangle. Fold the dough into thirds, like a letter. Pat the dough out again into a rectangle about 1 inch high. Lightly flour the top; cut biscuits with a 2¾-inch round cutter (or a glass of similar diameter), pressing the scraps together and patting them down to 1 inch, to get 8 biscuits. Place the biscuits in the greased skillet or Dutch oven. Brush the tops with milk.

In the grill or preheated oven, bake the biscuits until lightly browned on the top and bottom, about 14 minutes. In a campfire, using the chart on page 152 as a guide for heat, add coals under and on top of the lid of the Dutch oven or covered skillet, whichever you're using, to create an oven that is approximately 425°F. The biscuits are done when the bottoms are browned and the tops are lightly browned, anywhere from 14 to 18 minutes; this can vary with campfire cooking. Serve warm, with butter.

2 cups all-purpose flour, plus more for dusting

1 tablespoon baking powder

1 teaspoon fine salt

1 teaspoon freshly ground black pepper

2 tablespoons grated Parmigiano-Reggiano

8 tablespoons (1 stick) unsalted butter, chilled and cubed, plus more for greasing the pan and serving

¾ cup milk, plus more for brushing

PITA

MAKES 4 PITAS

---

1 teaspoon active dry yeast

⅛ teaspoon sugar

½ cup lukewarm water

1½ cups all-purpose flour, plus more as needed

½ teaspoon kosher salt

4 teaspoons olive oil, plus more for coating and cooking

MAKE AHEAD. *You can make dough and let it rise in the fridge overnight in a storage container, then bring it to the campsite already risen. Cook as directed above.*

This pita recipe is an accompaniment for the Venison Kofta Kebabs on page 276. If you're curious about making your own flatbread, this is a great place to start.

In a small bowl, combine the yeast, sugar, and warm water. Let stand until foamy, about 5 minutes.

In a large bowl whisk the flour and salt together. Pour in the oil, then stir in the yeast mixture with your fingers until a shaggy dough forms. Knead the dough in the bowl, grabbing up the stray bits as the dough forms a ball, until the dough is smooth and a finger indent slightly pushes back, about 8 minutes. If the dough is too sticky, add more flour, a little at a time, until it no longer sticks to your hands. Drizzle the dough with a little oil and turn to coat. Cover with plastic wrap and let rest for about 30 minutes to give the yeast a chance to start working. Transfer to a storage container or large plastic bag and refrigerate overnight to rise and double in size.

To cook, heat a cast-iron skillet on the grill grate over a medium-high fire for 5 to 10 minutes. Divide the dough into 4 even-sized balls. Lightly dust a work surface and roll the dough into roughly 7-inch rounds and cover with a kitchen towel. Once a flick of water on the skillet sizzles immediately, lightly oil the skillet and place a pita in it. Cook until you see bubbles forming, about 30 seconds. Flip and then cook until the pita puffs and the bottom has brown spots, 1 to 2 minutes. Wrap in a clean kitchen towel to keep the pita warm when it comes off the grill. Continue with the remaining dough.

SWEET TREATS

PEANUT BUTTER S'MORES

MAKES 8 S'MORES

S'mores have long reigned supreme as the number one dessert for outdoor meals. If you ever want to add a little depth to your s'mores, try slathering on some peanut butter. It's as simple as it sounds, so don't be insulted by the fact that we're actually gonna explain how to do it below. You never know, there could be someone out there who's never made a s'more and they've been too embarrassed to ask.

Break each of the 8 rectangular graham crackers horizontally into two squares. On half of the squares, spread 2 teaspoons peanut butter; reserve the other 8 squares as the lids for the s'mores. Divide the chocolate into 8 equal portions (about 4 squares of chocolate) and top each of the 8 peanut butter–covered squares with the chocolate.

Thread the marshmallows onto the sticks, one or two at a time, whichever you prefer. Over a campfire or hot coals, gently brown—or scorch and blister—your marshmallows. Again this is a personal preference. When done to your liking, lay the marshmallows on top of the chocolate and use the "lid" to help coax it off of the stick. Press the lid down to secure your s'more. Eat warm.

8 to 16 large marshmallows

8 whole rectangular graham crackers

2½ (1.5-ounce) bars milk chocolate

A heaping ⅓ cup peanut butter

SPECIAL EQUIPMENT

Green sticks with a whittled end for roasting marshmallows

NUTELLA AND BANANA IRON PIE

MAKES 1 SANDWICH

I love iron-pie makers and the sandwiches they produce. You can see some savory concoctions on page 170, but iron pies really shine when they're put to use for desserts. It's fun to have a few options when you're camping with a group. Peanut butter and jelly is a classic, and an iron pie full of cherry pie filling is spectacular. But nothing is as good as an iron pie made with Nutella and bananas.

TO ASSEMBLE. Separate your pie irons into two pieces, if attached. Wipe the inside of each pie iron with a wet cloth and dry well. Liberally coat the insides of the pie iron with the softened butter.

Press one piece of bread into each side of the pie irons (see illustration on page 169). Spread the Nutella onto one of the bread slices. Generously top the Nutella with overlapping slices of banana. On the remaining slice of bread, spread the peanut butter, if using. A fuller sandwich will make for a tighter press, allowing the bread to grill and become golden brown and delicious. Place the second piece of bread over the first, attach the two pieces of the pie iron, and lock them into place.

TO COOK. Prepare a hot campfire (or charcoal grill) for coal cooking. The campfire is ready when you have a sufficient bed of coals. With a coal rake, pull the coals out to the edge of the fire. Place the irons flat on the hot coals for an even transfer of heat (if using a charcoal grill, bank the briquettes to one side so that you can lay the pie irons in the grill on top of the coals). A good starting point is to cook for 2 to 4 minutes and then flip the iron and nestle it in the coals for another 2 minutes. Similar to cooking pancakes, you might burn or undercook the first one, but you'll know better how long to cook the second one. Pull the iron back from the fire, unlatch the handles, and carefully take a peek to see how browned it is (don't touch the actual irons as they're raging hot). If it needs more cooking time, close it up and throw it back on the fire. If it looks good, lay the iron on a log or board and remove the top half of the iron. Allow the sandwich to rest for a minute, then turn the iron holding the sandwich over and deposit it onto a plate. If it sticks, pry it out with a fork or metal spatula. The contents of the sandwich will be like molten lava, so warn any kiddos or unsuspecting adults to let the hot, oozing filling cool down some before eating. Eat whole as is or cut in half, if desired. Wipe out the pie iron if necessary, add a little softened butter, and start your next sandwich or pie.

1½ tablespoons softened butter

2 slices sandwich bread
(see Cook's Note)

1 to 2 heaping tablespoons Nutella

1 medium banana, cut into ⅓-inch slices
(use as much as you can fit)

1½ tablespoons peanut butter
(optional)

Pinch of kosher salt

COOK'S NOTE. *We like the consistency and ease of standard sliced bread, but to get fancy you can use sliced brioche bread or even biscuit dough in a tube. Half the fun of this dish is to play with variations and see which ones you and your family enjoy most.*

TWO MORE IRON PIES

We also like to mess around with various pie fillings. Keep in mind that these things are MOLTEN hot when they come out of the fire and really need to sit for a minute or two to cool off, especially if kids are involved.

Apple pie filling + slices of cheddar cheese: Use ½ to ¾ cup pie filling per iron pie and about 2 slices of cheese.

Cherry pie filling + cream cheese: Use about ¾ cup pie filling and 2 to 3 ounces of cream cheese per iron pie.

COAL-ROASTED BANANAS
WITH SWEET, DECADENT, OR BOOZY TOPPINGS

SERVES 4

4 bananas in their peels

DULCE DE LECHE OR CARAMEL

Makes 4 toppings

1 (4-ounce) can dulce de leche or a squeeze bottle of caramel, for drizzling

½ cup chopped salted pecans

Pinch of kosher salt or a flaky salt, such as Maldon sea salt

Splash of bourbon or whiskey (for adults if you've got it; optional)

SWEETENED CONDENSED MILK

Makes 4 toppings

1 (4-ounce) can sweetened condensed milk

1 fresh mango, seeded and diced (about 1 cup)

½ cup toasted coconut shavings (see Cook's Note)

Pinch of kosher salt or a flaky salt such as Maldon sea salt

Splash of dark rum (for adults if you've got it; optional)

COOK'S NOTE. *Here we're calling for the chunkier coconut shavings you can find in the grocery store. They come pre-toasted or you can toast your own. If you can't find them, shredded coconut or even roasted peanuts will work.*

I never knew about this preparation when I was a kid, but it seems like half the people that I hang out with have been making it their whole lives. In its most basic form, you split a banana down the center, jam it with M&M's or chocolate chips, and then wrap it in foil and chuck it onto the coals to get all roasted and gooey. This is a riff on that concept—with two versions of toppings that are a little more sophisticated but just as messy. There are also boozy variations for those who like bourbon, whiskey, or rum. Use our suggestions here, or come up with your own toppings.

PREPARE THE COALS. Make a campfire, a fire in a fire pit, or a chimney for a charcoal grill and burn until you have hot coals.

ROAST THE BANANAS. Place the bananas in their peels directly into the coals or just adjacent to them if the coals are crazy hot. (Bananas can also be wrapped in foil; both methods work.) Roast, turning a few times until the peels are charred, 6 to 12 minutes, depending on their proximity to the coals. Remove the bananas from the heat carefully with tongs and set them on a baking sheet or a rock to cool slightly.

Set each of the slightly cooled bananas onto plates. Using a knife, split the bananas lengthwise down the middle and spread the charred peels away from the interior roasted banana meat. Drizzle and spoon on your desired toppings. This is how we built ours: Spoon about 2 tablespoons of your gooey sauce of choice (either dulce de leche or sweetened condensed milk) onto the bananas and sprinkle with the crunchy toppings (either pecans or mango and coconut) and a sprinkling of salt. Splash with booze if you're into that (and of legal age).

Dive in with a spoon while it's warm.

COAL-BAKED FALL FRUIT
WITH GORGONZOLA AND WALNUTS

SERVES 4

This dessert featuring baked fruit is the antithesis of a marshmallow. It is on the savory side and has a much more sophisticated appeal. It makes a great finale to a meal around the fire, but it could just as readily start things off as an appetizer if you paired it with summer sausage or ham.

Prepare a fire to create coals. Once the coals are hot and glowing, quickly assemble the dish.

TO ASSEMBLE. In a cast-iron skillet, arrange the fruit, cut-side up. Distribute the cheese among the halved fruit and top all with chopped walnuts. Pour ½ cup water in the bottom of the skillet.

Cover the skillet with the lid or tightly with aluminum foil. Set the skillet among the coals and top the lid with coals; if you're using aluminum foil, don't top it with coals. Bake the fruit for 35 to 40 minutes, until soft when poked with a knife, checking after 20 minutes to be sure there is still some water in the bottom of the pan. Once the fruit is tender and the cheese has melted, allow it to rest for 10 minutes. Sprinkle with chopped chives and serve with crusty bread or breadsticks.

2 apples, halved lengthwise and cored with a spoon or knife

2 pears, halved lengthwise and cored with a spoon or knife

6 to 8 ounces crumbled Gorgonzola cheese, plus more as needed

¼ cup toasted and chopped walnuts, plus more as needed

½ bunch fresh chives, scallions, or wild garlic, chopped, for garnish

Crusty bread or breadsticks, for serving

SPECIAL EQUIPMENT

12- to 14-inch cast-iron skillet with lid (or heavy-duty foil) for cooking

MODULAR PANCAKE DRY MIX

MAKES 1 HEAPING CUP

1 cup all-purpose flour

2 tablespoons sugar

1 teaspoon baking powder

½ teaspoon baking soda

¼ teaspoon kosher salt

This dry mix was designed to be a flexible and versatile tool for making baked desserts and sweets when camping. Starting with a simple pancake mix (which we use for The Late Eugene Groters's Beer and Apple Pancakes on page 245), you can add cocoa, sugar, and an egg to make a chocolate cake (Steamed Moist Chocolate Cake, page 330) or you can use the batter to make a buckle, by loosening it up with milk and pouring it over assorted fruit (Peach and Raspberry Buckle, page 329).

We recommend making a few batches of this dry mix to keep in your RV or camping tote. Keep the instructions for these recipes handy—write them down or snap a photo. And break the recipes out to surprise your crew.

COOK'S NOTE. *We recommend using new baking powder and baking soda so there's no risk of keeping the dry mix past its expiration date.*

Whisk all the ingredients together thoroughly and place the mix into a resealable bag or an airtight container. Store at room temperature until ready to use.

PEACH AND RASPBERRY BUCKLE

MAKES ONE 10-INCH CAKE

This is a traditional buckle cake batter that is topped with fruit and a crumble topping. As the buckle cooks, the batter rises up around the fruit. The sugary almond crumble topping adds extra crunch and is a pleasing counterpoint to the gooey, tart flavors of the cooked fruit. You can substitute the type of fruit to suit the season.

Preheat the grill to 350°F or make a medium-hot reflector campfire (see page liv).

Grease the bottom and sides of the cast-iron skillet well with the extra butter.

FOR THE TOPPING. In a medium bowl, combine all the topping ingredients. Cut in the butter with your fingers or two knives until well distributed among the ingredients. You will still want to see some whole pieces of butter (larger than pea size). Set aside.

FOR THE BATTER. Whisk together the melted butter with the brown sugar until well combined. Add the egg and almond extract and whisk together thoroughly. Whisk in the pancake mix, then the milk, alternating dry and wet ingredients, beginning and ending with the dry, until the batter is smooth and well combined.

Pour the batter into the buttered cast-iron skillet. Top with the peaches and raspberries. Evenly layer the crumble topping over the fruit.

TO BAKE. Bake uncovered in the grill for 50 minutes (if using the reflector fire, cover with another cast-iron skillet or lid—you may want to top the lid with a few hot coals if conditions are cool or windy and the heat isn't steady; keep rotating the position so it cooks as evenly as possible.) Bake until it's slightly browned on top and a toothpick comes out clean when inserted into the center. Cool for at least 30 minutes or more before cutting into it or spooning it onto plates for serving.

TOPPING

4 tablespoons (½ stick) unsalted butter, diced

⅓ cup flour

½ cup granulated sugar

½ cup sliced almonds

¼ teaspoon kosher salt

BATTER

6 tablespoons (¾ stick) unsalted butter, melted or well softened, plus extra for greasing the pan

⅔ cup packed light brown sugar

1 large egg

1 teaspoon almond extract

1 recipe Modular Pancake Dry Mix (page 326), (1 heaping cup)

½ cup whole milk

2 medium peaches, peeled, pitted, and chopped into ½-inch cubes (about 2 cups)

1 cup raspberries

SPECIAL EQUIPMENT

10-inch cast-iron skillet

STEAMED MOIST CHOCOLATE CAKE

MAKES ONE 9-INCH-WIDE, 2-INCH-HIGH CAKE

¾ cup semisweet chocolate chips (about 4 ounces), melted and cooled slightly

6 tablespoons (¾ stick) unsalted butter, melted or well softened, plus extra for greasing the pan

¾ cup granulated sugar

1 large egg, at room temperature

1 teaspoon vanilla extract

½ cup unsweetened cocoa powder

1 recipe Modular Pancake Dry Mix (page 326)

1 cup whole milk

Confectioners' sugar, for dusting (optional)

SPECIAL EQUIPMENT

12-inch cast-iron skillet

9-inch cake pan

Large metal bowl or pot big enough (9¼- to 9½-inch diameter) to cover the cake pan snugly when inverted (see Cook's Note on finding a cover)

COOK'S NOTE. *Finding a cover for your skillet is key to this technique. I found a metal bowl with a diameter just larger than the edge of my 9-inch cake pan. It served as an ideal cover. If you aren't so lucky, you'll have to get creative; heavy-duty foil and a large bowl or an inverted pot could work. Use the foil to seal any gaps. You want a snug seal, but it doesn't have to be precise.*

This is an unusual but super-fun way to bake a cake outdoors. By steaming the cake, you get a very light and airy cake with a lavalike center. Cooking it seems almost like a magic trick, and the taste is just as good. You can bake this cake in an oven if you have access to one or would prefer the texture of a baked cake. Follow the mixing instructions and bake at 350 degrees for 40 minutes. This works well in a 10-inch cast-iron pan or a 9-inch cake pan.

Place the chocolate in a heatproof bowl and set it over a pot with an inch or two of boiling water. Do not let the water touch the bottom of the bowl. Stir once or twice to keep it from getting too hot. When the chocolate is about 75 percent melted, take it off the heat; the residual heat will melt the remaining chocolate.

TO PREP THE SKILLET. Pour 2 cups water in the bottom of a 12-inch cast-iron skillet. Place a round wire rack in the bottom of the skillet to raise the cake pan above the surface of the water; alternatively, find three flattish rocks to do the same. Grease the bottom and sides of the cake pan with the extra butter and set aside. Turn on the heat under the skillet and bring the water to a bare simmer while you make the batter.

FOR THE BATTER. In a bowl, whisk together the melted butter with the sugar until well combined. Add the egg and vanilla and mix well. In a separate container, whisk the cocoa powder and pancake mix together. Beginning and ending with dry ingredients, alternate adding the cocoa–pancake mix and the milk until smooth, then fold in the melted chocolate until well combined.

Pour the batter into the buttered cake pan. Place the pan on the rack (or stones) over the barely simmering water in the skillet. Cover and steam on medium-low heat for 30 to 35 minutes, until a toothpick comes out almost clean when inserted in the center. At this point, it will have a soft, light cake exterior and be slightly like a lava cake in the center. If you'd like it to be fully cooked throughout, steam it 5 to 10 more minutes, until the toothpick comes out clean when inserted in the center. Also check the water amount in the skillet about 20 minutes in; if there is very little remaining, add 1 more cup water to the bottom and continue cooking. When the cake is done, cool, covered, for 5 minutes before cutting into it.

Serve with a dusting of confectioners' sugar, if desired. The cake can also be frosted if desired with canned whipped cream, a soft store-bought frosting, or a homemade pourable glaze. The texture is delicate, so I don't recommend using a stiff frosting.

FIRE PIT MULLED CIDER

MAKES ABOUT 18 CUPS

This is the perfect cool-weather drink to be warmed over a fire or campstove. "Mulling spices" are considered warming spices and include cloves, star anise, orange zest, and cinnamon sticks. It's a fun one for kids, without the booze, of course. To make it a cocktail, add a glug or two of bourbon or whiskey.

Slice the apple into rounds crosswise about ¼ to ⅓ inch thick.

Pour the cider, orange juice, and maple syrup into a large Dutch oven. Add the sliced apple, ginger, cloves, star anise, and cinnamon sticks. Cover and bring to a strong simmer over a medium fire for 30 minutes to infuse the cider with the spices. The apples will soften but not fall apart. They are delicious to eat. Ladle into mugs and add 1 to 2 ounces of bourbon, if desired.

1 crisp apple, such as Gala or Granny Smith

1 gallon good-quality apple cider

1 cup orange juice

3 tablespoons real maple syrup

8 (¼-inch-thick) slices fresh ginger, unpeeled but washed

24 whole cloves

4 whole star anise

3 cinnamon sticks

Bourbon or whiskey, for serving (optional)

COOK'S NOTE. *This recipe can be doubled or tripled if you've got a large enough pot.*

PITCHER O' RED BEER

MAKES 8 CUPS; SERVES 8

BASE

1 (46-ounce) bottle tomato juice

½ cup orange juice

½ cup olive brine

¼ cup prepared horseradish

1 tablespoon Worcestershire sauce

1 teaspoon hot sauce, or to taste

¾ teaspoon celery salt

FOR SERVING

Ice

4 (12-ounce) beers

Large stuffed Spanish olives, for garnish

COOK'S NOTE. *To make these as Bloody Marys, mix the base as directed and add 1 to 2 ounces vodka to the glass. For "virgin" Marys, just serve the base over ice and garnish with skewered olives or celery sticks.*

This is one of my favorite cocktails. For some odd reason, I get mighty thirsty for these when I'm ice fishing. Especially on a nice sunny day when the fish are biting. It's similar to a michelada. You could use just tomato juice or Clamato, but this here is a fancier (and much better) version using a homemade Bloody Mary base. It's just as good with nonalcoholic beer—if that's your thing.

FOR THE BASE. Mix the tomato juice, orange juice, olive brine, horseradish, Worcestershire sauce, hot sauce, and celery salt in a large pitcher. Let it sit in the fridge covered for 4 hours, if you have time. It's still delicious if you want to drink it straight away.

FOR SERVING. Fill eight tall glasses with ice. Add 1 cup of the base mix to each glass, top with 6 ounces beer, and garnish with an olive.

CHARRED LEMON G&T

MAKES 10 CUPS; SERVES 10

It may seem absurd to grill a couple dozen lemons for a cocktail—but it's worth it. The grilled citrus creates a smoky, lemony, sour counterpoint to the simple syrup and gin. It's a unique, refreshing take on a summer cocktail—built for a crowd.

FOR THE ROSEMARY SIMPLE SYRUP. Combine the sugar, 1 cup water, and the rosemary sprigs in a small saucepan. Bring to a simmer over medium-high heat and stir until the sugar dissolves, about 5 minutes. Let the syrup cool with the rosemary to room temperature. Discard the rosemary before using. (This will make more than you need. Store any excess in the fridge for 2 to 4 weeks.)

CHAR THE LEMONS. Heat a grill to high heat. Place the lemons cut-side down and grill until charred, 5 to 10 minutes. Let cool slightly until cool enough to handle. Juice the lemons and reserve; discard the seeds and pulp. You're aiming for 15 ounces of juice. If you have more or a little less after squeezing all of those lemons, proceed with what you have.

FOR SERVING. Pour the gin, 15 ounces charred lemon juice, and the simple syrup into a large pitcher. Add the tonic water and gently stir. Fill glasses with ice, top with the cocktail, and garnish with a rosemary sprig.

ROSEMARY SIMPLE SYRUP

1 cup sugar

3 fresh rosemary sprigs, plus more for garnish

4 pounds small lemons (about 24), halved

FOR SERVING

20 ounces good-quality gin

5 ounces Rosemary Simple Syrup

40 ounces tonic water

Ice

CAMP COCOA

MAKES 32 OUNCES; SERVES 4

4 cups whole milk (to make it richer use 3½ cups milk and ½ cup half-and-half)

¼ cup sugar

¼ cup unsweetened cocoa

½ cup semisweet chocolate chips or chopped semisweet chocolate

Marshmallows, for garnish

Ready-made whipped cream, for garnish

COOK'S NOTE. *To make this into a cocktail for adults, you can add a splash of rum, Kahlúa, Bailey's, or crème de menthe to the hot chocolate.*

Hot chocolate can cheer up just about anybody, especially when fingers get cold. This recipe can be doubled or tripled, depending on the crew you're serving. The flavors can be adapted for kicks: Swirl a cinnamon stick to impart a fall flavor or a peppermint candy cane to make it a mint hot chocolate. Top it with marshmallows or whipped cream from a can.

Pour the milk into a 2-quart pot and warm the milk over medium heat on a camp burner, not allowing it to boil. Once hot, remove it from the heat and whisk in the sugar, cocoa powder, and chocolate chips until smooth. Pour into individual mugs and garnish as desired.

EXTRAS

**BRINES, MARINADES,
DRY BRINES, AND RUBS**

BASIC BRINE

A variation of this recipe is used in the Brined and Smoked Turkey Breast with Maple-Chile Glaze (page 128) and the Smoked Duck with Honey, Balsamic, and Chipotle Glaze (page 130) recipes. It's good for waterfowl, upland birds, and wild hog roasts.

Combine 1 gallon water, the salt, brown sugar, peppercorns, and bay leaves in a large pot over high heat and bring to a boil. Remove from the heat and let cool almost to room temperature. Transfer the liquid to a medium cooler and add the ice; there should still be ice floating in the water, but if there isn't, add more ice. Once cooled, add the meat to the brine, close the lid tightly, and brine for 8 to 24 hours.

1 cup kosher salt

1 cup brown sugar

10 peppercorns

3 bay leaves

8 pounds ice, plus more as needed

BASIC WET BRINE FOR SMOKING FISH

This brine will work for just about any fish or small-sized bird you plan to smoke.

In a nonmetallic container big enough to hold the fish, combine the salt, both sugars, honey, and water and whisk vigorously to dissolve the ingredients. Chill the brine. Thoroughly rinse the fish and submerge them in the brine, using a plate to weigh them down beneath the surface. Brine for 6 to 8 hours in the fridge.

¾ cup kosher salt

½ cup granulated sugar

¼ cup brown sugar

¼ cup honey

8 cups lukewarm water

STEVE'S BASIC BRINE FOR CURING A HAM

This is my go-to basic brine for curing a ham. Kevin Gillespie has another version on page 103 that is excellent for a bone-in hog leg.

In a large pot over high heat, combine 2 gallons water, the salt, brown sugar, Prague powder, mustard seeds, peppercorns, juniper berries, bay leaves, and garlic and bring to a boil. Remove from heat and let cool to room temperature. Strain the liquid into a container with a lid, discard the solids, and chill in the refrigerator until well cooled.

If you're brining a boneless ham, you can butterfly it and submerge it in the brine. You may consider injecting additional brine into thick portions of the muscle if you are brining a leg upward of 6 pounds. If you're brining a bone-in ham, take a quart of the brine and inject it into the muscle as deep as the bone. It's sufficiently saturated when the brine seeps from the injection and perforation holes. Then submerge the ham in the brine. Injecting the leg shortens the brining time to about 4 or 5 days for a 5- to 10-pound ham. If you're brining a bone-in leg without injecting, anything under 10 pounds should brine for 7 days, anything 11 to 15 pounds should brine for 10 days.

3 cups kosher salt

2 cups packed brown sugar

1 tablespoon Prague powder #1

2 teaspoons mustard seeds

20 black peppercorns

8 juniper berries

6 bay leaves

8 garlic cloves

RED WINE MARINADE

1½ (750 ml) bottles dry red wine (Cabernet, Chianti, or even a Syrah will work)

4 garlic cloves, smashed, or 2 shallots, sliced

2 fresh rosemary sprigs

3 whole star anise

10 black peppercorns

2 bay leaves

2 teaspoons kosher salt

Combine the ingredients in a medium to large bowl. Add the meat you are marinating; make sure the meat is submerged or transfer to a narrower container. Cover and let marinate for at least 6 hours or up to overnight.

AL PASTOR MARINADE

4 dried guajillo chiles, stems and seeds removed

½ large white onion, chopped

4 garlic cloves

1 chipotle chile in adobo sauce

3 tablespoons apple cider vinegar

2 tablespoons achiote paste (optional, but recommended)

2 tablespoons sugar

1 tablespoon kosher salt

1 teaspoon dried oregano, preferably Mexican

½ teaspoon ground cumin

⅛ teaspoon freshly ground black pepper

This is the same marinade used in chapter 5 in the scaled-up Hog on the Trompo (page 281). That recipe, built to feed a crowd, is made for 5 pounds of meat. Here is a smaller version for 1 to 2 pounds of meat, ideal for skewers or tacos serving about 4 people. Makes 1¾ cups.

Heat a heavy, dry skillet over medium heat until hot but not smoking. Toast the guajillo chiles until they blister slightly, about 15 seconds per side. Transfer the chiles to a large bowl and pour hot water over them to cover by 1 inch. If necessary, place a small plate into the bowl to keep the chiles submerged. Soak the chiles until soft, 30 minutes to 1 hour. The longer they soak, the easier they will be to blend smoothly. Pour ¼ cup of the soaking liquid into a blender jar. Drain the chiles and add them to the blender jar. Wipe the bowl dry and set aside.

Add the onions, garlic, chipotle, vinegar, achiote (if using), sugar, salt, oregano, cumin, and black pepper. Blend until a smooth, thick paste forms.

Transfer the marinade to a bowl and add your meat. Massage to coat it well. Cover and let marinate at least 8 hours or up to 48 hours.

JESSE GRIFFITH'S COFFEE CURE AND RUB

Jesse Griffith shared this dry brine/cure recipe with us. He uses it to confit game meat (see Cook's Note). But it's so good you could use it as a dry brine for any cut of big or small game or as a rub for grilling steaks. Makes ¾ cup.

Mix all ingredients together in a small bowl. Store in an airtight container for up to 1 year.

3 tablespoons kosher salt

3 tablespoons ground coffee

2 tablespoons brown sugar

2 tablespoons smoked paprika

2 tablespoons freshly ground black pepper

COOK'S NOTE. *For more information on how to confit, see the Beaver Confit Toasts recipe on page 20.*

ALL-PURPOSE BBQ RUB

Mix all ingredients together in a bowl. Store in an airtight container for up to 1 year. Makes 3 cups.

½ cup chili powder

½ cup kosher salt

½ cup brown sugar

2 tablespoons ground cumin

2 tablespoons granulated garlic

2 tablespoons dried oregano

2 tablespoons Hungarian paprika

1 tablespoon dry mustard powder

1 tablespoon smoked paprika

1 tablespoon freshly ground black pepper

2 teaspoons onion powder

1 teaspoon cayenne pepper

CREOLE SEASONING

This recipe is used in the Spicy Fish Cakes on page 207. Makes ⅓ cup.

Mix all ingredients together in a small bowl. Store in an airtight container for up to 1 year.

2 tablespoons paprika

1 tablespoon dried basil

1 tablespoon dried oregano

1 teaspoon cayenne pepper

1 teaspoon garlic powder

1 teaspoon onion powder

1 teaspoon dried thyme

1 teaspoon kosher salt

½ teaspoon freshly ground black pepper

LOW COUNTRY SEAFOOD SEASONING

4 tablespoons celery seeds

4 tablespoons black peppercorns

3 tablespoons coriander seeds

2 tablespoons whole cloves

2 tablespoons whole allspice

2 bay leaves

½ cup kosher salt

⅔ cup packed light brown sugar

5 tablespoons cayenne pepper

6 tablespoons garlic powder

4 tablespoons onion powder

6 tablespoons paprika

1 tablespoon dry mustard powder

4 tablespoons dried thyme

4 tablespoons dried oregano

4 tablespoons dried dill

Makes 4½ cups.

Place the whole spices and the bay leaves in a spice grinder and grind for 20 seconds, or until finely ground. Place these freshly ground spices in a medium bowl and whisk in the salt, brown sugar, and remaining spices. Store in an airtight container at room temperature.

TACO-STYLE SEASONING

2 teaspoons kosher salt

1 teaspoon black pepper

2 tablespoons oregano, preferably Mexican

1 tablespoon plus 1 teaspoon chipotle chile powder

1 tablespoon plus 1 teaspoon ground cumin

2 teaspoons ground coriander

1 tablespoon plus 1 teaspoon garlic powder

1 tablespoon plus 1 teaspoon onion powder

This recipe can be used in the Milanesa Torta with Wild Turkey (page 235) in place of the store-bought taco seasoning or in any ground game meat taco, iron pie, or foil packet combination you're cooking up at camp. Makes ½ cup.

Mix all ingredients together in a small bowl. Store in an airtight container for up to 1 year.

SAUCES, MOPS, GLAZES, AND CONDIMENTS

BBQ SAUCE

Whisk together the ketchup, vinegar, BBQ rub, brown sugar, molasses, lemon juice, Worcestershire, liquid smoke, mustard, salt, and pepper in a bowl. Store in an airtight container in the refrigerator, where it will last for about 1 week (or longer if you omit the lemon juice). Makes 3 cups.

2 cups ketchup

½ cup apple cider vinegar

¼ cup All-Purpose BBQ Rub (page 347)

¼ cup brown sugar

⅓ cup molasses

2 tablespoons fresh lemon juice

2 tablespoons Worcestershire sauce

1½ tablespoons liquid smoke

1 tablespoon Dijon mustard

1 tablespoon kosher salt

1 tablespoon black pepper

ALABAMA WHITE BBQ SAUCE

Whisk together all ingredients. Let sit for a few hours or overnight in the refrigerator before using for the flavors to marry. The sauce will keep stored in the refrigerator for up to 1 week. Makes 1¾ cups.

1 cup mayonnaise

½ cup apple cider vinegar

2 tablespoons prepared horseradish

2 tablespoons yellow mustard

4 dashes hot sauce, plus more to taste

2 tablespoons sugar

1 teaspoon kosher salt

1 teaspoon black pepper

PLUM GINGER GLAZE

If you can get your hands on plum preserves, make this glaze. Blackberry preserves will work in a pinch and are more readily available. Makes a little over 1 cup.

Combine all ingredients in a medium saucepan and simmer gently over medium heat, stirring frequently, until the mixture has reduced a bit, 3 to 5 minutes. Watch carefully so it doesn't scorch. Cool completely and store in the refrigerator for up to 1 week.

1 cup plum or blackberry preserves

1 (2-inch) piece ginger, peeled and grated

1 small shallot, finely grated

2 tablespoons soy sauce

1 tablespoon rice vinegar

6 dashes hot sauce

2 tablespoons sugar

¼ teaspoon five-spice powder

Large pinch of kosher salt

3 grinds of black pepper

GARLIC-CHIPOTLE FAUX AIOLI

1 garlic clove, plus more to taste

1 cup mayonnaise

1 chipotle chile in adobo sauce, chopped

1 teaspoon adobo sauce

½ teaspoon orange zest

Pinch of kosher salt

This is a "cheater" chipotle aioli, great to make at the last minute. If you don't have chipotle, substitute hot sauce to keep it spicy. Makes about 1 cup.

Finely mince the garlic in the bowl of a mini processor. Add the remaining ingredients and process until smooth. (Alternatively you can finely chop the garlic and chipotle and stir everything together.) Cover and store in the refrigerator for up to 1 week.

SALSA VERDE

4 large tomatillos, halved

2 serrano chiles, halved

3 garlic cloves

1 small white onion, halved

½ small avocado

½ bunch fresh cilantro

Juice of 1 lime, plus more as needed

Kosher salt, to taste

This would be excellent with the Milanesa Torta with Wild Turkey on page 235 or the Hog on the Trompo tacos on page 281. It's also fantastic with chips or smoked upland birds. Makes 1¾ cups.

Preheat the oven or grill to 400°F and place the tomatillos, serranos, garlic, and white onion on a baking sheet. Char and roast the veggies for 5 minutes to soften slightly and then transfer them to a blender. Add the avocado, cilantro, lime juice, ½ cup water, and ½ teaspoon salt. Pulse the blender five to ten times, until everything is broken down but not super smooth. Taste and adjust seasoning with more salt or lime, if desired. It will keep for about 1 week in the refrigerator.

CHUNKY PICO DE GALLO

Put the tomatoes into a bowl. Add the remaining ingredients to the tomatoes and mix thoroughly. Taste and adjust seasoning with more salt and lime juice, if desired. Enjoy within 24 hours for best flavor. Makes 3 cups.

1 pint cherry or grape tomatoes, quartered (2 cups)

½ large or 1 small white onion, chopped into ½-inch dice (about 1 cup)

1 serrano chile or jalapeño pepper, quartered lengthwise, seeded, and chopped

About ½ cup roughly chopped cilantro leaves

Juice of 1 lime (about 1 tablespoon), plus more as needed

½ teaspoon kosher salt, plus more as needed

GRILLED TOMATO SALSA

Grill, broil, or char in a cast-iron pan the tomatoes, onions, jalapeño, and scallions until they are well charred but not collapsed. Split the jalapeño and remove the seeds and ribs if you don't want the salsa too spicy. Chop grilled vegetables roughly and then pulse them in a food processor or blender with the lime juice and salt. Make this as chunky as you like. Makes 4 cups.

6 Roma tomatoes (about 1 pound)

1 large white onion, halved

1 medium jalapeño pepper

4 scallions, white and green parts, trimmed

¼ cup finely chopped cilantro stems and leaves

Juice from 1 lime, plus more to taste

1 teaspoon kosher salt

CLASSIC GREMOLATA

2 lemons

2 garlic cloves

⅓ cup finely chopped fresh flat-leaf parsley

Freshly ground black pepper

Flaky sea salt, such as Maldon

This is an excellent condiment for wild game and fish. I like to use either orange zest or lemon zest, and you can play with the herbs, too—parsley, mint, oregano, and basil are all possibilities. It's fantastic on grilled steaks and birds or even grilled fish. Use flaky sea salt for best results. Makes about ⅓ cup.

Using a Microplane, finely grate the zest of the lemons into a small bowl. Grate in the garlic. Stir in the chopped parsley and pepper and flaky sea salt to taste. This is best if used within 24 hours; store in an airtight container in the refrigerator.

CLASSIC BASIL PESTO

2 cups packed fresh basil leaves

⅓ cup pine nuts

1 garlic clove

¾ cup extra-virgin olive oil, plus more to cover

2 tablespoons fresh lemon juice

1½ teaspoons kosher salt

1 teaspoon freshly ground black pepper

Pinch of ascorbic acid (optional)

½ cup grated (optional) Parmigiano-Reggiano

Homemade pesto is another go-to condiment for me. This is the basic ratio you'll need. Feel free to swap some of the basil for other soft herbs and greens like mint, parsley, spinach, or kale, and likewise the pine nuts can be swapped for less costly walnut halves or even raw almonds. A pinch of ascorbic acid or smashed vitamin C tablet will help preserve the green color of the pesto; this step is recommended if you're making a large batch. Makes 1 cup.

Combine basil, pine nuts, and garlic in a food processor and pulse until coarsely chopped. Add 2 tablespoons of the oil and the lemon juice and process until smooth. Add salt, pepper, and ascorbic acid (if using) and, with the motor running, slowly pour in the remaining oil through the hole in the lid. Add cheese and pulse a few more times to incorporate.

Transfer the pesto to a container with a tight-fitting lid and add a thin layer of oil to cover the top of the pesto. Store refrigerated for up to 2 weeks or freeze for up to 3 months.

ITALIAN SALSA VERDE

This can be used in the same way you'd use a condiment like pesto or chimichurri. Italians use it for cooked seafood and on grilled or roasted poultry. Sometimes a soft-boiled egg is added to help emulsify it; go for it if you've got the time. Makes 1¼ cup.

Soak the breadcrumbs in the vinegar to plump them. In the bowl of a mini food processor, with the motor running, add the garlic through the chute to mince. Stop the motor, open the lid, and add the parsley, oil, anchovies, capers, black pepper, egg (if using), and salt and blend together. Taste and add salt or additional oil to get a pesto-like consistency as needed.

1 tablespoon breadcrumbs

3 tablespoons red wine vinegar

1 garlic clove

1 to 2 bunches parsley, roughly chopped

¾ cup extra-virgin olive oil, plus more as needed

4 anchovy fillets

1 tablespoon drained capers

½ teaspoon black pepper

1 soft-boiled egg (boiled 6 to 8 minutes), peeled (optional)

¼ teaspoon kosher salt, plus more to taste

RED WINE MUSTARD

This vibrant-hued mustard is delicious with the Brown Sugar Wild Hog Ham on page 103. It's ideal for sandwiches, roasts, and even fish dishes. Make some extra—it holds for about a month in the fridge. This recipe can be doubled or tripled as desired. Makes a scant ⅔ cup.

In a small saucepan, combine the wine and sugar over high heat. Stir to dissolve the sugar and bring the mixture to a fast simmer. Reduce the heat and simmer until syrupy and reduced by three-quarters to about ⅓ cup. Remove from the heat and let cool, then stir in the mustard. Store in an airtight container.

1⅓ cups dry red wine

4 teaspoons sugar

¼ cup Dijon mustard

MOSTARDA (MUSTARD-APPLE COMPOTE)

The traditional method of making mostarda involves a lengthy process of cooking fresh and dried fruit in syrup, but this version takes on the sweet-and-sour spirit of the original without the long cooking time. Makes 4½ cups.

In a 4-quart pot, combine all of the ingredients and set the pot over medium-high heat. Stir frequently but gently until the fruit and onions begin to soften, about 5 minutes. Lower the heat to medium-low and partially cover. Stir occasionally to ensure even cooking. When the apples have softened, about 10 more minutes, remove from heat. Serve at room temperature with smoked hog loin.

MAKE AHEAD. *The mostarda can be made in advance and stored in the refrigerator for up to 1 week.*

2 Golden Delicious, Fuji, or other semi-firm apples, cored and diced (about 3 cups)

1 red onion, sliced crosswise into half-moons (about 1½ cups)

¾ cup chopped dried fruit (such as dried apples, cranberries, and/or figs)

¾ cup dry red wine

¼ cup maple syrup

2 teaspoons kosher salt

2 tablespoons Dijon mustard

2 teaspoons mustard seeds

CAYENNE COMPOUND BUTTER

2 small garlic cloves

1 cup (2 sticks) unsalted butter, softened

1½ teaspoons cayenne pepper

½ teaspoon kosher salt

Zest of 1 small lemon

Juice of ½ small lemon

2 tablespoons chopped parsley or cilantro

This compound butter is in *The MeatEater Fish and Game Cookbook* and remains a go-to for me on any kind of grilled wild game or fish preparation. A simply grilled steak topped with a pat of this butter turns into a five-star meal. I've added a fresh herb (parsley or cilantro) to the recipe for this book. Makes 2 logs.

In the bowl of a mini food processor, chop the garlic. Add the butter. Add remaining ingredients and process until smooth. Scrape out and evenly divide the butter onto two pieces of parchment paper, roll it into logs with about a 2-inch diameter, and refrigerate until firm. Refrigerate for up to 1 week or freeze for up to 3 months.

BERRY COMPOTE

1 cup sweet red vermouth

½ red onion, finely chopped

¼ cup sugar

3 (¼-inch-thick) fresh ginger coins

1 cinnamon stick

Pinch of kosher salt

1 (6-ounce) container raspberries

1 (6-ounce) container blackberries

1 (6-ounce) container blueberries

1 thyme sprig

This is a classy accompaniment for any kind of grilled or smoked upland bird or big game. Its tangy, sweet flavors complement the complexity of game meat. It's also delicious on pancakes or waffles. Makes 1⅔ cups.

Add the vermouth, onions, sugar, ginger, cinnamon, salt, and ¼ cup water to a medium saucepan. Bring to a boil over medium-high heat, 4 to 5 minutes. Reduce to a simmer and cook until the liquid has reduced by half, 10 to 15 minutes. Add the berries and thyme and simmer for another 10 minutes. Let cool to thicken. Remove the ginger, cinnamon, and thyme. The compote will set up a little when cooled and will have the consistency of a loose relish. Cover and refrigerate for up to 1 month.

A FEW MORE BRINES, RUBS, SAUCES, AND CONDIMENTS

MORE BRINES

Enriched Brine (Brined and Smoked Turkey Breast with Maple-Chile Glaze, page 128)

Kevin Gillespie's Curing Brine (Brown Sugar Wild Hog Ham, page 103)

MORE MARINADES

Sour Cream Herb Marinade (page 77)

Shawarma-Style Yogurt Marinade (page 76)

Peruvian-Style Marinade (page 78)

Weeknight Butterflied Steak Marinade (page 45)

Bulgogi Lettuce Wraps Marinade (page 38)

Garlic Miso Shrimp Marinade (page 219)

MORE DRY BRINES AND RUBS

Dry Brine (Smoked Bone-In Hog Roast with Mostarda, page 124)

Rub for Braised and Smoked Wild Game Brisket (page 138)

Sichuan Spice Mix (page 265)

MORE SAUCES, MOPS, AND GLAZES

Sticky and Sweet Sauce (page 17)

Schlitz Whittington Small Game Basting Sauce (page 127)

Maple-Chile Glaze (page 128)

Peach Glaze (page 123)

Honey, Balsamic, and Chipotle Glaze (page 130)

MORE AIOLIS, MAYONNAISES, AND DIPPING SAUCES

Red Pepper Aioli (Hot-Smoked Fish Sausages, Chorizo-Style, page 115)

Harissa Aioli (page 275)

Anchovy Mayo (Smoked Venison Sandwiches, page 118)

Tomato Mayo Sauce (Spicy Fish Cakes, page 207)

MORE CONDIMENTS AND SAUCES

Chimichurri (page 71)

Ají Verde (page 78)

Pancetta-Onion Jam (page 55)

Sauce Chien Beurre Monté (page 59)

Peperonata (page 34)

Kimchi Slaw (page 33)

Chicago-Style Relish (page 34)

Maple-Sage Butter (Smoked Bone-In Hog Roast with Mostarda, page 124)

ACKNOWLEDGMENTS

Producing a cookbook is a massive undertaking with many moving parts. Without the talents of a small army of folks, you'd be holding a notebook with some half-written recipes in your hands.

First off, thank you to my publishing team at Random House: my editor, Ben Greenberg, for giving me the encouragement and room to do the best work that I can pull off; Leila Tejani, Azraf Khan, and Ted Allen for their help steering this project; and Debbie Glasserman, who designed this book, for her talent and her patience. And to the rest of our fine-tuned publishing team at Random House—Andy Ward, Tom Perry, Alison Rich, Windy Dorresteyn, and Steven Boriack—for their work in getting this book out into the world.

As always, thanks to Marc Gerald, my agent, who tracked me down twenty years ago and made me get to work.

Thanks to Krista Ruane, my collaborator on this project, who also served as the creative director, recipe developer, art director, and food stylist. Krista would take a bullet for her projects, and I'm constantly inspired by her passion and attention to detail. And a huge thanks to our internal publishing team here at *MeatEater*—Brody Henderson, Savannah Ashour, and Katie Finch. You guys do amazing work, but it's just as important that you make me laugh so much. Here's to a few thousand more pages. Together, the four of us owe a thanks to the generous and unflappable Kylee Archer for being a scheduling magician, an eel rustler, a party planner, and everyone's favorite person.

Much of the standout photography in this book is the work of John Hafner, with whom I've collaborated on three previous books. *MeatEater*'s own Seth Morris also contributed many terrific photos and was a huge help on the production of this book from start to finish. Thanks to Dave Gardner for his assistance on photo shoots. And thanks also to Brittany Brothers, Janis Putelis, and Brody Henderson for their producing skills on photo shoots. Additional photos (some plucked from the *MeatEater* archives) come by way of Garrett Smith, Justin Turkowski, Dave Gardner, Michael Mauro, Christopher Gill, and Jeff Stewart. For the top-notch illustrations, thanks to Ryan Frost.

Recipes take shape in all sorts of ways, ranging from mistakes to experiments to inspired creations. Thanks to the following folks for helping to get these into executable and replaceable form: Krista Ruane, Vivian Jao, Liz Tarpy, Jeannie Chen, Jon Heindemause, Koren Grieveson, Lish Steiling, and David Domedion. Thanks also to the professional chefs and home cooks who generously contributed completed versions of their own favorites and standbys for inclusion in this book, including my colleagues Danielle Prewett, Janis Putelis, Brody Henderson, Clay Newcomb, and fellow hunters and anglers Jean-Paul Bourgeois, Jessee Lawyer, Jeff Stewart, Jesse Griffiths, Kimi Werner, Parker Hall, and Kevin Murphy.

We could not have prepared these dishes for photography without the help of lead chefs Pancho Gatchalian and Koren Grieveson, as well as Austin "Chilly" Chleborad, Cory Calkins, Nicole Smith, David Braun, Austin Brown, Jasmine Lilly, Wyatt Hungate, Beau Linnell, Travis Barton from Barton Fabrication, and the hardworking firefighters Troy Brown and Dillon Smith. Also, thanks to Bodhi Farms, the Steiner family, and Sue Doss for help with shooting locations. And thanks to my colleagues Tracy Crane, Annie Raser, Valerie Ross, and Kristen McKellin for their behind-the-scenes support. And to Hunter Spencer for being such an incredible genius. If you want to know what something good would look like, ask him.

For your beautiful faces, thanks to Katie Finch, Jimmy, Rosy, Matty Meatball, Jennifer Jones, Aina, Mabel, Carrie Henderson, Hayden, Conley, Brett Archer, Kylee Archer, Mike Kmon, Christine Sawicki, Andre Brown, Brianna Stroebe, Corinne Schneider, Tressa Croaker, and Samantha Gilligan. I also appreciate the cameo photo appearances made by Rovin Alvin, Richard Martinez, Cameron Kirkconnell, Errol "T" Thurston Jr., Jesse Griffiths, Parker Hall, and Kevin Murphy.

ILLUSTRATION AND PHOTO CREDITS

INDEX

Page numbers of illustrations appear in italics.

ABOUT THE AUTHOR

STEVEN RINELLA is an outdoorsman, writer, wild foods enthusiast, and television and podcast personality who is a passionate advocate for conservation and the protection of public lands. Rinella is the host of the television show and podcast *MeatEater;* his most recent book is the #1 *New York Times* bestseller *Catch a Crayfish, Count the Stars*. His writing has appeared in many publications, including *Outside, Field & Stream,* and *The New Yorker*. Rinella lives in Bozeman, Montana, with his wife and their three kids.

themeateater.com
Facebook.com/StevenRinellaMeateater
Instagram: @stevenrinella and @meateater